59

13-50

GW00671743

MEN OF OUR TIME

THE HON. JULIAN M. GREENFIELD, C.M.G., Q.C., IN 1961
(Photo: Hay Wrightson, London)

TESTIMONY
of a
RHODESIAN FEDERAL

by
J. M. GREENFIELD
With a Foreword by Professor
Edwin S. Munger

MEN OF OUR TIME
Volume One

Bulawayo
BOOKS OF RHODESIA
1978

BOOKS OF RHODESIA PUBLISHING CO. (PVT.) LTD.

P.O. Box 1994, Bulawayo.

Publishers of Rhodesiana Reprints
and New Rhodesian Literary Works

First Published 1978

© J. M. Greenfield
© Foreword by Prof. E. S. Munger

ISBN 0 86920 172 7

PRINTED IN RHODESIA BY MARDON PRINTERS (PVT.) LTD, BULAWAYO

To my wife Florence
my constant support
and
to my son Ewen
in recognition of his many
courageous political fights against
heavy R.F. odds in the U.D.I. era.

Ambassadors cropped up like hay,
Prime Ministers and such as they
were like asparagus in May.

— W. S. Gilbert, *The Gondoliers.*

CONTENTS

ix

LIST OF ILLUSTRATIONS

PUBLISHERS' INTRODUCTION

DURING THE past ten years we have reprinted some sixty early Rhodesian works in our *Rhodesiana Reprint Library — Gold and Silver Series,* presenting to a new generation of Rhodesians a broad canvas of the historical landscape of our country. The contours of promise, the valleys of depression and pinnacles of achievement of the distant scene now stand more clearly delineated, and the panorama of the past is familiar territory.

We now turn our attention to our more immediate surroundings and, to extend the metaphor, have set ourselves the task of painting a record of our times by publishing the memoirs and biographies of persons who have influenced the course of our history and those who have contributed to the growth and development of national life in any of its many facets. To this end we have extended invitations to a number of persons from various walks of life to help sketch in some of the detail of the contemporary scene by recording their part in it. These memoirs and biographies will be published in a new series to be known as *Men of Our Time.* They will be produced as they become available and not at fixed intervals.

We have pleasure in presenting the memoirs of The Hon. J. M. Greenfield, C.M.G., Q.C., *Testimony of a Rhodesian Federal*,* as the first volume in the series. Appropriately his book is a convenient starting point for a study of some of the problems which bedevil Rhodesia today since it deals especially with our relationship with successive British governments during the Federal era. He leads evidence to show how the British broke faith with the white minority in Rhodesia in conceding the principle of majority rule in substitution of the accepted Federal policy of racial partner-

---

*The author has used the word Federal in its rare substantive form although it was colloquially employed in Rhodesia during the time of Federation, for instance, to distinguish between Members of the Federal House and those of the Southern Rhodesia House.

ship, thus bringing about a reaction which, in one of its manifestations, led to the taking of U.D.I.

This work will be followed by the memoirs of the late The Hon. A. R. W. Stumbles, G.L.M., I.C.D., which were all but complete at the time of his death on 2nd August, 1978.

We hope that *Men of Our Time* will receive the same generous support from the Rhodesian public that has been accorded to the *Rhodesiana Reprint Library Series* and that this new Rhodesiana-in-the-making series will serve as a useful and valuable medium for recording events of our times for future generations.

We hope, too, that the appearance of the first two named volumes will encourage many more Rhodesians to play a part in the project and to offer memoirs or biographies which may be considered for inclusion in the series.

LOUIS W. BOLZE

Bulawayo,
25th August, 1978.

FOREWORD

DIGNITY does not consist in possessing honours, but in deserving them. That Aristotlean epigram clothes the Honourable Julian Greenfield, a man of dignity.

As Rhodesia moves from white domination to a Zimbabwe that faces an uncertain future under some form of black majority rule, who does not grieve for the young and the old, the black and the white, who have died in the process of change and for those whose blood has yet to dampen the soil of their country.

How could it have been otherwise? That question will long haunt historians. This autobiography contains vignettes of key figures in the drama of post-World War II Rhodesia, and thoughtful judgments on the political process.

Julian Greenfield exemplifies the best of those Rhodesians of British stock. His reflections on his youth, in England as a Rhodes Scholar, and in greater detail on his legal and political career, cover most of the history of Rhodesia since European occupation.

I believe, although not all would agree, if he and men of his bent had played an even greater role in the history of his part of Africa, all the inhabitants would have fared better. Prime Minister Ian Smith and his government have come to a policy, after what some would say were twelve wasted years, that Julian Greenfield and others advocated many deaths ago.

It is easy to be wise after the event. There is no shortage of people and countries to share the blame. Although the United States has focused recently on the problems of southern Africa, its attention drawn there by the violence and by the Cuban presence, far less attention given at an earlier time could have meant far more. Britain, too—and one must include both the Conservative and the Labour governments—has not covered itself with glory over Rhodesia.

It is easily forgotten today that it was the Labour Party that launched the Central African Federation to draw Rhodesia northward and away from the influence of South Africa where the National Party was in its first term of office.

Living in Salisbury in 1952-53, this observer had a ringside seat as Rhodesians felt the first chill winds from the north. Julian Greenfield and his colleagues went into the Federation with high hopes. How these were dashed forms an important part of his book.

It was never ordained that Federation would fail. Among the many "ifs" that punctuate the history of that time and place, one may wonder if there had not been a change of government in Britain, if the suspicion of the British colonial officers in what was then Northern Rhodesia and Nyasaland had been less hostile, and if greater vision had not been had by all, the two northern territories might well have brought Rhodesia to majority rule at least a decade ago, and with far less trauma. Although at the time I asked the black Rhodesian leaders—among them Charles Mzingeli, Joshua Nkomo, Jasper Savanhu, Mike Hove, and the Reverend Sithole—I have never understood how Africans in Rhodesia would benefit from the failure of the Federation. In time it may appear that the independence leaders of the north and the Labour Party in Britain turned their backs on black leaders in Rhodesia lest the independence of Zambia and Malawi be delayed.

Welensky and Greenfield had to contend with a predominantly white electorate that they felt—and probably rightly —was not prepared for change at the rate the situation demanded. I believe that the white Rhodesian leadership in the Federation made a gallant effort at a successful multiracial society. When it did not succeed, they had spent too much of their strength and idealism that they lacked the energy to try again in Rhodesia alone.

But they were certainly not colonialists in the traditional sense, albeit some of the British settlers after World War II contributed a colonial mentality that was a brake on progress.

The voters in Rhodesia, all white for many years and then with a somewhat broadened franchise, at one stage supported a Garfield Todd to the left of Greenfield, but then turned against moderate Edgar Whitehead for Ian Smith.

Julian Greenfield's younger son, Dr. Thomas Greenfield, who was a student of mine at the California Institute of Technology and who was resident in the United States in the critical years, comments on how the white leadership in Rhodesia, fearful of white backlash, found it so difficult to appreciate fully the gathering storm in the world on the side of majority rule. As a Rhodesian abroad, he himself came to understand this.

This autobiography is the story of Julian Greenfield's fight to bring change without chaos. His temperament is always liberal with respect to race relations but conservative as to the rate of change. As Macmillan's "Winds of Change" howled down the African continent, it was not easy for Greenfield, especially with his love for the law and for ordered change, to mesh his personality with the times. One cannot say that he failed in spirit or that he succeeded in fact. Life cannot ask more than that he strove with integrity and compassion against heavy odds.

The new Zimbabwe will not be a palimpsest. Memories of events described in this book are fresh and too often bitter. United States Senator S. I. Hayakawa told me that on his first visit to Rhodesia in 1978 his most discouraging observation was that the political leaders—Nkomo, Smith, Sithole, Muzorewa, and others—spoke too much of the past. They spoke of what the whites had done for—or done to—blacks. The American semanticist encouraged Zimbabweans of all races not to look back but to think forward. Julian Greenfield looks back in this book but looks forward in spirit.

PROFESSOR NED MUNGER

Pasadena, California
August, 1978.

Preface

IN DEFERENCE to the promptings of several friends, I here set forth my political testimony, preceded by background information of boyhood and family against which readers may test veracity.

From 1933 to 1963, I engaged in active politics in Rhodesia. In the first half, I was a back-room party worker (unpaid). In the second, I was an M.P. for 15 years, in over 13 of which I was the legal member of the Cabinet. I participated in most of the conferences and constitutional discussions, affecting the formation and dissolution of the Federation of Rhodesia and Nyasaland. I was sent on several missions to London connected with changes in territorial constitutions. Thus, though Lord Blake has recently published his impressive *A History of Rhodesia*, I think that I can add something to accounts given by him and others which may be of use to a future historian. For example, political partnership, a corner-stone of the Federation, gets barely a mention by Lord Blake.

My task has, unhappily, revived memories of a shameful and shabby period in the history of a once proud nation whose Ministers in faraway London submitted to intimidation by black demagogues and cynically substituted premature majority rule for partnership between the races in breach of solemn pledges on which the white minority relied.

I wish to express my appreciation to an old friend, Ned Munger, for the kind sentiments so generously recorded in his Foreword.

I thank Mrs. Rose Heard for typing my first manuscript and my niece, Mrs. Hazel Shaul, for typing a revision; also Mr. W. E. Arnold for much useful advice.

J. M. GREENFIELD

30th May, 1978

My Forbears

MY FATHER was born in 1868 at a little village called Nottawa Saga in Ontario, Canada. He was christened Cornelius Ewen, after his maternal grandfather, the Rev. C. E. Maclean, one of the many thousands of Scottish Highlanders who emigrated to Canada in the nineteenth century. His paternal grandfather, James Greenfield, was a sea captain from Jamaica who gave up the sea and settled in Eastern Canada where he carried on a contracting business. He married a Highland woman, Mary MacCrimmon, a descendant of the famous piper. Their son James, my grandfather, was born in 1831 and he like his father-in-law became a Presbyterian minister. After his marriage to Elizabeth Maclean he accepted a call to the Free Church in Stornoway, Island of Lewis. Most of their children were born there; including Father who was the eldest son, eleven survived infancy.

The Rev. James Greenfield was somewhat of a patriarch, and an eccentric. He had an idea that there was a fortune to be claimed in Jamaica, and eventually he journeyed to that island in quest of it. I have in my possession a few rough notes he made of his investigations, consisting chiefly of items relating to the sale of slaves on various plantations, presumably once owned by his ancestors. There is nothing else to show for his expedition.

Father had all his schooling in Stornoway. He excelled in swimming, athletics and cricket, and learned to handle boats, rod and line. He, too, was destined for the Church, and went to Edinburgh for his theological training, taking with him the proverbial bag of oatmeal. He had to live very frugally; learning did not come easily to him so his course was somewhat prolonged, but eventually he was ordained in 1894. He then took various assistantships in Scotland. In the course of one of these he came to Hawick in the Scottish borders where he met my Mother, Jeannie Henderson, second daughter of James Henderson, the founder of a woollen mill which used to produce the famous Braemar knitwear.

Two people more unlike in temperament and upbringing than my parents it would be difficult to find. Mother was of Lowland stock, careful, clear-headed and practical. Father was imaginative, carefree and fond of people. Mother generally had much better judgment, both of people and of affairs, and a completely logical mind. She excelled at school and should have gone to university, but in the naughty nineties her father did not think this would be at all proper. She pursued her literary studies by correspondence, and read very widely. Mother's father was a twin and she herself was a twin, but her twin sister died in infancy. Her mother, Elizabeth Cruickshank, died before the children were in their teens. There were four sisters and a brother who followed his father in the woollen business. He became Sir Thomas Henderson and was for a few years a Liberal Member of Parliament. The Henderson household was a deeply religious one, and in this respect Mother was well fitted to be the wife of a minister.

In 1896, shortly after the Jameson Raid, Father accepted a call to minister to a flock of miners at Boksburg in Kruger's South African Republic. In 1898, Mother went out to the Transvaal accompanied by her father and the marriage was celebrated on the 2nd June. She had grown up in an affluent home in the beautiful border country and the contrast of life in Boksburg, a small, hot, dusty mining town where church and manse were of corrugated iron, was almost more than she could take. One of her sore trials was a smoky wood-burning stove which her father described as the "furnace of affliction", but her duties as Minister's wife kept her from repining and she took a lively interest in her new surroundings and the people of both British and Afrikaner extraction, most of whom were quite unlike anyone to be encountered in the Scottish borders.

My eldest sister, Elizabeth Cruickshank, was born on 26th March, 1899 not long before the outbreak of the second Anglo-Boer War. Mother and the young babe returned to Scotland when the war was imminent. Father stayed till the last moment, and then went into camp at Wynberg, Cape, as Chaplain to the Royal Scots Greys. He served in that famous cavalry regiment in the Transvaal throughout the war. His knowledge of that country was, of course, vastly superior to that of his brother officers and his service to the regiment extended well beyond the line of a chaplain's duty. Early in 1901, he was sent from the Eastern Transvaal to Durban to collect stores for the battalion's commissariat.

It was a notable journey during an exceptionally heavy rainy season. He trekked to Pietermaritzburg and back in charge of several wagons in a convoy of several hundred, floundering through endless mud and numerous flooded rivers, sometimes coming under enemy fire. Later he contributed a very lively description of his adventures to the *Scotsman* under the caption "Wait for the Wagon". Here is a short extract :

> *It was a terrible time at the drift in the darkness and rain — such toil for transport people and brutes. My teams were taken to help others, one of them was eventually freed and I thought I would go on to camp with it and let the others come on with the conductor. I waited for the wagon but it came not. I went back. After going half a mile I came on an upturned wagon, the four wheels silhouetted against the dark skyline like a pair of bicycles. Alas, it was mine. On a broad way, half a mile from camp after a long journey since 3.30 a.m. the wretched driver had tumbled over a small precipice. The goods were littered over the veld. This was the climax. I didn't see how the wagon could be righted. However, in the darkness and the rain the boys put the team at right angles to the wagon and pulled it over onto its feet . . . the hood was all bent to one side.*

Father gained first-hand experience of Kitchener's "scorched earth" policy and the guerilla tactics of the Boers. While he was campaigning with the Greys in the Transvaal one of his younger brothers, Jack, arrived from Canada with "C" Battery of the Royal Canadian Artillery and participated in the relief of Mafeking.

The Canadians with their guns, and a party of Queenslanders, landed at Beira on 23rd April, 1900. They went by rail to Marandellas, thence by stage-coach drawn by mules to within 25 miles of Bulawayo where oxen were substituted. They continued by train from Bulawayo to Ootsi in Bechuanaland (Botswana) and marched for three days, fighting their way to Mafeking where they were given a great reception.

Jack returned to Canada at the end of 1900 and was given a hero's welcome in the little Ontario town of Thorold. His brother Jim wrote a graphic account of it from which it appeared that Jack "was presented with a handsome gold watch valued at $75, also a purse of $100 in gold by the people of Thorold. Tonight the Thorold firemen are giving him a reception and are going to present him with a diamond ring. He is going to another reception tomorrow given by the Veterans Association." Jack, however, had itchy feet and in March, 1902 he was back in the Transvaal, this time with the Canadian Mounted Rifles. When the war came to an end Father returned to his flock at Boksburg, and Jack became a rigger on the gold mines. Mother and Elizabeth returned to the manse and, on 30th September, 1903, Emily was born, followed by the twins, Cornelius and James on the 2nd May, 1906, and myself on 13th July, 1907. I was ushered into the world by a violent dynamite explosion. Meanwhile, Uncle Jim had also arrived at Boksburg from Canada, and entered the printing industry. The youngest of Father's brothers, Ben, also came to Southern Africa, but whether to the Transvaal first or direct to Rhodesia I never knew.

Father went to Rhodesia for the first time in 1905 for the opening of the Victoria Falls bridge. Perhaps he intended to spy out the land. At all events, in 1909 he accepted a call to the Bulawayo Presbyterian Church.

Mother was delighted at the prospect of leaving Boksburg, but the problem of how to get the family and our goods,

chattels and livestock to the railway station began to exercise
her mind. To Father with his memories of the trek to Natal
in 1900 this was a small worry. Mother kept on questioning
him about his plans and eventually in response to her persistent question he replied, testily "Well, I suppose we'll have to
get a wax-oggen". He was never allowed to forget this
spoonerism.

2

Bulawayo Boyhood — 1909 to 1916

WHEN the Greenfield family arrived at Bulawayo in June, 1909 I was too young to take note of my surroundings, but I began to be aware of them from 1910 onwards. We were then living in a house in Abercorn Street, near the Presbyterian Church. The celebrated wide streets were unpaved and on windy days a wall of red dust would often blow up the avenues. Most of the shops kept their doors closed with a notice reading "Come in, closed on account of dust". There were many empty stands across which one could take "short cuts". Motor cars were very few. I remember one belonging to Mrs. Redrup, wife of a pioneer and later a prominent town councillor. Anyone who was anybody, including us, had some form of equipage. We kept a cow, in addition to the horse, in the backyard. Periodically, a wagon-load of hay was delivered for the benefit of these animals, and we children had fun building houses for ourselves with bales of hay. Surprisingly, the town was lit by electric light, in fact Bulawayo was one of the first towns in the world to be so lit. The water supply, however, was precarious, depending as it did on two very small dams at Hillside which only filled in an exceptionally good rainy season. When they ran dry the town fell back on boreholes near the present Hillside bowling greens.

Uncle Jack had preceded us to Rhodesia; he worked on various gold mines including the Globe and Phoenix at Que Que where he erected the headgear and was known as "Jack the Rigger". Periodically he and Uncle Ben would come to stay with us. I suspect that Mother had the task of nursing them through bouts of malaria. We children were very fond of our uncles, though we went in some awe of Uncle Jack because he had a fearsome moustache and was somewhat of a sergeant-major. In fact, this was his military rank throughout the Kaiser's war.

One of my earliest memories is associated with Jenny, the baboon which Father bought one Saturday morning at the auction sale at the Market Square. He frequently went to these sales in search of bargains. Mother strongly disapproved of this purchase, but there was nothing she could do about it. Jenny was chained to a post in the backyard. Our next-door neighbour was the pioneer doctor, Dr. Vigne, who shared Mother's dislike of Jenny, and let this fact be known. So eventually a plan was made to take Jenny to Khami, twelve miles from town, and to cast her loose among her kindred in the kopjes in the hope that she would revert to her natural state. In those days Khami with its ruins was a favourite camping place for Bulawayans on occasions such as the Easter or Rhodes and Founders holidays. I have a vivid recollection of Uncle Jack sitting on the driver's seat of a mule wagon in the backyard at Abercorn Street with Jenny seated beside him on the point of setting out for Khami. The rest of us went in the governess cart drawn by Tommy, a Basuto pony we had brought up from Boksburg. The plan as regards Jenny misfired, because she had not lost what ancient Roman lawyers called the *animus revertendi* which was their way of distinguishing wild from tame beasts. She made her way back to Bulawayo, touching en route at a house on the outskirts and alarming its occupants by knocking on their door.

Among my other early memories was the coronation of George V in 1910. The Town Council gave a fireworks display in the South Park at the point where the fountain now plays. We children were taken there by our coloured driver John, but when the fireworks began Tommy became restive. He plunged and reared between the shafts of the cart so I was filled with alarm and the fireworks themselves left no impression.

Not long after this we went for a seaside holiday to Natal leaving John and his brother William in charge of the house and livestock. On our return the governess cart was found to be in a very dilapidated condition. It transpired that John and William had made a practice of taking the cow to the municipal dip tank on the commonage by attaching it with a riem* to the cart and driving through the streets in grand style.

Another early memory is of Halley's Comet which made its appearance nightly for a period in the year of 1910. I am hoping to see it again in 1986.

As I grew older I occasionally joined my brothers and their friends in expeditions out of town to the cold storage works where a leaky pipe provided a drinking place for birds. There, I regret to say, we laid straws coated with bird-lime, and caught many birds. I never quite overcame my natural aversion for this cruel sport and I became somewhat of a stay-at-home. Consequently, I was usually at hand when Father required the services of a boy to hold the horse while visiting members of his flock or when conducting funeral services at the cemetery. On such occasions, we generally travelled immediately behind the hearse which was drawn by two horses with nodding plumes, driven by Jock McKeurtan. In those days malaria and blackwater fever took a heavy toll. A pleasanter aspect of church life was the annual Sunday school picnic, usually held at Forestvale, where we went in mule-drawn wagons. Fizzy drinks were not as commonly dispensed to children then as they are now but we thought the lemon syrup provided by the ladies of the congregation to be the most delicious drink imaginable.

From time to time ministers or missionaries from other parts came to stay with us. One such whom I remember, probably because of his long flowing beard was John Smith Moffat, son of the celebrated Robert Moffat and father of H. U. Moffat who succeeded Sir Charles Coghlan as Prime Minister of Rhodesia. In 1912 I had my first trip to Rhodes' grave in the Matopos, when someone visiting us at the time hired one of the few available taxis, a Napier, and I was

---

*Afrikaans word meaning thong or rope made from oxhide.

included in the outing. The World's View and the Shangani Memorial made a deep impression on my boyish mind.

In that same year my youngest sister, Jane, was born. She was called "Little Jane" to distinguish her from "Big Jane" who had come out from Hawick to Boksburg to help Mother with her growing family, and accompanied us to Bulawayo. Big Jane was a very religious person who distributed tracts in her spare time and became a strong influence on our early lives.

A date that stands out in my memory is 4th August, 1914 when Great Britain declared war on Germany. I remember a conversation between Father and Mother about "war stores". Father with memories of food shortages in the Anglo-Boer War, insisted on Mother laying in a stock of *boermeal* and sugar. Food never became very scarce in Rhodesia but, when rationing was enforced in Britain, Mother decided that our family should voluntarily adhere to the British ration scales, so we had meatless days and sugarless tea. We were not allowed to eat newly-baked bread until it was at least a day old.

One of the immediate consequences of the outbreak of war was the hurried departure of Uncles Jack and Ben, who set off at the first opportunity to join General Smuts' invasion of German South-West Africa. Jack joined the Natal Light Horse and Ben the Imperial Light Horse, and soon we received picture postcards from Swakopmund when that town fell into the hands of the South African invaders. After the short campaign was over, Jack and Ben, like many other Rhodesians, paid their own fares to England. Jack enlisted in the Canadian forces and held the rank of company sergeant-major. Ben was commissioned in the Royal Engineers, and survived the war only to die just after the Armistice, of Spanish influenza at Thurso in the north of Scotland where his sister Mary, Mrs. Galloway, was living. Jack, to the great grief of his nephews and nieces, returned to Canada. I paid him a visit in 1931 at Niagara Falls.

Father, on coming to Bulawayo, joined the Southern Rhodesia Volunteers, a mounted regiment, and took a full part in all the exercises of his company. When my brothers and I went to the Milton School, in 1914 and 1915, there was an atmosphere of tension in the matriculation class, most of whom were eager to be off to the war. As the years rolled on we became part of the Milton cadet company, and were brought up in the traditions of King and Country. We learned how to march and shoot, and signal in semaphore, and we attended cadet camps and sham fights.

3

Ruberslaw

———

I WAS five years old in 1912 when I first saw the kopje on which the two houses Kaya Pezulu and Harthill now stand among the boulders. Father bought the land, comprising about forty acres, at an auction sale of stands in the township of Hillside some four miles from the centre of Bulawayo. The township owners were Colonel Napier, a well-known pioneer, and his partner, Percy Weir. There were perhaps forty families living in Hillside at this time but they were scattered far and wide. Our nearest neighbour was about half a mile away. The Hillside road was an unpaved dusty and stony track through the bush. In Hillside itself there were very few internal roads, so Father and Uncle Jack, who had a share in the purchase, had to cut a track through the veld to get to the kopje. Napier and Weir had provided a communal water supply for residents, consisting of an iron tank fed by a windmill from a well some distance away. This tank was also about half a mile distant from the kopje. A few of the residents were connected with the town's electric-light supply but most of us depended on candles and paraffin lamps.

Father and Uncle Jack soon set about building a very large stone rondavel and a small rectangular storeroom, the latter with a flat roof of unceiled corrugated iron. These buildings were sited on a small shelf of comparatively level ground about half way up the kopje, accessible by a rough track which formed a water course in the rainy season. The builder was a black gentleman called Makonze, a name which Big Jane corrupted into "Macscones" probably because of his propensity for scrounging. He used the rough stones and rocks which came to hand with white antheap for mortar.

The floor was of beaten antheap coated with tar. It was barely level and indeed several rocks were incorporated in the floor and projected above it. Uncle Jack erected the roofs himself.

It was always a great thrill for the younger members of the Greenfield family to spend a night or two at Ruberslaw, a name derived from the Borders near Hawick. After outspanning the horse we would climb to the Big Precipice, from which one looked down on what in those unenlightened days we called a "Kaffir kraal". The inmates had cattle and we shouted to them in "Kitchen kaffir" in this sort of style : *"Hey wena. Tina lambile. Buyisa lo melek."*

In response a piccanin would shortly make his appearance with a bottle or billy can of milk for which he would receive a sixpence. It would then be necessary to get some water, which involved an expedition to the public supply. One of our friends described these outings in the following terms when writing a tribute to Mother in 1948 :

> *Well do I remember the week-ends spent with the Greenfield family at their Hillside home, then only a small week-end camp. I remember the long absorbing days on the kopje in the shade of huge granite boulders, excitingly near what seemed to us an enormous ravine known as the "Big Precipice" only a little way from the "Little Precipice" over which we peered with delicious terror; I can still see us all eagerly gathering jugs and buckets towards sunset and walking in single file, led by Mrs. Greenfield, along the grassy veld path to the tank that I suppose must have supplied all Hillside residents — very few then — with water. That evening procession in the warm dusk, with one or two stars just beginning to peep through, was a thrilling adventure to us and we'd have hated to find water on tap in the big thatched hut we slept in.*

The evening meal was usually taken outside around an open fire. Fridges had not been invented so it was difficult to keep the milk from going sour and to keep ants out of the food, but these trifles did not spoil our pleasure. There were more serious hazards in the form of serpents, large and small. I can remember an occasion when one of my brothers went to pick up what he thought was a piece of piping which fortunately slithered away before he laid hold of it. On another occasion a large snake was seen to crawl under a boulder. Uncle Jack advised us to put out a saucer of milk for it. Not long afterwards the snake was found asleep near the empty saucer and was easily dispatched with a spade. Then there was the time when Uncle Ben told his nephews to gather green grass for Tommy. We were disconcerted to find a puff-adder coiled up around a succulent tuft of grass.

Ruberslaw was not quite virgin territory in 1912. At both ends of the kopje someone had quarried granite, probably for the foundations of houses in Leander Avenue (called after Leander Starr Jameson). To this day one can see jumper holes in some of the rocks, drilled in some cases to a depth of more than three feet. But centuries before the "hammer boys" had drilled these holes there were other human dwellers in the kopje. They left crude stone implements and potsherds, and some of them left pictorial evidence. In an overhanging rock near the present tennis court there is a small panel on which some squatting human figures are crudely painted. At the base of Big Precipice there is a line of roan or sable antelope heads. In a crevice on this same precipice there is embedded some lead from Martini Henry cartridges; we used to find cartridge cases in the same vicinity, relics perhaps of some skirmish in the 1896 Rebellion.

In 1967, we found a fine clay pot almost intact, hidden behind a rock in a small cave beside Little Precipice. The Keeper of Antiquities at the Museum pronounced it to be of Rozwi manufacture, probably about the seventeenth century. Not very far away in a crevice near Norman's Rock some human bones were found which the same authority said were of a Boskopoid man. In 1917, we had found a bangle made of copper plated with gold in an old mealie land where Weir Close is now. Mother was keenly interested to know about our predecessors in title at Ruberslaw. She used to question some of the older fruit and vegetable vendors about a legend that Lobengula had a kraal for one of his queens at

Matsheumhlope near our part of Hillside. At one time we employed a man called Jim Nyati, who subsequently joined the Salvation Army. I append a letter received from him which refers to this kraal and to the daughter of a Princess who came from Gazaland to marry Lobengula. It was typed on paper headed "Director of Bible Training".

> *Mr. Greenfield*
> *Hillside*   *May 8, 1937.*
>
> *"Matjamhlope was King.Lobengula s" which he put his doughter her Name was Mhlumela she was a Girl wherefore was five mens looking her. this kraal was Built before the Government House ko.Bulawayo) the Majtamhlope is the first kraal which he started when he arrive in this Country his chiefs was no allowed to enter inside, their being staing? on the Huts out side Majtamhlope.s" Kraal. Himself the Late King Lobengula he was sleep in small hut. this Hut was for the rest. it was cald a King.s" Farmer. also the (Umganini) was likened Majtamhlope. where the Bellevue is sitting also was small Kraal. I hpe you will understood the few explanation.*
>
> *"I have the Honour to be sir yours obetient sarvant*
>
> *MVIMBI, NYATI*
> *FORT. USHER. MATOPOS.*
>
> *"AND THEREFORE. MHLUMELA SHE WAS. WHO BREWERRY KING LOBENGULA. BEER."*

About a mile to the south-east of Ruberslaw there is a rocky pool in the Bushman's Spruit which is the source of the Matsheumhlope River. This was known in my boyhood days as Queens' Pool, no doubt because one or more of Lobengula's ladies were wont to bathe in it. North-east of Queens' Pool are some boulder-strewn kopjes which overlook the Hillside Dams. In the Matabele Rebellion there was a police outpost there, and later this place became the property of R. N. Hall, an archaeologist who had once been Curator of Zimbabwe. He called his property Bushman's Haunt. There are some Bushman paintings on the rocks in these kopjes.

In 1917, I had the strange experience of guiding an unknown traveller to Bushman's Haunt, which used to be noted in a little guide book as one of the places worth visiting near Bulawayo. This strange man arrived at Ruberslaw wearing an outfit which bore a close resemblance to the garb worn by David Livingstone on his travels, including the explorer's hat with a cloth flap behind to protect the neck. He informed me that he had crossed Africa from east to west. When we returned from this expedition he rewarded me with a florin. I was too shy to ask his name. The memory of this excursion still haunts me, and I sometimes wonder whether it was not a reappearance of the great explorer himself.

The outbreak of the Kaiser's War in 1914 had a very significant effect on the history of Ruberslaw. Father had hankerings to return to the life of a chaplain. In 1916, he could restrain his ardour no longer and decided to go to London, after making arrangements for a *locum tenens* to occupy the pulpit in Abercorn Street. The arrangement involved Father's salary of £500 per annum being shared with the *locum*. To make ends meet it was decided that Mother and the family should move out to Hillside, thus saving £10 per month which was the rent of the house in Abercorn Street. Elizabeth at this time was at college in Cape Town. Emily became a boarder at the Eveline School and my brothers and I, with Little Jane, accompanied Mother to Ruberslaw. In preparation for this move, Father had engaged a Dutchman, as Afrikaners were called then, Mr. van Eeden, to build a stone kitchen in front of the storeroom. Below the kopje he built stables surrounded by a dry-stone wall or kraal. Behind the stables was a lean-to boy's kaya. Next to the stables was a P.K. but these letters were not then in general use to describe a "wee hoose". This building became known in the family as the "Blue Sea" which was Little Jane's first attempt at "W.C." It was, of course, devoid of water. Before setting off for England, Father called his three sons together and assigned various duties to us. Jim and Niels were to attend to the horses, cows and poultry. My chore was to see to the removal of the week's accumulations of the "Blue Sea".

On Father's departure, Mother made the following entry
in her diary on 8th March, 1916 :

> *Ewen left this morning at 8.40. Great crowd of*
> *people saw him off. Came home to Ruberslaw. First*
> *of all a shindy with piccanin. Unpacked Ewen's goods*
> *and stowed them away. The children came home with*
> *McCalmans as arranged, very hot and tired. After-*
> *noon Emily and I darned stockings. John ironing in*
> *kitchen. Then watched the cow milking and animals*
> *feeding which went on till a late hour. Got to bed at*
> *10 after a hot bath but the dog kept up a barking. At*
> *last went out to find Tommy loose out of stable and*
> *the calf at the cow. Roused up the boys with lantern,*
> *got the horse etc. stabled again after which peace.*
> *Slept till morning.*

Mother divided the rondavel with a curtain so that half
of it was a bedroom for herself and Jane, and the other half
a living-room. The three of us boys had the storeroom for
a bedroom and the kitchen was used for dining and bathing.
Hot water for the weekly ablution was boiled in a paraffin tin
on top of the wood stove. The main drawback was the lack
of shade, and the heat generated in the kitchen by its flat
iron roof and the ever-burning wood fire in the stove, which
was used for baking bread in addition to heating water and
cooking generally, including the making of quantities of Cape
gooseberry jam and marmalade. There were no trees of any
size on the kopje except some large euphorbias near the Big
Precipice and at Leguaan Rock where Harthill now is. They
cast no shade around the dwelling.

One of the main problems in the early days at Ruberslaw was the perennial one of getting to school. It was a
long and tedious journey by horse and cart. We outspanned
on a vacant stand near the school and tethered the nag to a
thorn bush. The return journey was uphill and in the hot
season we seldom had much inclination for lunch in the hot
kitchen when we got home. We often resorted to "the
shadow of a great rock", in this instance "Mouse Rock", for
a picnic lunch. As the year wore on we all began to feel the
need of a seaside holiday. Mother had somehow contrived

to save enough money to pay the fares of the family, plus one of our school friends, to Umkomaas, on the Natal South Coast. We spent the Christmas vacation there and were joined by Elizabeth who travelled from Cape Town. At the end of the year Father landed at Cape Town, his arrival being announced in a telegram to Mother "Wire me £5", which she did. He joined us at Umkomaas and a few weeks later we all returned to Hillside. Looking back now, I think it is surprising that on our return we continued to live at Ruberslaw instead of going back to Abercorn Street. It must have been exceedingly difficult for Father to attend to the duties of his parish from a base four miles away, when we were entirely dependent on horse transport. The position was somewhat alleviated when Uncle Tom Henderson sent out from Scotland a motor cycle as a present for Father. It was one of the variety that had to be pushed to start; when the engine fired the rider had to take a flying leap to mount his iron steed. Father had several spills and on the whole he was not sorry to part with his motor cycle when, in 1919, he resigned his charge at Bulawayo.

4

O'Connor, Mtagati, Hep & Tembo

WHEN we all got back from Umkomaas in 1917 the living quarters at Ruberslaw which had been very cramped were even more so now that Father was also with us. He soon set about enlarging the accommodation. Unlike Uncle Jack he had few practical skills, at any rate in the way of building operations. Van Eeden was not available, so Father engaged an Irishman called O'Connor, alleged to be a stonemason, who at the time was an inmate of the Salvation Army Home. O'Connor was very probably the pioneer who, as related by Selous in his *Sunshine and Storm in Rhodesia,* was nearly murdered at Essexvale in the Rebellion. Certainly he had acquired a large thirst for whisky. Father, who must have known this, was careful to pay O'Connor's wages into a savings bank account, but periodically he broke out, and building operations were held up. While he was on the job he was accommodated in the stable building, probably not a new experience for this son of Erin, but he had his meals with the family. In the evenings he would regale us with Irish stories.

The building erected by O'Connor was intended as a dining-room/sitting-room combined, with a "lean-to" behind as a new bedroom for us boys. It was built in the space between the rondavel and the kitchen, and shared the eastern wall of the kitchen, but O'Connor decided that this wall was not sufficiently plumb so he built a new wall alongside, with the result that the mutual wall is three feet in thickness. His efforts at masonry are notable for their solidity rather than the accuracy of his right angles. The dining-room was supposed to be square but turned out to be oblong. The roof — in the form of a pyramid — was erected by Jock McKeurtan, the well-known Bulawayo undertaker, assisted by another Scot called Alexander Cockburn. They probably completed their efforts before the Spanish 'flu hit Bulawayo. Jock had a busy time during the 'flu epidemic, but Father had an even busier time, because the volume of business that came Jock's way deflected him from the waterwagon to the whisky bottle, so Father had sometimes to assist in nailing down the coffins. During the 'flu epidemic I think Father must have ridden on the hearse with Jock, as our horses could not cope with these extra journeys.

Mrs. McKeurtan was a character in her own right. She disapproved of Jock's addiction to the bottle as she was from time to time president of the Women's Christian Temperance Union (W.C.T.U.), alternating in that office with my Mother or Mrs. John White, wife of the Wesleyan minister. Mrs. Mac was a determined feminist and committee woman, and was constantly urging that there should be more "meetns". She did not approve of some of the celebrations that occurred from time to time, such as the annual St Andrew's Nicht banquet, which she referred to as "one of they orgies". No doubt Jock was wont to indulge rather freely in the national beverage on such occasions.

When Jock and his mate had erected the timbers of the new dining-room the roof had to be thatched. The thatch was obtained from black ladies who carried bundles of it on their heads and were paid one shilling per bundle delivered to the door. It was then broken down into smaller bundles after being combed by means of a line of nails driven into a plank.

The "lean-to" which became our bedroom had a flat corrugated iron roof and was in consequence somewhat hot. Its walls remained unplastered, no doubt because money had run out, and O'Connor's services could not be continued. However, it was a great improvement on the old storeroom. The completion of these buildings did not solve the problem of accommodation for my sisters, so within a year or two Mother decided to build rondavels for them. Jim Nyati, the subsequent "Director of Bible Training", was at this time our gardener, but Mother observed that he had a certain skill at building stone walls. She put him on to erecting the walls of the rondavels. Cockburn was engaged to erect the roof timbers of the first rondavel. When the second was built my brothers and I were able to attend to this. The thatching was done by another of our employees who rejoiced in the name Mtagati, a name which seemed to fit him well. It means "witchcraft" or "bewitched". He was an old soldier in both senses of the term and a veteran of the German East-Africa campaign. Like O'Connor, he regaled us with many stories of his exploits, and I discovered that he had once been employed on the diamond mines at Kimberley. I was anxious to test the veracity of his statement to this effect and I questioned him about I.D.B. It ran like this :

"Did you ever steal a diamond? — Yes.

How? — I walked off with it between my toes.

What did you do with the diamond? — I sold it to a trader.

For how much? — £90.

What did you do with the £90? — I bought nine heifers at £10 each.

What became of them? — They were swept off in the rinderpest."

I think Mtagati stood up reasonably well to cross-examination. I taught him one or two tricks such as floating a needle on water. I believe that he subsequently used this skill to acquire some goats by laying bets with their owners that a needle could be made to float. By the time these new rondavels were built our dwelling at Ruberslaw bore some resemblance to a sizeable kraal.

While O'Connor was with us we often had visits from another pioneer, George Hepburn, eldest son of the missionary who wrote *Twenty Years in Khama's Country*. Little Jane called him "Hep". He had fought in German East Africa and when we first got to know him he had probably been invalided out of the army. Hep seldom came empty-handed; he usually brought a hare, a leg of venison or a guinea fowl. He invariably came attended by several dogs which I believe were the forerunners of the breed that became famous as Rhodesian Ridgebacks. Their domicile of origin was probably Botswana. They had perfect ridges but their colour was not up to the best standards. Jupiter was brown but Juno was white. Inspired by Hep, Mother bought us a 16-bore shotgun from a former Bechuana missionary, the Rev. S. S. Dornan, and Hep took the three of us boys out into the veld and taught us to shoot. We occasionally bagged a hare or even a duiker or steenbok on our 40-acre domain. We shot our first guinea fowl — a sort of combined operation — near the Hillside Dam. To make sure of the bird we waited till it had gone to roost in the evening. There was no thought in our boyish minds of such action being unsporting — cartridges were expensive and could not be wasted.

Living as we did on what amounted to a very small farm, we had a constant succession of African servants to attend to cattle, horses, garden, well-sinking and building. I have already referred to one or two characters, among them Jim Nyati and Mtagati, but the star of them all was Tembo, our cook and man of all work in the house. Looking back on it I am amazed at how he managed to cope with attending to a family such as ours, doing most of the cooking, washing, ironing and general housework, and collecting and chopping firewood. He was at times assisted by a piccanin. Tembo was blessed with a sense of humour; perhaps his limited command of English made some of his remarks even funnier than he intended. For example he would ask Little Jane, "Whasamatter steak? Wantee stew, wantee fly?" Then there was an occasion when he informed Niels that he was "maningi gentleman", pointing out to him that the seat of his trousers had become worn out, the inference being that gentlemen sit around more than non-gents.

One of Tembo's earlier employers rejoiced in the name of van Niekerk but Tembo spoke of him as Mr. Vinegar. Tembo also baked bread when required to do so. He would draw attention to the fact that another baking was required by producing a loaf and saying "Rista rast roaf". We boys would occasionally try to pull Tembo's leg. On one such occasion when we were engaged in this occupation we heard Father's stentorian voice call out, "Boys leave the blackamoor alone". We were somewhat surprised but it transpired that Father had been reading from Struwel Peter to Little Jane.

During the early years at Ruberslaw there was only one butcher who served the Hillside area. There were then no shopping centres outside the town limits of Bulawayo. Meat was delivered by a "boy" who brought with him an order book and one could study what the other residents of Hillside were to have for dinner next day. On one occasion Mother noted the following in the order book :

Mrs. Black: No order, killing a fowl.
Mrs. Hepburn: No order, some game has been sent.
Mrs. McCalman: No order, observing meatless day.
Mr. Philpott: No order, sending to Cape Town.
                   See back of book.

On reference to the back it was revealed that the book was supplied by a Cape Town stationer, a fact to which Mr. Philpott, founder of the stationery business of Philpott & Collins, rightly took exception.

5

Animals

———————

LIFE at Ruberslaw was very much bound up with animals.
Pride of place must go to Witch, our blue Persian cat
which came with us from Boksburg. Once, when she had
a litter of six she managed to catch a bird for each of the
first five, and then finally brought in a leaf for the sixth. She
soon settled down at Ruberslaw and became a noted snake
hunter. She slew several and gave timely warning of others.
In the end, alas, she succumbed to snakebite. At the foot
of Big Rock is the legend painted in 1917 in tar by myself:
"Here lies Witch".

Horses were all important. Tommy had a mate called
Peggy who foaled in 1917. The foal was called Thomasina,
or Sina for short. Soon after this event Peggy was gored
in the flank by Bess, one of the cows, and nearly died. A
few months later Tommy, who had supposedly been "salted"
died of horse sickness.

For veterinary services we relied heavily on our friends
Mr. and Mrs. D. L. Black. Mr. Black was the local Hillside
Police Trooper, his wife was the daughter of pre-pioneers and
she could speak Sindebele fluently. Mr. Black was known
throughout Hillside as "Lo Blek". If a piccanin gave trouble
he was sent with a note to Lo Blek who could be relied upon
to mete out the necessary correction. If an animal went lame
or sick Lo Blek was called in. If a horse had to be broken
in he threw it. He did this for Sina, but she was not the
best advertisement for his skill in training horses. One of her
less endearing habits was to take her rider to the nearest
thorn tree where she would do her best to scrape him off
her back. Mr. Black had a fine stable of police horses, the

largest of which was a strawberry roan which he often lent
to Mother. She rode side saddle, having learned to ride in
the Transvaal. This was her favourite mode of transport
until late in life.

One of Mr. Black's occasional duties was to guard the
gate at the Agricultural Show and he so far neglected this
duty as to let in members of the Greenfield family free. In
fact, the benefactions that we derived from the Blacks were
unending. An extract from Mother's diary on 10th March,
1916 reads :

> *Such a day with the cow. In the morning, piccanin
> announced she was "maningi sick, aikona melek".
> Found something wrong with the udder. Sent Emily
> on horseback for Mr. Black but he could not come
> then. Got milk from Moffats.* Busy unpacking books,
> etc. Went to town for children. Met Mr. Black on
> road back. He came over and pronounced cow seriously
> sick, festered udder. Applied liniment of grease, paraf-
> fin, linseed oil, etc. Later in the evening he came
> again. Lots of fuss. Got to bed late and tired.*

Our stock book records the birth to Bess on 12th
January, 1918 of Andrew the Ox. A year or two later, on
our return from school one day we found Mrs. Black awaiting
us with the news that Mother had been tossed by Andrew,
and was in bed. She had gone down to the cattle kraal just
as the herd was emerging and got in Andrew's way.
Fortunately, Mother was little the worse for this shattering
experience except that she suffered for some years from a
stiff neck.

When first we went to live at Ruberslaw we had only
one or two milk cows. Father had the idea that dairying
could be made profitable and it would be a suitable invest-
ment for his sons to own some cows. We each had a few
pounds in the Post Office Savings Bank and he persuaded us
to invest this money in the purchase of dairy cows.
Unfortunately, when it came to the point, he bought for us

---

*H. U. Moffat, the subsequent Premier, who lived in Hillside at
this time.

two rather expensive stall-fed cows which were sent up from the Eastern Cape. They did not easily adapt to our primitive conditions. Mother was tactless enough to call them the "Pearls of Great Price". However, for a few months they did produce a good deal of milk and this we carried to the dairy on our way to school. On the whole it was not a very profitable venture.

On one occasion our little herd had gone out to graze in the surrounding veld as usual but returned at midday and set up a great lowing and bellowing. The herd boy later turned up with the news that one of the cows had been killed by a "schelm" the nature of which seemed obscure. When Father got home towards dusk he and I set off with the herd boy to see what had happened. Eventually, when we got near to an electric power pole, there was a sizzling noise and a smell of roast beef. We did not linger as the light was failing. While we were moving away from the scene the herd boy gave out a dreadful shriek. His sleeve had come into contact with a live wire but luckily he was able to spring back unharmed. In the growing darkness Father and I made a long detour to avoid any further brush with death.

The cattle had considerable nuisance value at times, apart from their ailments, as they sometimes broke into neighbours' mealie patches. We also grew mealies, and the harvest, in the form of cobs, used to be spread out to dry on the flat roof of the bedroom I shared with my brothers. Unfortunately, the cattle discovered that by climbing up the back of the kopje on to some rocks beside the bedroom they could crane their necks and reach the cobs on the roof. On several occasions they broke out of the kraal at night and I would awake with the sound of pounding on the roof. My brothers always seemed to be sound asleep on these occasions, and I perforce had to get up and drive the cattle back to the kraal.

Our cattle-keeping venture came to an end in 1924 when there was an outbreak of East Coast Fever and the Government decided that cattle in the infected area must be slaughtered. Fortunately for us, compensation was assessed by Major Robert Gordon, an Australian known as

Boomerang, who was reputed to be able to kill snakes by catching their tails and cracking them like a whip. His assessment erred, I think, on the generous side and we recouped some of our expenditure on the Pearls.

Like everyone else in Hillside, we kept poultry of various kinds, never very profitably. Then Mother got the idea that bee-keeping might pay better dividends. Starting with one or two hives bought from a neighbour and conveyed home under cover of night in the wheelbarrow, we gradually accumulated an apiary of a dozen or more hives. When I say "apiary" this is not a very apt description. The hives were dotted about at all sorts of odd corners among the boulders. Each hive was called after some famous queen. One was a particularly vicious hive generally called "the mad hive" but officially known as Queen Jezebel. The Rhodesian bee is much more vicious than its counterpart in Europe. We did not then appreciate that bees ought to be housed in a cool building. There was little or no shade for our hives and we soon found that to attempt any work in daylight was to court disaster. Supers had to be taken off at night. Working in the dark with a hurricane lamp in one hand and a smoker in the other we somehow managed to get a good deal of honey, mostly in the form of "sections". We found, however, that the Bulawayo public had no great interest in comb honey, and we then acquired an extractor and produced "run honey". One of the most ambrosial scents in the world comes from the extractor when the combs are whirled around. Even working at night as we did, the bees might be left in a very angry state and it was not altogether unusual for the kopje to be in a state of siege the following day. Many a time I arrived at school looking like a case of mumps as a result of a sting near the eye. Our bee-hives attracted other nocturnal visitors in the shape of ratels or honey badgers. These animals must be related to the polecat because when disturbed at their work they emit an all-pervading stench. As a protection against these depredators each hive had a sheet of corrugated iron on top, held down by a heavy stone.

Bee-keeping in the way we did it was a dangerous occupation and looking back on it I am surprised that our horses suffered no fatal stings. Bees need much more attention than we were able to give them and after I went off to college the swarms gradually died out. As I write, we still have one hive, but it is in the natural state in a hole under a rock.

Perhaps the most notable animal to live at Ruberslaw was a bird. In 1928, Mother acquired a green Brazilian parrot on her return by sea from a visit to Scotland. She called him Nicky and loved him dearly but alas, a cat was his undoing. A year or two later he was replaced by Nicky-two. At the start he was caged, and his wings clipped, but later he was given his freedom and grew his wing feathers. He became a strong flier and would circulate freely around Hillside; fortunately he had the *animus revertendi*. Occasionally, however, he was lost, and then Mother would set up a great lamentation. One such occasion occurred in 1946 when Nicky fell into our water supply tank at Harthill. The story of his plight and rescue by my eldest son, Ewen, is best told in Mother's own words :

At last a singular sound is heard
A sort of scratching splutter
Is it, oh can it be my bird
Not answering, not saying a word
But struggling in the water?

Quick, bring a ladder. Can he last
Till back to life we draw him?
We must get there and get there fast
An hour must at the least have passed
Since near the tank I saw him.

The tank is filled to three feet nine
But in the close connection
By which the parts together join
There's just above the water line,
A very slight projection.

On this the bird has hooked his beak
He tries his wings to flutter
He cannot raise his voice or speak
Impossible to call or shriek
Suspended in the water.

What then?   A fishing rod — a stick
With cord attached, says Ewen
With luck that might just do the trick
But time is short, we must be quick
Delay might prove his ruin.

Can it be done?   Yes, clever bird!
He's snatched the lowered line
A nearer thing I never heard
They haul him up and on my word
We're only just in time.

6

A Scottish Visit

————◆————

AS I HAVE already mentioned, Father resigned from his Bulawayo charge in mid-1919 and sought pastures new in South Africa. Although he was able to get temporary "supply" work at Cape Town, East London and Kimberley he did not receive a "call". His remuneration averaged £30 per month out of which he had to pay board and lodging, with "washing extra". Nevertheless he managed to send home about £15 per month. Mother was able to supplement this by teaching, although she had never been trained as a teacher. This occupied all her mornings; shopping and W.C.T.U. activities had to be done in the afternoons, which often entailed the horse in a second journey to town.

One of the recurrent expenses at Ruberslaw was payment of annual quit-rent. The land had been bought on a form of tenure, now obsolete, which entailed an initial payment together with an annual payment of quit-rent, which latter could be redeemed by paying ten times the amount thereof at one time. The quit-rent amounted to about £75 per annum so that a capital sum of £750 was required to redeem the property. It was difficult during Father's absence in South Africa to keep up the quit-rent payments, a fact which Uncle Tom Henderson became aware of, and he decided to pay us a visit early in 1921 to see what was what. He was accompanied by his sister, Aunt Jessie, and his business partner, Willie Innes, a boyhood friend of Mother's. They intended to stay at a hotel, but Mother would not hear of this, so the accommodation at Ruberslaw had to be stretched to include three extra people, added to which Father paid us a visit so as to be on hand for discussions with Uncle Tom.

Our visitors chose to come during the rainy season which meant that the problem could not easily be solved by putting camp stretchers outside. We three boys were turned out of our bedroom and lodged in some odd corners. Our room had never been plastered, and it was decided to try to furbish it up for our titled relative and his friend. We proceeded to plaster it ourselves using for the purpose "daga", consisting of antheap and water. Unfortunately, the mixture contained no sand nor any cement or lime, and as a result the plaster was full of cracks and resembled the bottom of an earth dam when the water has dried out. However, it was daubed with whitewash and our visitors probably did not notice its imperfections as much as we did ourselves. Willie Innes was intrigued by a nocturnal visitor in the shape of a large *chongolola* (millepede). During this visit, Mother invited her friends to an "at home", and among those attending were Mr. and Mrs. F. Issels, Pioneers, who rejoiced in the possession of a Model T Ford. Unfortunately, a heavy rain storm came on and the stream nearby came down in spate. The Issels' Ford was bogged down in the vlei and the male guests of the "at home" spent the greater part of the afternoon digging it out, up to their ankles in water.

All things considered, the Scottish visit was a success and Uncle Tom generously produced the £750 required to redeem the property. Father spent the next year or two between Salisbury and Umtali in "supply" work.

At last, in 1923, he was appointed Superintendent of the Presbyterian Missions in Matabeleland at a salary of £35 per month plus £5 by way of transport allowance. From this time on he was able to live with his family at Ruberslaw. What is more, he returned home one day in triumph in a new Model T Ford which cost £200, with a case of petrol, i.e. two four-gallon tins, into the bargain.

The Ford was an unqualified success and was probably the best bargain Father ever made. Mother was not so happy when, in 1923, he bought a large 8½-inch reflecting telescope from a neighbour who was suffering from a temporary financial embarrassment. The price was £30, which amounted to three-quarters of his monthly emoluments. Included in the bargain was a white canvas cover through which part of the drum of the telescope protruded. The general effect was not unlike that of a white elephant which was the name Mother promptly bestowed upon the object, but not only for that reason. Many years later my younger son, Tom, became an ardent astronomer, and the instrument was conveyed to Salisbury and surmounted by a revolving dome. Tom's astronomical interests were in a measure the cause of his going to California to pursue his studies. So Father's purchase of the white elephant had incalculable results.

7

Following the Plough

———————

IN MY boyhood days in Bulawayo every householder had a patch of mealies on his stand. Hillsiders who were more dependent on horses and cows tended to have larger patches of mealies. At Ruberslaw we had abundant land. At the east of the kopje there was an old African mealie land about an acre in extent. Further away, there had been an old cattle kraal, rich in manure. We surrounded these areas with a thornbush fence or "scherm" and hired the services of an African ploughman. Thus, in a good rainy season, we were able to reap a few bags of mealies and some potatoes.

As time went on we stumped and cleared more land; gradually the thornbush fences, which were never very effective in keeping the cattle and horses out of the crops, were replaced by wire fencing mounted on wooden posts cut on the spot. Despite the application of carbolineum, these wooden posts were constantly under attack by white ants and borers, and had frequently to be replaced.

Fencing wire was obtained in odd lots bought on the Market Square. Eventually, after the property was surveyed, Jim erected a first-class fence with steel poles and new wire. After Andrew and another ox, called Eland, had been trained we acquired our own plough and grew mealies on quite a large scale. Besides reaping the grain, we turned the stalks into ensilage which was made in a very large pit in the ground, covered over with corrugated iron with about eighteen inches of soil or gravel on top. There were no Young Farmers Clubs in our day but my brothers and I learned to milk the cows (though we did not regularly do this operation), and we shared with our African labourers all the tasks of ploughing, planting, stumping, weeding, reaping and shelling mealies, making ensilage, lifting potatoes, planting fruit trees and fencing. We never lacked occupation in school holidays.

I must not, however, give the impression that it was a case of all work and no play. In the dry season, as soon as homework was finished in the afternoon, my brothers would be off with their "catties" into the veld to shoot birds. They became accurate shots, with the result that at the usual time of their return home in the evening the cats would go out to meet them and receive an offering of small birds. On one occasion Jim shot a cobra with his catty, and on another Niels secured a hare. I was no use whatever at catty shoot-ing. The only thing I ever managed to hit was my own thumb.

In the rainy season when the Bushman's Spruit came down in flood we were allowed to bathe in it. Bilharzia did not have quite such a hold as it does now, and so long as the stream was actually flowing it was regarded as safe.

Following the example of one of our school friends, we made a canoe out of a 10 foot sheet of corrugated iron. The stern piece was formed from the end of a wooden petrol case. We had quite a lot of fun with out boat. When marulas were thick on the ground and we could gather some friends together we engaged in marula fights. We fortified Mouse Rock and Lizard Rock and these were vantage points from which to hurl marulas at people down below. We also played shinty with a tennis ball, using knobkerries instead of hockey sticks. As we grew older and more sophisticated, together with some friends, my brothers and I organised ourselves into a soccer club. Without seeking permission from anyone we cleared and stumped the bush off a section of the Bulawayo Commonage near the Hillside Tennis Club. There we erected our own goal posts from trees cut on the spot, surmounted by long gum poles for cross bars. There were barely enough of us to field a full team of eleven, but we did manage to do so once or twice for matches with a similar group at Bellevue.

My brothers and I did not engage in horse riding for pleasure. We rode when it was necessary to do an errand, such as collecting the post, or searching for a lost cow. My sisters, however, did ride for pleasure. They frequently went off for long rides with our neighbours, the McCalmans. Isobel was a keen horsewoman and a good linguist. She informed us that our house was known to Africans as Kaya Pezulu — the house high up. This name gradually superseded Ruberslaw.

After Elizabeth had completed her studies at Cape Town University she became a schoolteacher, and in 1922 she was teaching at Plumtree School sixty-five miles from Hillside. At this time, most of her colleagues had steeds of one sort or another and Elizabeth decided to buy a horse of her own. Having done so she wanted to ride it to Plumtree. Jim and I volunteered to accompany her, and we set off one morning early. We had intended to camp out for the night but were persuaded by a gentleman we met at Figtree to call in at a farm belonging to people called Montgomery to spend the night there. We arrived at the Montgomery's unannounced at dusk and they hospitably took the three strangers in. Next day we arrived at Plumtree after nightfall. The following day Jim and I set off on our return; we spent the night camped at a spot near the railway line. It was an eerie feeling to wake in the night with the lights of a passing passenger train blazing in our eyes. I can well understand the tremendous impression made on an African child, now the Rev. Ndabaningi Sithole, when he first saw a passenger train. He recounts this experience in his book *African Nationalism*.

In the morning as we resumed our journey we lost our way and trespassed on the farm of a woman less given to hospitality than the Montgomery's. She sent us on our way with a severe rebuke. We arrived home late in the evening somewhat saddle sore but none the worse for our long ride.

8

Water

———————

I HAVE already referred to the public water supply on which
we depended in the early days at Ruberslaw. In 1916, we
had a rainwater tank connected to the kitchen roof. This had
been one of Father's bargains at the Market Square but it
had a propensity for leaking. We boys had not then acquired
the art of soldering, and so the leaks were patched up with
soap and, later, in our bee-keeping days, with propolis, a
substance that bees make for sealing up apertures in their
hives. During the rainy season this tank, and another connected to the stable roof, held sufficient water for our domestic
needs. When the tanks gave out a piccanin was sent with a
wheelbarrow to the public supply, taking with him four
paraffin tins. After filling these about three-quarters full he
would put in a bunch of leaves from a bondo tree to help
prevent the water from splashing out. On returning with
his load the water was poured into a forty gallon oil drum.
His morning was fully taken up with several trips to the
water tank where he might have to queue up with others on a
similar errand. There were times when there were scenes
at the tank reminiscent of the quarrels between Abraham's
and Lot's servants, and sometimes the piccanin would come
home with little water and a sore head.

After some years had passed, Mother was able to
arrange with a friend who lived about a mile distant to
let us have water from her well. By this time Andrew the
Ox was mature. Mother bought a trained ox, called Eland,
and we decided to fetch the water in the oil drum mounted
on a sleigh which would be drawn across the veld by Andrew
and Eland. There was no difficulty in making the sleigh out

of a forked tree and making a yoke and *skeis** from another
tree, but we had some difficulty in breaking Andrew in to his
new life. When yoked in with Eland he would charge for
the nearest tree and get it between Eland and himself. After
many hard tussles he accepted his lot and the sleigh made a
daily journey along what is now Weir Avenue and through
the Bushman's Spruit at a rather steep drift. This arrangement worked very well for some months until our friend's
fence was broken. Although Jim repaired it to her satisfaction relations were a bit strained. Mother decided that at
all costs we must have a well of our own. She selected a
site conveniently near the kopje and the stables. A gang of
well boys under a "foloman" was engaged and well-sinking
operations began. After going through about eight feet of
gravel, hard rock was struck. A windlass with miner's
bucket was erected over the pit and the hammer boys drilled
into the rock with jumpers and hammers. The "foloman"
charged the holes with dynamite and lit the fuses. After the
blast, time had to be left for the smoke to clear before the
resultant rubble could be removed. Work was disappoint-
ingly slow and the shape of the hole as it descended became
increasingly irregular. Water was struck at about forty feet
but turned out to be "surface water" of considerable nuisance
value. Month after month the work went on, the footage
dwindled and money to pay the boys dwindled also. Eventually we gave up at ninety feet. For a year or two the well
filled up in the rainy season and relieved the necessity of
fetching water by sleigh for part of the year, but it was a
bitter disappointment to Mother.

Father was away during this period but on his return
he pointed out that one of the stands he had bought in 1912
was a "water stand". It was in a vlei about 350 metres
from the house. Well-sinking was begun again on this site.
The going was much easier, a neatly shaped well was sunk
and good water was struck at eighty feet. For a year or two
the water was conveyed to the house in petrol tins loaded
on a scotch cart. Eventually in 1926, Mother was able to
afford the luxury of a windmill and piping. A tank was

---

*Afrikaans word meaning yoke-pin.

installed behind the kitchen and so after a decade at Kaya
Pezulu we had a piped water supply when the wind was
favourable. The windmill served us for twenty years before
municipal water was eventually reticulated in Hillside.

In 1923, Mother engaged a surveyor to locate the
boundaries of the Ruberslaw estate and then we discovered
that the first dud well was exactly in the centre of Stornoway
Road. When the Bulawayo City Council took over Hillside
they filled it up.

From the well boys, my brothers and I learnt how to
blast with dynamite, and this knowledge was put to good use
later in quarrying stone for building the new Kaya Pezulu
and Harthill.

Now that we had water on tap at the top of the kopje
Mother had an incentive to build a bathroom. Sigogo the
gardener had built a stone house for the ducks and the work
looked so good that she tried him out to build an outdoor
bathroom. The old water barrel was converted into a boiler
and we then had hot and cold laid on. Sigogo's efforts were
so successful that next he was given the task of building a
new bedroom for my brothers and me. We quarried the stone
at the south end of the kopje, using home-made gunpowder
for our blasting operations, having learned at school that a
mixture of saltpetre, sulphur and charcoal were the constituents. We bought the first two ingredients from the
chemist and made our own charcoal on the spot. Quantities
of it were needed also for sharpening jumpers, the drills used
for drilling into the rock. During well-sinking operations we
had acquired a forge and learnt to do our own blacksmithing.

9

Building a House

L IVING in a conglomeration of round and square "hawels" on a rocky kopje may be picturesque but in the rainy season it had grave disadvantages. Our dwelling was perched some distance from the cattle kraal and stables, and access between these and our dwelling was a tiresome scramble among the boulders. Mother was an agile, energetic and wiry person, and she determined to improve the access. She got a crowbar and set to work making steps and paths, and removing rocks that were in the way, a process Scots describe as "howking". Our bee-keeping venture was a further incentive to terracing part of the kopje so that the hives could be made more accessible and easier to work at night. During school holidays, my brothers and I assisted in these operations and gradually we acquired some skill in manipulating the crowbar and building massive terrace walls out of huge boulders. As these terraces became more extensive, it became evident that we had an elevated site on which there was room for a fair-sized house. Mother decided that the rectangular buildings already in existence could be incorporated in the new layout. Sigogo was entrusted with the erection of the walls, a slow and laborious operation. First, a new kitchen was built. Then, a large sitting-room was added. Eventually, the original rondavel was pulled down and three bedrooms were built in its place. Building in stages, Jim, who was by this time employed in one of the banks, was able to erect the roof and install floors and ceilings with some help from me during my college vacations. I also assisted in quarrying the stone.

The entire operation was spread over a period of three or four years, during which time, of course, Father and

Mother and some of the family were living on site. After
the first half was completed, we were able to get connected
to the town's electricity. Throughout my school days, we
had depended on paraffin lamps and candles for illumination,
and the first electric light that ever shone on the kopje came
from the headlamps of the Model T Ford. Such things as
fridges were, of course, completely unknown until the 'thirties.

Basically Mother's plan for the house was excellent.
When she died in 1948, and I took over Kaya Pezulu, I was
able to make a number of improvements. The most recent
of these was the extension of the eaves and superimposing
Tile-Lite tiles on the corrugated iron.

The terrace which extends in front of the house to the
north has been converted into a lawn, something undreamed
of in Mother's day, when the surrounds were of gravel and a
windy day brought a large quota of dust on to the verandah.

10

School

————◆————

MY SCHOOL career began at the Eveline High School for Girls which had a mixed kindergarten. Elizabeth, then in the matriculation class, took me on the first day on the carrier of her bicycle, and when I emerged at noon Uncle Jack was there and we repaired to an ice-cream shop, a very rare treat in those days. My two brothers were already at Milton School, where I also went in 1915. After a term in Standard I, I was promoted to Standard II. From then on the three of us were in the same class, which had its complications. We were, in any event, somewhat conspicuous on occasions because, unlike the rest of our classmates, our Sunday best took the form of kilts surmounted by Eton jackets and collars. There were occasions, such as the advent of the school inspectors, or some visiting luminary, when pupils were expected to wear their Sunday best which generally consisted of a school blazer and grey flannel trousers. Nothing would induce the three of us to go to school in our kilts, and we felt somewhat "spare" on these occasions in our usual khaki attire. It was not until 1923, in my last year that I acquired a blazer and was able to merge with the crowd.

Horse transport to school had its drawbacks. If Peggy went astray or cast a shoe, we might have to walk the four miles to school. In the rainy season, we might be held up by Kinnear's Spruit, near the present Bradfield, or an unnamed stream between the Showground and Grey Street, when these came down in spate. On such occasions, when the three Greenfields trooped into the classroom late, one of the wags in the back of the class would sing under his breath "There is a Greenfield far away without a motor car".

REV. C. E. GREENFIELD

MRS. C. E. GREENFIELD

REV. C. E. GREENFIELD, PADRE OF ROYAL SCOTS GREYS, ANGLO-BOER WAR, 1899

MRS. C. E. GREENFIELD, RIDING SIDE SADDLE IN THE HILLSIDE AREA, BULAWAYO

TEMBO

ORIGINAL HUT, KAYA PEZULU, 1913

(Centre): KAYA PEZULU IN 1923, FROM BIG ROCK.
(Bottom): TERRACE WALL BUILT BY THE AUTHOR AND HIS BROTHERS
AT KAYA PEZULU IN ABOUT 1921.

When this was reported to Mother she took the opportunity to point out that the word "without" when used in the hymn is used in quite a different sense from that conveyed in the parody.

Memories that stand out in my decade at Milton are chiefly those concerning aspects of the Kaiser's War. In the years from 1915 to 1918, there were departures, at not infrequent intervals, of senior members of the school to join the war. On such occasions, Mr. E. B. de Beer, the headmaster, would assemble the school to bid farewell to the departing soldiers, some of whom, alas, were destined never to return. I remember clearly the occasion when Tommy Lewis, whose brother Jack was in our class, was reported missing. Fortunately, we were able to rejoice later at the news that he was alive, though a prisoner of war. In the closing stages of the war, Northern Rhodesia was invaded by the Germans from German East Africa (now Tanzania), under their brilliant General Von Lettow Vorbeck. There was great excitement in the Milton Cadet Corps and speculation whether our services might not be needed in defence of our country. We were quite disappointed to find that our help was not needed. Those were the days when we were proud to sing "Land of Hope and Glory". German South-West and German East Africa were added to the Empire, albeit as mandated territories, and we saw in this the fulfilment of the prophecy, "Wider still and wider shall thy bounds be set".

Towards the end of 1918 Bulawayo, like the rest of the world, was smitten by the dread Spanish influenza epidemic to which I have already referred. During this time, or perhaps it may have been the occasion of some other epidemic, the Eveline School where Emily boarded, was closed. Miss Langdon, the headmistress came to an arrangement with Mother whereby a party of the senior girls came out to Hillside and camped at a spot where there is a very large wild fig-tree just about a hundred yards from Kaya Pezulu. They spent about a week camping in the open, and relied on us to organise water supply, firewood and sanitary arrangements. It did not seem to occur to anyone that there was any risk to the girls or their teacher chaperones from "black peril" or other marauders.

When finally the Kaiser was defeated on 11th November, 1918, we celebrated the event at Kaya Pezulu by flying three flags which Father, in his capacity as chaplain to the S.R.V., had procured from the Drill Hall. The Scottish Lion was flown from Mouse Rock, the Union Jack from Big Rock, and the Royal Standard from Leguaan Rock. We kept the flags for future celebrations, which included the arrival of the first aeroplane ever seen in Rhodesia, the *Silver Queen*, piloted by Quinton Brand and Pierre van Ryneveld, in May, 1920. My brothers and I were at the racecourse with the rest of the Milton School, and most of the citizens of Bulawayo, when she arrived. Alas, the following morning we saw her crash. We had heard the roar of her engines, and we climbed Big Rock just in time to see her take off, only to hit a thorn tree near Winnie's Way on the edge of the golf course. We rushed off to the scene on foot and joined a crowd of spectators engaged in picking up scraps of the fuselage as souvenirs. There was a large pool of petrol on the ground which miraculously did not ignite despite the cigarettes of some of the onlookers. The two airmen, fortunately, had no serious injuries. They were able to continue their journey to the Cape a few weeks later in a smaller plane called the *Voortrekker*.

Membership of the school cadet corps entailed attending camp at Gwelo or in the Matopos. Catering arrangements at one such camp I attended in the Matopos were by present-day standards a little primitive. Each section of twelve cadets was issued with a loaf of bread, a pound of butter and a tin of melon and ginger jam, and had to make its own dispositions to keep the butter from melting and the jam and butter from being inundated with flies and ants. However, hot food in various forms was also available. In the year 1920, a highlight was the funeral of Sir Leander Starr Jameson. Milton cadets travelled by train to the Matopo railway terminus. Thence the younger members, including myself, were taken on mule wagons to the lower Outspan. We arrived there at about midday on a very hot day. After a light meal of bread and jam, helped down by strong tea boiled in dixies, we made the ascent of the Hill for the service. Several cadets were overcome by the heat and emotion. When the service was over, those who had marched in the morning were too exhausted to march back, and refused to do so. The younger fry who had come in the wagons had perforce to march back. It was quite late by the time we got back to Bulawayo, and later still when three tired Greenfields got home to Kaya Pezulu from the railway station.

In 1922, Rhodesia was about to undergo a momentous constitutional change after a referendum in which the electorate was given a choice between joining the Union of South Africa and "going it alone" under Responsible Government. Our parents were convinced Unionists, and so was I. Feelings ran high not only on the hustings but also on the playing fields of Milton. In those days there was no turf. The rugby fields were covered with small but sharp pebbles. Some of us Unionists, being in the minority, found the ground very hard during the school breaks, and it could be said that the referendum was fought on the playing fields of Milton. The Responsible Government (R.G.) party won but I felt that the electorate had made a disastrous mistake.

The year 1923 was a memorable one for me. Early that year I acquired my first bicycle. I had won a small scholarship of £7 given by the Bulawayo Caledonian Society. Mother allowed me to spend the money on a bicycle. I was a complete greenhorn and the owner of the cycle shop must have seen me coming because he persuaded me to buy a second-hand racing bicycle with a fixed wheel and low handlebars. A few weeks later I was cycling home from the post office with two parcels held on the handle bars. In front of me as I pushed up the Hillside Road was the late Mr. Tom Meikle, driving his pony cart. I put on a spurt to pass him, but as I did so the chain of my bike broke. It wheeled around in front of Meikle's horse and I fell down. Next moment the horse put its hooves through the back wheel and then came down on its knees. Mr. Meikle, not knowing the cause of my collapse and being a bit shaken himself, managed to get the horse to its feet and drove off while I pushed my broken cycle home disconsolately on its front wheel.

Within a week or two of this occurrence, I returned from school one day with a tremendous pain in the stomach which intensified as the afternoon advanced. At night it was plain that I was desperately ill. Fortunately, this was after the acquisition of the Model T Ford and Jim was despatched in it to fetch Doctor Mitchell. He arrived at about 10.30 p.m. and I was whisked off to hospital and operated on forthwith for a burst appendix followed by peritonitis. I remained in the old Memorial Hospital for seven weeks. In consequence, I did not write the matriculation examination at the end of 1923 as my brothers did, but stayed at Milton for an extra year. A long stay in hospital is in itself quite an educative experience for an adolescent separated temporarily from his family, so when I look back upon this experience I do not count it all as loss.

At the end of 1923, my sister Elizabeth invited me to accompany her on a trip to Beira in what was then Portuguese East Africa, and thence by sea to Lourenço Marques, now called Maputo. On the rail journey to Beira, I stopped for a day or two in Salisbury which was at that time a smaller town than Bulawayo. Beira was interesting because whites travelled through the streets in trolleys pushed by Africans along tram lines laid in the sandy streets. Beira in December was hot but the bathing was lovely as the water was so warm. The trip to L.M. was my first sea voyage and I was violently seasick as soon as I got aboard, with the consequence that I spent the whole voyage on deck and was able to study the deck passengers, mostly Indians from Kenya. I was fascinated by Lourenço Marques and its continental cafes. This was my only visit to Mozambique.

Milton School in my day was not the ideal seat of learning, though I am still grateful for a succession of devoted teachers who did their best in difficult conditions. One of the drawbacks was the age range in my class which invariably included a number of boys several years too old for the rest, who could with advantage have given up the unequal struggle before they did eventually leave. However, the main disadvantage was that whatever cultural activity there was at Milton, in the way of music or debating or speech occasions, occurred in the evenings and was not available for boys like us who lived out of town, dependent on horse transport.

The motto of the Milton School was in Greek, which the headmaster translated for us "Quit ye like men". That was the only Greek I learned, my Latin was adequate for subsequent translating of Justinian's Institutes but I never acquired any facility with Latin verse and gained no insight into any of the classics. We were well grounded in English grammar, mathematics and general science, though what we learnt at Milton in the 'twenties seems rudimentary when compared with what is now learnt at secondary schools. In English literature we "did" Scott's Marmion and two of Shakespeare's plays. The school library did not extend beyond the works of G. A. Henty, R. M. Ballantyne and the like.

Some of my schoolmates sprang from Afrikaner stock and were not entirely at home in the English medium of instruction. This lead to an amusing incident after we had been making an intensive study of Tennyson's immortal poem "The Brook". The lessons, like the brook, seemed to go on for ever. As it happened a school inspector arrived and proceeded to examine the class. He put to a boy near me the pertinent question "What is a brook?" To the consternation of the teacher the boy replied, "A pair of trousers." (*Broek* is the Afrikaans word for trousers).

At Kaya Pezulu we had such a variety of interests of a practical sort that apart from attention to the necessary homework one felt little inclination for reading to occupy one's time. Both my parents were very widely read, and it is perhaps surprising that they did not insist on my following their example. Unfortunately, I usually sat somewhere near the top of my class, and on paper I may have appeared to be receiving an education; the superficialities of it, alas, became all too evident to me as the years went on.

11

College Days

I MATRICULATED in December, 1924 aften ten years at Milton School and won a Government bursary of £80 for three years with which I proceeded to the University of Cape Town in March to study law with the object of going to the Bar. At this time, University fees to live in residence amounted to £60 per annum and tuition and other fees to about £40. I was lucky enough to be awarded a further scholarship for Presbyterian boys, amounting to £30, also tenable for three years, so I was covered for my fees for three years. When Father had ministered at Cape Town in 1920 a benevolent woman gave him £200 as a contribution towards the cost of educating his family. Father handed this money over to me and I banked it on fixed deposit so that it was available for my two final years. I count myself extremely fortunate that I was able to get through my course at Cape Town without financial worry and without imposing a burden on my parents. I did not have a great deal of pocket money but I had enough to get by. Fortunately, at the residence in which I lived, University House, few of my fellow students were affluent.

Among Rhodesians ahead of me in the LL.B. course were Hugh Beadle, W. H. Phear, B. D. Goldberg and H. J. Hoffman. Beadle took a prominent part in student activities and was an all-round sportsman. I saw him in the boxing ring when U.C.T. were ranged against Rhodes University College. He showed himself to be a most courageous fighter. Goldberg subsequently established a very successful attorney's practice at Umtali but his first love was the conservation of natural resources and regional development. In

1953, he became Umtali's representative in the Federal
Assembly and later succeeded me as Minister of Education.
He had the misfortune to lose an ear in a car crash during a
ministerial tour. When next he met his constituents he was
able to exhort them as Mark Antony did in Shakesperian
lines. Hoffman, a most lovable man, crowned a successful
career at the Bar as a Water Court Judge and Workmen's
conciliator. Phear's legal career was interrupted by war
service. On returning to civilian life he found the law less
congenial and turned to tobacco farming. He transformed
a large tract of virgin bushveld into a highly productive farm
with energy and ingenuity which amazed his friends.

On the whole, my five years at Cape Town were happy
but uneventful. At Varsity House more than half the residents were of Afrikaner descent. I had no difficulty in making
friends with them; I am only sorry now that I neglected
opportunities of learning to speak Afrikaans. I returned
home each year for the two annual vacations, a month in
July and three months in the summer. During such vacations,
I frequently accompanied Father on his missionary journeys
to various kraal schools sited at different points within a
range of thirty miles of Bulawayo, and approached by way
of extremely bad roads or tracks through the veld.

In 1927, we went further afield, to the Zimbabwe Ruins,
and in 1928 I made an expedition to the Victoria Falls in
convoy with Mrs. Russell and other members of her family
who drove a Buick. I followed behind in the Model T Ford
enveloped in the dust of the Buick. The journey was spread
over three days. There was no tarmacadam outside the
towns of Bulawayo and Salisbury at this date; strip roads had
not yet been invented, so long journeys of this kind were
quite an adventure and one acquired a good deal of facility
in changing wheels and repairing punctures. When driving
in heavy sand it was a help to the car's engine to deflate the
tyres a little. We arrived at the Falls at night and knew we
were in the vicinity, about five miles before reaching there,
not because of lights, for the whole place was in darkness,
but because of the mighty sound of falling water. We
encamped on the railway reserve, there being at this date no
recognised camping site or national park facilities. Next day

a policeman tried to get us to remove but desisted when he found that Mrs. Russell was the wife of the judge, who had made the necessary arrangements with the railway authorities. We signalled our safe arrival at the Falls by a telegram pre-arranged with the judge : "Right as a trivet".

Apart from these excursions, I usually found plenty to do at Kaya Pezulu in the vacations, assisting in various stages of building operations, or with bee-keeping activities.

In my third year at U.C.T., Mother began to urge me to apply for a Rhodes Scholarship. The idea of going to Oxford had no appeal for me. During my college days at Cape Town I always longed to be back in Rhodesia and I invariably returned twice a year for the winter and summer vacations. To me the prospect of three years in a country as remote as England seemed an unnecessary exile. Accordingly, I resisted her persuasions until 1928 when I was prevailed on to apply and was successful. By rights I should have taken up residence at Oxford in October, 1929, but I was allowed to delay entry until January, 1930 to enable me to sit my final LL.B. at Cape Town in December. Having obtained that degree, I was qualified for admission to practise at the Bar in South Africa and in Southern Rhodesia.

I selected University College on the recommendation of a South African who had recently come down, and was lucky enough to be accepted by this college which claims to be the most ancient in Oxford. There were about eleven Rhodes Scholars there in my time, mostly from South Africa, among a student population of only 180. I continued to study law, and was much impressed by several professors whose lectures I attended but rather less impressed with the celebrated tutorial system as unfortunately Univ was without a law tutor in my first year and I had to go out to one else-where, and when we did acquire a tutor of our own he was inexperienced.

Shortly after I arrived in Oxford I had a visit from a Bulawayo attorney, Mr. H. T. Low (later Sir Henry) who urged me to get myself called to the English Bar with the object of acquiring a qualification to practise in Northern Rhodesia, which used the English legal system. He pointed out that large copper mines were being opened up in the North and that there might be good prospects in a legal practice there. I was impressed with his advice but my Rhodes Scholarship, though adequate for my needs at Oxford, would not stretch to cover the full cost of admission to Gray's Inn. I appealed to Uncle Tom Henderson for help and he very generously paid what was required to enable me to enter the Inn, and I managed out of my scholarship to save enough to pay the fees and costs entailed term by term. I got a 2nd class in the Honours B.A. in Jurisprudence in July, 1931, and also passed Part I of the Bar examinations. In July, 1932 I got a 3rd class pass in the B.C.L. I was becoming somewhat bored with writing examinations but still had Bar final to do. My scholarship held good until the end of the year. The Rhodes Trustees gave me permission to spend my final term in London so as to have the experience of reading in chambers. Through Hugh Beadle, who had preceded me to Oxford in 1928, I had an introduction to Sir George Jones, M.P. and I read in his chambers at 1 Essex Court for a few months before passing my Bar final. During this period I lived at London House, Mecklenberg Square. At this time there were about a hundred residents from all over the Commonwealth.

I enjoyed my time at Oxford at Univ. Apart from fellow Rhodesians, my closest friendships were with an Australian whose father was Bishop of Grafton, two South Africans and a Chinese man from Hong Kong. Like the majority of my Rhodesian and South African contemporaries, I did not find it very easy to make intimate friendships with the indigenous undergraduates. This was hardly surprising as we "colonials" had all had several years at another university before going up to Oxford and were to some extent blasé, and our outlook was rather different from that of home-born Englishmen. I found my membership of Gray's Inn very rewarding; it gave me a *pied a terre* in London, the atmosphere of the Inn even from a student's point of view was charged with the practical application of the law. I participated on two occasions in student moots at which the judges were an impressive array of "benchers", in fact the bench before which I appeared on these occasions was more formidable than any I was to encounter in later life.

At Cape Town in my final year, I had enjoyed the privilege of reading in chambers with Advocate (later Mr. Justice) C. Newton-Thompson. This was a pleasurable experience but hardly as instructive as my shorter term with Sir George Jones in whose chambers there were of course several other barristers and pupils, not to mention the barrister's clerks who played an important part in the pupil's education. One of the advantages of reading in chambers, to a young barrister who intends to practise in England, is the occasional opportunity of meeting solicitors from whom he may hope subsequently to obtain briefs. The only time Sir George ever introduced me to a solicitor it was in these terms: "Mr. Smith, this is Mr. Goldfield of New Zealand."

My vacations, while I was up at Oxford, were spent to a great extent with several relatives in different parts of Scotland and two who lived in England in places as different as Malvern in Worcestershire and Whitehaven in Cumberland. My cousins in Malvern had a lovely house filled with beautiful *objets d'art;* those at Whitehaven were also affluent and included a somewhat eccentric but exceedingly kind first cousin of my mother who was also a temperance enthusiast. On occasions, however, I went to stay as a guest in the homes of perfect strangers in England under a scheme organised by the Lady Frances Ryder assisted by Miss Celia MacDonald of the Isles. These visits were of considerable interest to me and a way of getting further insight into the English way of life, that is to say the way of life of certain "gentlefolk" living in easy circumstances in various beautiful villages or country places. The people with whom I had the good fortune to stay appealed to me greatly because of their easy manners, their kindness to and interest in young men from the dominions and colonies. One sensed a great integrity of character among Lady Frances Ryder's hosts and hostesses. Some of them on occasion must have had to put up with somewhat *gauche* behaviour on the part of their guests, but they were very understanding.

In the summer vacation of 1931, with a fellow Rhodes Scholar from Bulawayo, John Pitt, I crossed to Canada by way of the St. Lawrence and thence by rail to St. Albans, Vermont, in the U.S.A. where we bought an old Chevrolet touring car for $50 and in it paid visits to several aunts and uncles living at Buffalo, Grand Rapids and Duluth. We finished the journey at New York where we sold the Chev for $5 and embarked on the gigantic ocean liner *Leviathan,* 3rd Class, to return to Southampton. This ship was nicknamed the Levi-Nathan. It was built in Germany and formed part of that country's war reparations following the 1914-18 War.

My years at Oxford coincided with the great depression. This had not been very much in evidence at Oxford, though I saw signs of it in Whitehaven's mining community. It was very obvious in the course of our journey in the U.S.A. Incidentally, Prohibition was still in force — to the extent it ever was in force — when we were there. A cousin took us into a "speak easy" but the experience was not very memorable, and on another occasion I attended the trial of a "bootlegger" in a court in Vermont.

The most important event of my Oxford career was my meeting for the first time in Aberdeenshire, and subsequently at Somerville College, with the girl who was to become my wife in 1935 — Florence Couper. She was reading Italian, and one of the highlights of my Oxford days was an expedition by way of a "reading party", which I made with her and a cousin of mine from Aberdeen and several other friends, to a village on the Italian Riviera — Diano Marina — in the spring of 1931. We stayed at a *pensione,* which we had to ourselves, at the cost of three shillings and fourpence per day, wine included, also occasionally octopus.

One of my contemporaries at Oxford, with whom I had also overlapped for a year at the University of Cape Town, was Braam Fischer who won the Orange Free State Rhodes Scholarship in 1930. He had great ability and was one of the most charming and delightful people I have ever known. He was a cousin of Hugh Beadle and like him had a first-class mind allied to great will power and courage. During an

Oxford vacation he went to the U.S.S.R. where he was converted to communism. At Oxford he founded a small club among South Africans called the Saamwerk Club, the object of which was to encourage white South Africans to work together with Africans. On returning to South Africa, he practised as an advocate at Johannesburg where he soon made his mark. From the outset he took a leading part in a movement known as the Joint Council which formed a meeting ground between whites and educated blacks. Although he made no secret of the fact that he was communist he acquired a leading commercial and mining practice and as a silk was much in demand in capitalist litigation. When the National Party gained power in 1948 curbs were put upon his activities but they failed to stop him.

Though I did not share his belief in communism I kept in touch with him whenever I had occasion to visit Johannesburg until about 1958. He was held in very high esteem by many of his fellow advocates until he broke the terms of his bail bond during his trial on charges under the South African laws relating to the suppression of communism. He spent a long period in the underworld having disguised himself to the extent of undergoing plastic surgery to his face, but was eventually arrested and detained for several years, only to emerge on his death bed in, I think, 1973.

While still up at Oxford I watched from a distance political events at home in Rhodesia. The Hon. J. W. Downie who was the Rhodesian High Commissioner in London took a lot of trouble to help Rhodesian students and we were asked to various functions at Rhodesia House in the Strand. Rhodes Scholars were invited to honorary membership of the Royal Empire Society (now the Royal Commonwealth Society) and I availed myself fully of this privilege. There was little at this period to suggest that the Empire was in decay, except for the activities of Mr. Gandhi and others in India. One of my fellow-Rhodesian Rhodes Scholars at Univ had decided on a career in the Colonial Office, and enjoyed a fourth year at Oxford doing the Tropical African Course under the auspices of the Colonial Office, as a prelude to a cadetship in Northern Rhodesia. There were several others at Univ doing this course, among them Rob Moffat, nephew of H. U. Moffat.

As the great depression had now struck Southern Rhodesia, I was also attracted to the idea of a fourth year at Oxford, with the prospect of a career in the service of the Empire to follow. But because of the depression the number of posts on offer was greatly reduced. I survived my first interview but was eliminated in the second round, even though I had signified my willingness to go to the Gilbert and Ellis Islands, sometimes described in those days as the Gilbert and Hellish Islands.

Two Rhodesian Rhodes Scholars who overlapped with me were more successful a year or two later, Evelyn Hone who finished up as Governor of Northern Rhodesia, and John Ingham who became Chief Secretary of Nyasaland for a period before he incurred the displeasure of Dr. Banda.

12

Return to Africa

———————➤———————

A S MY time in England drew to a close when I was living
at London House, preparing for my Bar final, I decided
to return to Bulawayo by an unusual route. The era of long-
distance air travel had not yet arrived but a new railway had
recently been constructed linking Lobito Bay, on the west
coast of Angola, with Elisabethville in the Katanga province
of what was then then the Belgian Congo. There the railway
linked up with the Rhodesia Railway system to the south.

In Aberdeen I had met Sir Robert Williams, a former
associate of Rhodes, who was the builder of the Benguela
Railway, and he kindly gave me letters of introduction to
officials of his company at Lobito and Elisabethville to help
me on my way. At this time Portugal did not encourage
tourists to visit Angola. To get a visa one had to get a
medical certificate from a Portuguese doctor, and a certificate
of "good morals" from a British J.P.

Armed with these I landed at Lobito in February, 1933,
only to find that on the previous day eleven inches of rain
had also landed there and had almost obliterated the railway
line between that port and Benguela some twenty-four miles
away. Lobito was intensely hot, and I did not enjoy the
prospect of spending a fortnight there while the railway was
being repaired. Fortunately, I was able to divide my time
of waiting between Lobito and Benguela, having got a lift
on a motor truck to the latter port, where I stayed for some
days with a shipboard acquaintance who managed a mineral-
water factory there.

Lobito and Benguela were both very unimpressive towns
and I was glad when eventually I boarded the train for the

Congo Belge. After ascending the steep coastal escarpment by rack railway we got into a mountain pass, and the train was hit by a minor avalanche which I had noticed coming down the side of the mountain as we wound our way through a cutting. Fortunately, no significant damage was done and we continued unharmed. Next day, we travelled through bushveld with kopjes strongly resembling parts of the Matopos in Matabeleland.

At Elisabethville, I was shown over the Katanga copper mines. The town was humming with the news of some further progress by Adolf Hitler on his way up the ladder of infamy. I stayed a day or two with friends at Livingstone and saw the Victoria Falls for the second time before catching the night train to Bulawayo. My journey from London to Bulawayo had taken six weeks and I could now claim to have crossed Africa by rail from west to east, having gone from Bulawayo to Beira in 1923 as previously related.

At this time none of my sisters or brothers was married and three of them, Elizabeth, Jane and Jim, were still living at Kaya Pezulu with my elderly parents, a situation which was unusual in 1933 and would be inconceivable a generation later. Jane was about to celebrate her 21st birthday. Emily had taken her medical degree at Cape Town in 1926 but remained in South Africa where, during the war, she attained the rank of Major in the S.A. Medical Corps. Niels, after a brief period with Coghlan and Welsh, followed by a few months with Barclays Bank, joined the civil service. In 1953, when the Federation was formed, he became Secretary to the Treasury in Southern Rhodesia, and like me became involved in constitutional talks with the British government. He acted as adviser to successive Prime Ministers whom he accompanied to London and, in the case of Ian Smith, also to Gibraltar for the *Tiger* talks. He was knighted at the instigation of Winston Field, and now uses the longer version of his name, Cornelius.

In 1933, Elizabeth was acting headmistress of her old school, Eveline High. During that year she happened to be in a butcher shop and the proprietor demanded to know whether she was still a teacher. When she replied in the affirmative he sharpened his knife and said: "Ach! Teaching children! I can tink of nodings vorse!" Perhaps this verdict on her profession turned Elizabeth's thoughts to matrimony as in 1934 she married John Wightman, son of an 1894 pioneer, and became the mother of three children. Their home was just across Stornoway Road from Kaya Pezulu. When the children's education was complete she returned to her old profession, riding to work on a motor cycle.

Jim, on leaving school, joined the Standard Bank, and on retirement was appointed to a senior post in the civil service in Bulawayo. He followed in Father's footsteps in that he devotes much of his time to his church and to lay preaching. His son is a medical missionary at Morgenster.

Jane excelled at sport and represented Rhodesia at hockey. She lived at Kaya Pezulu and was the joy and solace of our parents throughout their declining years.

When I became engaged to marry in 1935, my financial resources were slender. Father suggested that I should build a house on the northern half of the kopje and I gladly availed myself of this site and a loan of £1 000 from Mother. With the experience gained in the building of Kaya Pezulu I was confident of being able to organise the building of my own house. As will appear later I was then a somewhat briefless advocate and so had plenty of time to spare.

I quarried the granite myself and supervised the African stonemasons. When the walls were complete I engaged a contractor to put on the roof, do the floors and finish off the building, while I sailed off to Scotland for my wedding. I carried my bride over the threshold on New Year's Day, 1936. When I made up the final accounts for Harthill, as we called our house, the entire cost, including a large water tank, came to £950, leaving me £50 to pay Mother a year's interest on her loan.

We found life at Harthill very pleasant in proximity to my parents with whom Florence established a very happy relationship. She had a specially close bond with Father. Our son, Ewen, was born in 1938, followed by Caroline in 1941, and Tom in 1943. In 1944 we were saddened by the

THE AUTHOR WITH HIS FATHER, REV. C. E. GREENFIELD (centre),
AND (left to right): 'UNCLE JACK', NIELS (CORNELIUS), JIM, AND
'UNCLE BEN' (GREENFIELD), C. 1917.

RHODES LOOKS NORTH FROM THE INTERSECTION OF EIGHTH AVENUE
AND MAIN STREET, BULAWAYO, TAKEN IN ABOUT 1922.

THE AUTHOR WEARING
HIS CHARACTERISTIC
WIDE-BRIMMED HAT

SIR ALLAN WELSH, C.M.G.
SPEAKER OF THE SOUTHERN
RHODESIA PARLIAMENT

A PICTURE TAKEN IN APRIL, 1946 IN FRONT OF THE HIGH COURT,
BULAWAYO, OF THE FIVE RHODES SCHOLARS WHO WERE ENGAGED
AS COUNSEL IN THE CIVIL ACTION BETWEEN THE BULAWAYO
MUNICIPALITY AND THE RHODESIA CREAMERIES (1936) LTD. THEY
ARE (from left to right): THE AUTHOR, ADVOCATE T. H. W. BEADLE,
JUSTICE R. C. TREDGOLD, ADVOCATE A. SHACKSNOVIS AND MR.
W. H. PHEAR. THE RHODES SCHOLARS COMPRISED FIVE OF THE
SEVEN LEGAL PERSONALITIES ENGAGED IN THE CASE.

(Photo: *The Chronicle*, Bulawayo)

loss of Florence's only brother, David, in the landing at Walcheren.

Father had retired in 1934 with serious heart trouble. He spent most of his time in his rondavel study or in strolling the terrace past the "White Elephant". When the Rhodesian Presbytery assembled in Bulawayo its moderator would call on him as a revered elder statesman of the church. On one of these occasions the late Rev. Dr. Kennedy Grant arrived to be met by Father at the top of the flight of steps leading to the house. "Grant," he said, "Did you know that the scientists have discovered that the apple was not the fruit which caused disruption in the Garden of Eden?" "What did they find?" asked K.G. "A green pair," replied Father, delighting himself and his visitor with this pun.

In 1939, he wrote and published privately a small book entitled *From Afric's Sunny Fountains*. This includes a prophetic address he gave as Moderator of the General Assembly in 1927, about the awakening from slumber of the African giant. It consists mainly of stories based on African folklore told to the boys of Plumtree School. They affectionately dubbed him the pirate captain. On 6th January, 1940 he fell asleep in his study and did not awake. He was buried at the western foot of Big Rock. The funeral procession wound through a rocky passage to the strains of a lament played by Pipe Major Matabele Mac, a Macdonald clansman from Stornoway.

Mother survived a further nine years. Hers was a retiring disposition, much given to unostentatious hospitality. An instance was the case of a schoolmate of mine who boarded the train in Botswana when I was returning home for my first vacation. He was going to join the Standard Bank, so I invited him home with me for a bath and breakfast before he reported for work. Mother ascertained that he had made no plans for lodgings so he returned to spend the night. He remained under her roof till he married in 1934. He ended his banking career as a deputy general manager.

In her earlier years at Bulawayo, Mother had produced two pantomimes very successfully in aid of church funds. In

1933, for the same purpose, she produced Tilly of Blooms-
bury in the old Empire Theatre. She lived to see me elected
to Parliament but died a few months later, at the end of
1948.

I note that Lord Blake affirms that Rhodesia is a
cultural desert. I wonder if it was less so in the era of
Mzilikazi or of Lobengula and whether things will improve
under majority rule. Probably Lord Blake would agree that
there were some oases in the desert, and perhaps I can claim
that Kaya Pezulu was one of these.

13

The Rhodesian Bar

———————

ON MY return to Bulawayo in March, 1933, my eight
years of university studies behind me, there were no
prospects of employment in the local civil service, so depression or no depression there was nothing for it but to try
my fortune at practise at the Bar. For this I was academi-
cally more than usually qualified, but like other newcomers
to the Bar ill-equipped from a practical stand-point. The
High Court at this time had two judges resident in Salisbury,
while the Chief Justice, Sir Fraser Russell, anomalously was
alone in Bulawayo. He had originally been appointed in
1915 from the Cape Bar when he was still in his thirties. He
and his family were intimate friends of my family. There
were perhaps seven or eight advocates in Salisbury and three
in Bulawayo, all of them former Rhodes Scholars. R. C.
Tredgold had been in practice since 1923; his practice
extended to Northern Rhodesia where he had been an acting
judge, at Livingstone, towards the end of the decade. W. H.
Phear and T. H. W. Beadle had been in practice for two
years. It was soon apparent to me that Beadle would make
his mark at the Bar. Phear subsequently became an attorney.

Admission to the Bar in Rhodesia is secured by application to the High Court when one has acquired the necessary qualifications in Roman Dutch law and Statute Law.
The petition for this purpose is drawn by an attorney who
briefs an advocate to appear *pro amico* for the applicant.
Having in mind the friendly interest Mr. H. T. Low had
shown in my career while I was at Oxford, I asked him to
draw my petition and to brief my friend Hugh Beadle to
appear for me. In choosing Low, I made an error of judgment or so it might be thought, because another leading

attorney, the Hon. A. R. Welsh (later Sir Allan), who up to then had been a very close friend of my father, took umbrage at my having bypassed his firm. This caused a serious rift in his friendship with my father, and also had the result that no brief came my way from the firm of Coghlan and Welsh until it was unavoidable, all other advocates being out of town or otherwise unavailable. Welsh was a partner of Sir Charles Coghlan until the latter's death in 1929. He was a very able attorney and had great charm when it pleased him to exert it, but was inclined to be very much of a partisan. After Coghlan's death, he became a member of Parliament but was eventually sidetracked by Huggins into the Speakership in which capacity he ruled Parliament with a stern discipline.

After I had been in practice for several years, my relationship with Welsh improved though I never found it an easy one. Earlier in my account of Kaya Pezulu I have quoted from a tribute paid to my mother by Mrs. Marion Munn. She was Welsh's eldest daughter and inherited his many good qualities and was always a very good friend to my wife and me.

Until 1938, the High Court at Bulawayo was housed in a handsome stone building in Main Street, called Agency Chambers, which had been erected before the end of the nineteenth century. Unfortunately, it was destroyed by fire some years ago. The interior of the Court was not particularly impressive; one of its features was a punkah, which was worked by a wallah from the prison. Advocates rented chambers in the same building, which also housed Messrs. Coghlan and Welsh, and the Chamber of Mines.

The marathon Globe and Phoenix case dealing with important aspects of the gold-mining laws had ended shortly before my admission to practice, save for a subsidiary argument about the costs. After that had been disposed of there was little contested civil litigation until 1935 when the depression began to lift. However, I shared with the other junior advocates in the *pro deo* criminal defences of alleged murderers of which there were usually about fifteen or twenty per annum, if one included the circuit sessions at

Gwelo and Umvuma. I also had a share of the uncontested divorce cases and "motion" work.

It was not until I had been in practice for nearly two years that I was briefed for an opinion, and then only because both Beadle and Tredgold were away for the Christmas vacation, or on shooting trips. My gross earnings in my first year of practice amounted to about £139 from which had to be deducted rent of £3 10/- per month for my chambers. I had virtually no other expenses, because at that time advocates employed no clerical assistants and did not have telephones. We wrote our pleadings and opinions in manuscript and delivered them ourselves by hand to the attorneys who had briefed us. My earnings during the first few years included an occasional guinea for devilling for Beadle, and remuneration for adapting South African correspondence course lectures for the needs of Rhodesian students. I also did some sub-reporting for various law reports and very occasionally was asked to review a newly published legal text book, the remuneration consisting of the reviewer's copy. Another source of income was tutoring articled clerks for their law exams at ten shillings per hour.

During my years at college I had neglected many opportunities of learning to speak in public, but during my final year at Gray's Inn I took part in two moots at that Inn. This was virtually the only practical training I had in the forensic art. It was therefore very fortunate for me that some friends of mine invited me to join them in the formation of the Bulawayo Debating Society. I was appointed Secretary and in that capacity was provided with a telephone, thus becoming the first advocate in Bulawayo, if not in Rhodesia, to be so equipped.

My learned friends were not particularly pleased at this innovation, but in 1934 when Tredgold and Beadle both stood as candidates in the general election they found my telephone very useful. Tredgold was successful in winning the Shabani seat for the United Party and very soon afterwards he took silk and transferred his practice to Salisbury.

During the time he practised in Bulawayo he was often briefed for cases in Salisbury and in Northern Rhodesia.

When my practice overlapped with his I always found him friendly and helpful. Before leaving he presented me with some valuable numbers of the Southern Rhodesia Law Reports, thus enabling me to complete my set of these rather scarce volumes.

It was not long after that he succeeded Vernon Lewis as Minister of Justice. Tredgold's departure from Bulawayo resulted in much more work for Hugh Beadle and my practice also took an upward turn. I usually found myself on the opposite side to Beadle in any contested matter, but occasionally we were on the same side against an opponent specially briefed from the Johannesburg Bar.

In 1935, a grateful client, a woman mining magnate with an impressive personality, showed her appreciation by laying on a camp for us in a place where Hugh could indulge his appetite for buffalo hunting. I knew his reputation as a fearless and tireless hunter of these dangerous beasts. Nevertheless, armed only with my Boer War Mauser carbine, I had the temerity to accompany him on one of these hunts.

Starting at sunrise and taking with us only an apple for sustenance we tramped at least twenty-four miles in pursuit of our quarry, only occasionally visible in fearsome thorny thickets. When we got back to camp at sunset, after a fruitless trek, I was somewhat exhausted, but the distant call of a guinea fowl roused Hugh at once. He dashed off at high speed to return an hour later with something for the pot.

We became firm friends and close associates in the political sphere. In November, 1935 I went to Scotland to be married by which date my income was about £360 per annum. At the outbreak of war in September, 1939, I was earning about £900 a year, and a year or two later I paid war-time excess profits duty on a small surplus over £1 000. Even at this stage, a substantial portion of my income was made up from law reporting and similar extraneous activities.

By this time Harry Davies had joined the Bar in Bulawayo. Hugh Beadle and the fourth member of the Bar were on active service so Harry and I between us shared all the work of the Bar. Harry supplemented his income by running a scheelite mine. He had persuaded me that we ought to afford the luxury of an African messenger. We were not very lucky in our choice of the first such person, because a few months afterwards I found that he had been milking my bank account. Fortunately for me, the cheques he had presented were all bad forgeries as he had spelt my name "Greenfeild", and the bank accepted responsibility for the loss. The next incumbent of the post bore the name "John Horridge", presumably called after a well-known English judge. The work of attending to our messages did not occupy the full time of John Horridge, and in between times Harry occupied him in pounding up the scheelite ore on the verandah outside our chambers.

I cannot claim to have participated in any very noted cases during my early years at the Bar. One of the most interesting perhaps concerned the Watch Tower Bible and Tract Society, now known as Jehovah's Witnesses. This Society had achieved a certain degree of notoriety, especially on the Copperbelt of Northern Rhodesia as Zambia then was. Tredgold had been engaged professionally in certain cases in the aftermath of Watch Tower ceremonies and had formed an adverse opinion of the activities of this religious body. When he became Minister of Justice he introduced into Parliament a Sedition Bill, the main purpose of which was to curb the activities of this society and, in particular, to prevent the distribution of its literature.

The Bill was duly passed and it enabled the Minister to declare certain publications to be seditious. However, a loophole was provided enabling the would-be importer of the "literature" to test the declaration in Court. Hugh Beadle appeared for one, Kabungo, who had endeavoured to import a set of about fifteen books and booklets all of which had come under Tredgold's ban. I appeared for the Crown, and my first task was to peruse the voluminous literature in an effort to identify seditious passages. However, I was unable when the case was presented to persuade Hudson, J. that there was anything seditious in the books.

Government took the case on appeal to the Appellate Division of the Supreme Court of South Africa at Bloemfontein. I was led by Hoexter, Q.C., later a Judge of Appeal. It was disappointing for me, in my first appearance before that very distinguished Appeal Court, to find that my leader had little faith in our case. The early South African Law reports are studded with cases on sedition and treason but these were of sterner stuff than the Watch Tower books, and in the result the decision of Hudson, J. was affirmed. I had conducted the case in Bulawayo for a fee of 25 guineas and at Bloemfontein my fee was two-thirds of the 50 guineas marked on Hoexter's brief. I was somewhat annoyed to discover a few months later that the attorney for the Watch Tower had been allowed a fee of over £100 for "perusing the record on appeal" which included the fifteen books. I am very doubtful whether, in fact, the attorney ever perused this "literature" — a task that occupied me many laborious and unprofitable nights.

14

The British South Africa Police

ONE OF the most difficult but most interesting of the briefs I held, was to represent the non-commissioned and other ranks of the British South Africa Police before a Commission of Inquiry set up in 1946 to go into their grievances. Perhaps I should mention that the B.S.A.P. is Rhodesia's police force, in case readers not conversant with the nomenclature should be misled, as Mrs. Barbara Castle was, into thinking that the force was an offshoot of the South African Police. It was established before Rhodesia got her name, when the country was administered by the British South Africa Company, and it has over the years acquired a fine tradition and won many laurels

From its inception the force was organised on military lines with similar ranks and a stern discipline. During the Hitler War, many of its members served with distinction abroad, in some cases attaining high commissioned rank, but returning to civilian duty with perhaps the status of N.C.O. With the return of peace, it was not surprising that many of the men became impatient with the somewhat military style of discipline which pervaded the system. Up to the outset of the war, and indeed for some years after its conclusion, the majority of recruits came from the "Old Country", many of them products of public schools. In some cases, promotion to commissioned rank had been very rapid and in some quarters it was thought that certain officers lacked the tact and experience to have authority over men with long service in Rhodesian conditions.

The main grievances aired before the Commission related to discipline, promotion, and rates of pay. The chairman was a former Secretary for Agriculture who used the prefix, Major, and was something of a snob, though a man of keen intelligence and high integrity. It was soon apparent that in regard to pay and conditions of service we were pushing at an open door, but on the question of abolition of military ranks and discipline it was very different. It was difficult to get instructions from my clients as the local Bulawayo committee, from whom initial instructions came, did not regard themselves as fully representative, and I had to interview committees in several other centres. The men's leaders were in an awkward position, some of them worried in case there should be victimisation. I had to avoid giving the impression to the Commissioner of Police or the Commission that I was myself an agitator helping to stir up a mutinous band. Then I had the unpleasant task of leading a considerable body of evidence tending to show that certain officers had abused their position by excessive zeal calculated to humiliate the men under them. We led evidence to show that antiquated practices still obtained, for example in the inspection of small rural stations where, on a surprise visit, the member in charge might have to go through the motions of putting his handful of men through barrack square drill, to the amusement of members of the local community who happened to be around.

As I foresaw, the commission at the end of the day recommended a general rise in pay and material improvements, but praised with faint damns the military style in which the force was being ruled. My clients were to a great extent mollified by the improvements in pay and conditions but the committees I had worked with were disappointed with the minor concessions in other respects. Before long, however, it became manifest that the evidence we had led had made an impact on the Commissioner of Police or his superior in the Ministry of Justice. The irksome practices began to be alleviated, and a few years later a new Commissioner took the initiative in recommending the abolition of army ranks. A further outcome of the enquiry was that my friend Hugh Beadle asked me to chair a Police Advisory Board, an office I held only for a few years before succeeding Beadle as Minister responsible for the Police. They came under my jurisdiction in my capacity as Minister of Justice for over three years, in the period 1950 to 1954, and I took great pride in my association with the British South Africa Police whose reputation was second to none among the police forces of the Empire.

15

Northern Rhodesian Interlude

WHEN Tredgold entered the Government, I hoped to inherit his practice in Northern Rhodesia but it was not till 1940 that I began to get briefs there. The Chief Justice resided, and usually sat, at Livingstone but another judge was stationed at Ndola. The Court only occasionally sat at Lusaka. In the North, no distinction was made between barristers and solicitors but I only undertook cases when the brief was arranged by a local practitioner. I appeared on several occasions at Ndola where there was also a resident judge, and once at Lusaka where the Court held periodical sittings.

The Northern judges, whom we in the south always referred to as Colonial Office judges would, before their elevation to the Bench, usually have served in one or more Crown Colonies or Protectorates as Crown Counsel, rising to Solicitor- or Attorney-General. On occasion, they had been senior magistrates. All of those before whom I appeared, with the exception of one who in my time was only an acting judge, were charming gentlemen, but one could see that they were mostly more at home in the realms of criminal law than in civil litigation. Shorthand writers were not employed, and in witness cases the pace was consequently slow. In my day, all the legal practitioners were whites, but the Government was trying to encourage one or two African clerks to qualify for the Bar in London, with, I believe, disappointing results.

On one occasion, I was briefed to defend the reigning Mayor of Ndola who was charged with offences under the income tax laws. In a preliminary examination, the Crown had engaged a chartered accountant to report on the books of account which formed exhibits in the case. I advised that we ought also to engage an accountant to examine the exhibits. As it turned out, this was unfortunate advice, as our accountant went to inspect the exhibits at the High Court and arrived in the nick of time to disturb the white ants which were busy demolishing the evidence. Enough was left to prove the Crown case.

On another occasion, I was in Lusaka to defend in a murder case before the High Court. Before my case came on, the Court had been dealing with an appeal by a young white man who had been convicted by a magistrate whom I knew quite well, and sentenced either to corporal punishment or to a term of imprisonment, I do not now remember which. At all events, the conviction was sustained but the sentence was altered by the substitution of a fine. While still in Lusaka, I met the magistrate who had inflicted the original sentence. He told me that the assault had been a particularly brutal affair, and that after conviction it transpired that the accused had a previous conviction for a similar offence, and had received a warning from the Bench that a repetition would probably result in a sentence of corporal punishment (or it may have been imprisonment). My magistrate friend felt impelled to give effect to this warning. He told me that the judge who heard the appeal had sent for him and had told him that there was nothing wrong with the sentence imposed but that "political considerations required that the sentence be reduced". I had, of course, only the word of the magistrate for this extraordinary story but as he was later elevated to the Bench I am prepared to believe that he told me the truth.

The most notable trial in which I took part was in 1947 at Fort Jameson, in a case known as "the murder in the mosque". The deceased had been shot with a pistol on the steps leading from mosque to courtyard at noon on a Friday when the congregation was dispersing. There were literally hundreds of eyewitnesses. Four men were charged with the crime and each was being separately defended. My client was an old gentleman called Munshi and he was alleged to have fired the shot, incited thereto by the other three, one of whom was a wealthy merchant on whose behalf a well-known South African silk, Advocate Robin Stratford, had been briefed.

Stratford and I were acquainted and we flew together from Bulawayo to Salisbury and thence to Livingstone through quite appalling thunderstorms in a tiny Fox Moth plane. In Livingstone, we were joined by a solicitor and flew on to Fort Jameson in a Dragon Rapide which managed with some difficulty to get through. Rain poured down incessantly and several days elapsed before the Acting Judge and party got through from Ndola. While we were cooling our heels, I discussed matters with Stratford in the hope that we could co-ordinate our defences. He had other ideas. When I informed him that there would be no shorthand writer he was visibly shaken as the case would obviously go on for at least a week. The upshot was that Stratford persuaded me to apply for a separation of trials. My application was supported by Stratford and the case against his client was deferred to await the outcome of the case against the remaining three. Next day Stratford was lucky enough to be able to fly back to Johannesburg.

At the outset of the trial, when Munshi was called on to plead, I asked that the indictment should be interpreted into his own language. The Acting Judge had obviously anticipated my request because he had open on the Bench beside him the Immigration Ordinance, a section of which he proceeded to read. From this it appeared that immigrants to Northern Rhodesia were required to have a knowledge of a European language. His Lordship demanded to know why, in view of this requirement, Munshi needed an interpreter. This somewhat acrid and irrelevant intervention did not inspire me with any confidence in the further proceedings, and as the case proceeded and I cross-examined the first witness the judge in a sarcastic snarl asked whether I seriously expected him to record my questions. However, the trial went on at the halting pace required for longhand notes.

Whenever the Court adjourned, I was surrounded by a throng of Munshi's supporters who made embarrassing offers to procure witnesses on any point I cared to mention. They were most disappointed when I elected to call only two short witnesses besides the accused. I addressed the Court on lines which Stratford had suggested. The solicitors appearing for the other two seemed content to leave it at that and all three accused were acquitted.

Munshi and his supporters saw me off at the airport and I was presented with a watch for myself and a phial of scent for my wife which one of the solicitors told me was Attar of Roses worth at least £10. On my return home, I gave it to my wife but she did not think much of the perfume and said that she would rather have the £10. Subsequent enquiry from a chemist elicited the information that the phial contained Attar of Geraniums worth one and sixpence. Satisfaction in my forensic triumph was short lived, as friends in Ndola took care to inform me that the Acting Judge, whose name in those parts was "Orrible Orace" had been seen in a jeweller's shop selecting some valuable silver plate, the implications of which were not lost on me.

Procedure in criminal trials in Northern Rhodesia conformed to the English practice. One aspect of this seemed to me to be very unjust, namely that when evidence had been fully led and included witnesses for the defence, apart from the accused himself, it was incumbent on defence counsel to address the court first, thus forcing him to anticipate the line to be taken by the prosecutor. When reading a biography of the late Lord Justice Birkett, I learned that he too had regarded this rule as being unfair. I do not know whether it has since been changed.

My experience in the North fortified me in my opinion that the administration of justice in the courts of my own country showed up extremely well in any comparison.

16

Irons in the Fire—1933-1950

DURING the first two or three years of my practice in Bulawayo, Rhodesia was very slowly emerging from the great depression. Memories were still fresh of "bob-a-day Leggate" who, as Minister of Internal Affairs in Moffat's Government, had inaugurated a scheme of relief work for unemployed whites and had been tactless enough to express the opinion that one could live on a shilling a day. Leggate was also a farmer, and the story is told of a farm manager he appointed whose emoluments were carefully prescribed, and included a pint of milk a day. On the first day the manager collected his milk ration in a large Ellis Brown's coffee tin. Next morning he found that a nail hole had been punched in the tin at the pint level. In fairness to Leggate I should point out that the road relief-workers were paid five shillings a day.

Briefs were few and far between in my case, and I had ample leisure to devote to pursuits, some related to the law and others remote from it. I have already touched on the Bulawayo Debating Society. It ran with moderate success for a couple of years after which, to keep interest alive, we converted it into a Parliamentary Society. We found a Speaker, divided ourselves into parties and I assumed the rôle of Parliamentary draftsman besides being Leader of the House. We went through the motions and enacted sundry laws, including a Bill to repeal some ancient Roman legislation known as the *Senatus Consultum Velleianum* and the *Authentica si qua mulier* which survived in Roman Dutch law to prohibit women from undertaking suretyship, and especially so in cases where the principal debtor was the woman's husband. The real Rhodesian Parliament did not emulate this venture into the sphere of Women's Lib until the lapse of two more decades. It was all good clean fun and in my case it helped to bring to life some of the musty themes of constitutional law which had formed a large part of my studies.

Another sideline on which I embarked was the compilation of an index to the Statute Law of Rhodesia which, by 1935, amounted to about 16 volumes. The Law Society paid for the printing and I sold about eighty copies at £1 each which helped to pay for my boat ticket to Scotland where I went to be married towards the end of 1935. An outcome of my venture was that Tredgold appointed me as a member of a commission chaired by Sir Fraser Russell, the Chief Justice, which brought out the first Revised Edition of the Statutes in 1939. This entailed numerous visits to Salisbury and I gained a familiarity with the statutes which stood me in good stead both in my practice and in my subsequent political career. Most of my work on the statutes was done in office hours, but during the time available afterwards I soon became involved in matters affecting the African community in Bulawayo. During the early nineteen thirties, some of the leading citizens, including my father, were giving thought to the plight of urban Africans living in the so-called "location" west of Lobengula Street, and for whom the only amenity, if such it could be called, was the municipal beerhall which dispensed "kaffir beer" by the gallon to men who under its influence sometimes became beasts. The location sported no recreational facilities, and medical treatment was only available for the more serious cases involving hospital treatment, which was given in an annexe to the Old Memorial Hospital.

The outcome of this was the formation of the Bulawayo African Welfare Society. It established a clinic in the location under a white nursing sister, with a black medical orderly to minister to minor ailments. Africans were still reluctant to take the white man's medicine but they soon recognised the value of the clinic, and its functions were extended to maternity services. Sporting facilities were organised, including a soccer league, a boxing ring and athletic track.

Initially, most of the work was done by Detective Inspector R. S. Perry whose achievement was beyond praise.

Very soon after my return from Oxford, my father suggested my name as honorary secretary of the Welfare Society and thus began a long and happy association with other stalwarts of the society, including Arnold Carnegie, a son of the pre-pioneer Hope Fountain missionary, and the Reverend Percy Ibbotson, a Methodist missionary. Percy was a human dynamo, interested in all aspects of social justice and welfare. The society was not confined to white "do-gooders" but included several of the leading members of the urban African community, one being an interpreter in the Native Department called Bradfield J. Mnyanda. I got to know him extremely well as we were also associated in my professional work; he often accompanied me to the Bulawayo Prison when I interviewed *pro Deo* clients, mostly those charged with murder. It was sometimes difficult even with Mnyanda's help to persuade the alleged murderers that my services were being paid for by a benevolent Government in order to help them to escape the rope; on occasion the accused remained convinced that my purpose was to extract a confession for the benefit of the prosecution.

Some years after meeting Mnyanda we became associated as advocate and lay client when he had the misfortune to be charged on four counts of a serious offence. At the trial in the Magistrate's Court, he was defended by an able attorney and was acquitted on two counts. I was briefed in an appeal to the High Court on the other two counts but only succeeded in having one of the convictions quashed, and the remaining one left a nasty stigma. Mnyanda could not afford to brief counsel in a final appeal to the Appellate Division of the Supreme Court of South Africa at Bloemfontein. At my suggestion he presented his appeal in person and succeeded in eliminating the final count. Years later when I met Centlivres, the South African Chief Justice, he told me that Mnyanda had made a powerful impression on the Court. Mr. Mnyanda has since retired to the land of his birth, and has an important post in an industrial concern at Port Elizabeth.

The Welfare Society also raised funds for a recreation hall, and eventually a modest building was erected and officially opened by the Governor who gave it his name — the Stanley Hall. It is still in use but seems insignificant now when compared with newer halls built by the City Council of Bulawayo, which eventually took over much of the work pioneered by the Welfare Society.

In Salisbury, the Anglican and Roman Catholic Bishops, Paget and Chichester took a leading part in a similar society and gradually welfare societies were also started in all the larger towns. A move was made to federate the societies and I was at different times secretary or chairman of the federation. Its activities centred mainly on administrative and legislative reforms in matters affecting Africans, especially in regard to health, education, labour relations and housing. The federation's council met from time to time at different centres and the Government was usually represented at the meetings by senior officials from the Native Department, and the Department of Health. Thus I got to know some of the leading personalities throughout the country. The federation gradually made its influence felt on the Government and on local authorities. As its work expanded the need for a full-time secretary became apparent. Percy Ibbotson volunteered and was seconded by his church for the post which he held with great distinction until his election to the Federal Parliament in 1953 as the European representative of African interests in Southern Rhodesia. He made a number of intensive surveys on juvenile delinquency, housing and the poverty datum line, and his work led to the setting up of remand homes, the appointment of probation officers and so forth. In 1947, when there was a period of industrial unrest, the Government recognised the work of Percy Ibbotson and myself by appointing us to the National Native Labour Board which was required to prescribe minimum rates of pay and conditions of service on the railways and in industries.

On the whole, the Federation of African Welfare Societies steered clear of the more controversial aspects of party political questions, but it did become involved in the question of the electoral franchise. Inevitably, the leading members of the executive were divided on this subject but we did not quarrel over it.

Ibbotson's place as secretary was taken by Dr. E. M. B. West who did excellent work, and converted the federation into an Institute of African Affairs. Unfortunately, interest declined, and with Dr. West's retirement in about 1960 it ceased to exist, although some of the constituent societies are still active.

The African townships of Bulawayo have expanded and increased out of all recognition. The medical, social and sporting activities, previously undertaken in a modest way by the Welfare Society, have in a great measure been taken over by the Housing and Amenities Department — now the Housing and Community Services Department — of the Bulawayo City Council which was under the inspiring administration of Dr. E. H. Ashton until his retirement in 1977. The work that he and his officials have done deservedly wins high praise from visitors from all parts of the world.

My Presbyterian upbringing with its latter-day missionary bias gave me some contact with mission churches and schools in my boyhood, and during my first university vacation in July 1925 I drove a newly-appointed and very raw missionary in the family Model T Ford to the place which has since become the David Livingstone Memorial Mission. There I dumped him and his belongings on the bare veld, on a bleak windy and drizzly day. The buildings which the missionary erected were of a rather poor standard, but a primary school was established. In 1936, the mission got its name as the result of a windfall. The Federated Caledonian Society of Southern Africa erected a statue of the famous explorer which overlooks the Devil's Cataract at the Victoria Falls. The fund collected for the memorial was considerably over-subscribed and Father persuaded the society to devote the surplus to a living memorial. The Caledonians stipulated that a Scottish architect, Donald McGillivray, should be employed to design a new school building to be visible from the Salisbury road, and this was done.

I soon found myself on the committee responsible for this institution, and for the Gloag Ranch Mission and about ten or a dozen kraal schools situated on remote farms or at points in the Tribal Trust Lands in the Bulawayo district. The kraal schools were usually primitive buildings of pole and dagga or Kimberley brick, catering for sub-standards and possibly standards 1, 2 and 3. Usually there would be a single male teacher who had to cope with a range of pupils of all ages and both sexes. I had often visited these schools when Father was missionary superintendent, and I got to know some of the teachers and I realised that they did a difficult job with credit.

Gloag Ranch was bequeathed to the Church by a Matabeleland pioneer who had received 2 000 morgen (about 6 400 acres) as a pioneer grant and called it Half Ration Ranch. The bequest included a substantial, but not vast, sum of money and the testator stipulated that it should be used to establish a school for teaching agriculture and other practical subjects. As the name of the ranch was hardly likely to attract pupils the committee changed it to commemorate the pioneer. Several years elapsed before the buildings and water supply, necessary for a school of this kind, could be erected, and war had broken out before the first pupils were admitted. During the war, it was difficult to find suitable European staff for the David Livingstone and Gloag Missions, and the committee had many problems. For some years the school at Gloag had as its principal Mr. Wellington Manoah Chirwa, who had been born and educated in Nyasaland. When I visited the school, I was always impressed with the tone which was suggestive of a very effective discipline.

Chirwa aspired to higher education and I was able to help him to get a bursary, and with some assistance from the Nyasaland Government he went to Fort Hare in South Africa to take his B.A. degree. From there he went back to Nyasaland, to reappear in 1953 as one of the Africans from that territory appointed to the Parliament of the new Federation of Rhodesia and Nyasaland. He was an able and persistent critic of the Federal Government who by this time had become somewhat militant. Despite his strenuous opposition to the Government, he incurred the displeasure of Dr. Banda by the very fact of his having accepted a seat in Parliament, and in 1958 he declined further nomination. Later he served on the Monckton Commission and signed a minority report. He sought a reconciliation with Dr. Banda but failed, and for many years now he has been an exile in London.

As time went on, I became chairman of the committee and retained that responsibility until 1950. In about 1947, on my return from a trip to the North, I found awaiting me at home a Gloag pupil aged about fourteen who had sinned, and was due to receive a moderate correction with a cane. The boy, whose name was Herbert Chikhomo, decided to appeal to me, as the chairman of the committee, against the sentence. I persuaded him to return and face the music. He did so, and the upshot was that during several vacations he came to my home where we gave him accommodation and work. Subsequently, when he had gone as far as Gloag could take him I helped him to further his studies, and he is now an ordained minister of the Presbyterian Church and responsible for a secondary school in Mashonaland.

I have dwelt, perhaps at undue length, on my association with Messrs. Mnyanda, Chirwa and Chikhomo because I have found that many of Rhodesia's critics, and especially visiting Members of Parliament from Britain, are wont to assume that Rhodesians like myself have no contacts with Africans except their domestic servants.

As chairman of the committee, I had to give periodical accounts of my stewardship to the Presbytery of Rhodesia, and also the General Assembly which met annually at different cities in Southern Africa, as far afield as Cape Town. The venerable General Assembly is not only a court of the church but is a legislature enacting ordinances, debating overtures and adopting deliverances. It has some resemblance to a Parliament and in its heyday its delegates included men of powerful intellect who in other circumstances might well have graced the legislatures of Rhodesia or South Africa. The presentation of a mission's committee report to the Assembly could be something of an ordeal, but the experience so gained no doubt helped to enable me to withstand the slings and arrows that were to come in my subsequent political career. The Assembly was somewhat remote from the day-to-day running of its missionary enterprises in Rhodesia and on occasion showed little understanding of the problems of the men on the spot. In like manner, I was to find that members of the British Government and the House of Commons had a lack of comprehension of political problems in Rhodesia, a lack that was seldom rectified by fleeting fact-finding tours of the Kissinger type.

The Assembly's missions and schools were perennially short of money and, worse still, short of dedicated and capable men and women qualified to administer them. Christian forbearance was not always the most notable attribute among those who laboured in the vineyard, nor of myself who laboured outside. Occasionally, there were wrangles which degenerated into quarrels. I cannot say that the considerable time I spent on the committee's affairs was the happiest of my times. But I must add that among those who served at the David Livingstone and Gloag Missions there were some very devoted men and women of considerable talent who had to work in isolated places, and uncongenial surroundings, subject to the frustrations of inadequate finance and the sometimes irritating control of a committee which seemed as remote from them as the Assembly seemed remote from me. I salute the work of John and Jean Stakesby-Lewis and the Reverend Thomas Erskine, the Reverend John Manod-Williams and their wives who were stationed at David Livingstone or Gloag during my time on the committee. Their work was consolidated by the Reverend A. G. Leask under whose direction both institutions have made notable strides.

Another of my extramural activities during my early years at the Bar was concerned with tribalism. When Matabeleland was occupied in 1893, Scotsmen among the Pioneers lost no time in founding the Bulawayo Caledonian Society and electing Leander Starr Jameson as their first Chief. In 1938, I became one of his successors. One of the main functions, of course, was the annual St Andrews' Nicht banquet.

In earlier years the Government sometimes used the occasion to make policy pronouncements, and generally the speeches took on a political flavour. In 1942, it fell to me to propose the principal toast to The Government and the Land we live in. As a compliment to Sir Godfrey Huggins, I pointed out that he had managed to carry on the Government for eight years without the benefit of a single Scotsman in his Cabinet. As it turned out, he carried on for another eight years before inviting a Scot to join his Cabinet, and then it was I who had the honour.

17

Local Government

———————

IN THE years up to and during the Hitler War, Hillside
had changed comparatively little from the straggling
township set in bushveld interspersed with granite kopjes,
which I had known as a boy. It lay outside the boundaries
of the city of Bulawayo. There was no local authority and
no community or sanitary services though there was a tennis
club, a police station and a primary school. The old common
water supply, provided by Napier and Weir, had long since
fallen into disuse; household water came from rainwater
tanks, wells and boreholes. Roads were dusty and stony
tracks, maintained, if at all, on a do-it-yourself basis.

In 1934, when Hugh Beadle intended to stand for
Hillside, where he lived, he and I discussed a project which
might help to bring him to the notice of the voters.
This was to macadamise the main Hillside road which inter-
sects the township and continues as the Hope Fountain Road.
Hugh Beadle interviewed the Government Road Engineer
who agreed to lay tarmac strips on this section of the road
provided the residents defrayed half the cost. We had to
get £250, a considerable sum to raise among a poor community hit by the depression. Each of us went around with
the hat and we collected £245, but had seemingly exhausted
every source except the late Mr. Tom Meikle who we were
reluctant to approach, although he was probably the
wealthiest man in Rhodesia and lived in Hillside. Eventually,
I went to see him accompanied by a mutual friend, the late
Mr. R. M. Nairn. Meikle at once pointed out that the strips
would be of no use to him as he invariably rode a horse, and
in any event the road to his house turned off before the point

where the strips would be laid. Nairn reminded him that he had bought a piece of land up the Hope Fountain Road as a burial ground, as the old pioneer had no desire to lay his bones in the Bulawayo Cemetery. "When the time comes," said Nairn "you will have a much more comfortable journey on the strips." With that Meikle took the list from us, ran his eye over it and then wrote his cheque for £5.5.0. It is only fair to add that Meikle was a very generous man, but he preferred to do good by stealth.

In the ensuing election campaign, Hugh and I laid stress on the initiative thus taken, but the constituency remained loyal to the sitting member, H. H. Davies, although by a very narrow margin.

By 1942, conditions in Hillside were becoming increasingly difficult and I started a campaign to set up a town management board. The residents reluctantly agreed and I became chairman of the board which started its life without a penny in the coffer, in fact we owed the Government the midwife's fee for bringing us into the world. Dog and bicycle taxes were levied immediately, followed by a rate on land and buildings. A board member donated a cator hut as an office, and a part-time secretary was appointed. When next the post fell vacant, the Mayor of Bulawayo, E. J. Davies, who happened to be the brother of H. H. Davies, M.P., applied for the vacancy and we gladly appointed him. He undertook this humble job at an insignificant salary as a simple service to the community in which he lived. Oh! that all men were like him.

When the board got into its stride we employed a qualified engineer to deal with the roads. Priority was given to constructing a bridge over the Bushman's Spruit; quite a small affair. When completed a notice was erected on either side: Load not to exceed five tons. We arranged an opening ceremony at which Lady Mary Baring, wife of the Governor, Sir Evelyn Baring, graciously cut the tape and was driven across the bridge. Within a week it was brought to my notice that the bridge had subsided, but on inspection I found that our engineer had already had a stone pier erected to support it in the middle; ever since then it has continued in constant use. The cause of the subsidence was a lorry with a heavy load, the combined weight of lorry and load exceeding five tons. The notice was an object lesson in ambiguity.

The City Council had been somewhat contemptuous of the local authority on its doorstep, but after a few years it deigned to negotiate a take-over. Possibly, the incongruity of the city's Mayor being the board's factotum was the motivating force. In any event, incorporation has been a blessing and Hillside now ranks as the most attractive suburb of Bulawayo.

I turned my local government experience to good account in 1948 when I stood as the United Party candidate for Hillside in the general election. The township of Bellevue formed a large part of my constituency. It had not followed Hillside's example of establishing a board and lacked the most elementary services. One of the main planks in my platform was the benefits to be obtained by taking a little initiative, such as I would do, and the sitting Member had failed to do for Bellevue. In due course, I was able to help Bellevue to get organised, and its board completely transformed that suburb. When I look back on my Parliamentary career I derive some satisfaction from the improvements which came about in Bellevue, by self help and hard work on the part of a handful of residents at my prompting.

Before recalling events when I was personally involved in politics I shall review briefly the constitutional and political developments which occurred in my boyhood and when I was a young man.

18

The 1922 Referendum and following decade

IN 1909 when I arrived in Bulawayo as a two-year-old white settler, an historical convention was deliberating at Durban on the formation of the Union of South Africa out of the Cape Colony, Natal, the Orange River Colony (better known as the Orange Free State) and the Transvaal. Rhodesia was represented by Sir Charles Coghlan, leader of the unofficial members of the Legislative Council. He had been an attorney in Kimberley, before founding the Bulawayo firm of Coghlan and Welsh.

Rhodes had been passionately keen on the unification of South Africa, and he contemplated the inclusion of Rhodesia as part of the grand design. This appears from the clause in his will relating to burials in the Matopos in which he stipulated that the authority to decide who should lie near him at Malindidzimu should be the "Federal Government of South Africa". In 1909, Coghlan had a narrower vision and did not press for Rhodesia's inclusion. The representatives of the Transvaal and the Orange Free State thought that Rhodesia would turn the scales in favour of the more liberal "native policies" of the Cape and Natal, so they did not want Rhodesia to be included. In any event, the opportunity was lost for Rhodesia to get in on the ground floor.

In 1922, another opportunity was afforded by Winston Churchill who, as Colonial Secretary, gave the Rhodesian electorate the choice of linking up with the Union or "going it alone" as a self-governing colony. By this time, General Smuts, who had followed General Botha as Prime Minister of South Africa, was keen to draw Southern Rhodesia into the Union fold, hoping that its Parliamentary representatives in the South African Assembly would join his party and help to keep him in power at the general election which was then looming up.

In the referendum campaign Sir Charles Coghlan led the Responsible Government party (R.G.) against Union. They made much play upon the racial prejudices of the voters but on this occasion the races involved were not white and black but British and Afrikaner. Joining the Union would have entailed bilingualism for Rhodesia, and much was made of this bogey, added to which the voters were told that Rhodesia would be flooded with poor whites, of whom there was at that time no dearth in South Africa. Spokesmen for R.G. even managed to assert that Rhodes, had he been alive, would have been on their side.

The Unionists suffered from the disability of having no popular leader. Their case was based on economic considerations, and the fact that Southern Rhodesia on its own would be a landlocked country dependent on the Portuguese port of Beira. As a broad generalisation, with some very obvious exceptions, the Unionists were the intelligentsia among the electorate. Coghlan drew much of his support from those who subsequently formed the Rhodesia Labour Party. He carried the day but not by an overwhelming majority — 8 774 voted for self-government and 5 989 for Union.

Churchill himself was believed to favour Rhodesia joining the Union, and I think it is a great pity that he did not assert himself instead of leaving the decision to the voters upon whose emotions such play was made. I always believed that the decision to go it alone was a disastrous mistake. Apart from Rhodesia's own selfish interests, her junction with South Africa at this critical stage could have maintained Smuts in power and changed the whole course of South Africa's history. As it was, in 1924, General Hertzog made an alliance with the South African Labour Party and was able to oust Smuts under the pact. In Rhodesia, at the general election which followed the referendum in 1923, Coghlan did not have to rely on the Rhodesia Labour Party.

His Rhodesia Party included several prominent Unionists, among them Mr. Godfrey Martin Huggins, the Salisbury surgeon who had not voted at the referendum because he paired off with his wife, Blanche, who was anti-Union.

Coghlan included in his Cabinet one or two Ministers who had not campaigned with him for Responsible Government, notably R. J. Hudson (later Sir Robert Hudson, Chief Justice).

Until 1923, the status of Southern Rhodesia was a protectorate. As a prelude to becoming the Colony of Southern Rhodesia it was annexed to the Crown. During the next thirty years, no stigma was attached to the word "colony", and "colonialism" was a word yet to be invented. It was usual for the Government, and the public alike, to refer to the country as "the Colony" in contradistinction to "the Union". Although technically a colony of Great Britain, in reality Southern Rhodesia was a colony of the Cape Colony, whose Prime Minister, in 1890, was the founder of Rhodesia, and whose legal system and laws she followed. Southern Rhodesia was never a charge upon the British taxpayer. The best the British Government could do for the new Colony, in 1923, was to lend it £2 million.

Long before Responsible Government, indeed before the end of the nineteenth century, Southern Rhodesia had a rudimentary parliamentary system, namely a legislative council, some of whose members were elected by the general public, that is to say the white general public. The voters rolls were open to members of all races but there were income and property qualifications and, in practice, few, if any, blacks sought registration. In the 1923 Constitution, the B.S.A. Company's Administrator was replaced by a Governor appointed by what used to be called the Imperial Government, and the Legislative Council was replaced by a parliament of thirty elected members. The Governor had certain rights of veto which in practice were never used. The executive was a Cabinet whose head was called the "Premier", until 1933 when "Prime Minister" was substituted. It became fashionable when Britain began to grant independence to numerous former colonies to speak of Parliaments on the "Westminster model". Southern Rhodesia's Parliament from

1923 onwards fell within this description. In forms and ceremonies there was a strong resemblance to the House of Commons, but in practice a House of thirty members, none of whom has ever the least difficulty in catching the Speaker's eye, is somewhat different from an assemblage of over 600 members.

Coghlan died in 1927 and was accorded a burial at the Matopos, not quite as near to the founder as Jameson. He was succeeded as Premier by H. U. Moffat. There were two opposition parties, the more numerous of which was at times called the Progressive Party, and at times the Reform Party. The other was the Rhodesia Labour Party led by H. H. Davies whose most notable henchman was L. J. W. Keller, a railway trade unionist. Its main purpose seemed to be the protection of the white worker against black competition and consequently it drew much of its support from the less affluent sections of the white community.

19

Back - Room Politics—1933 Onwards

SOON after putting up my plate at Agency Chambers in Bulawayo I was invited to the 1933 annual congress of the Rhodesia Party. H. U. Moffat had resigned from the Premiership, and George Mitchell led the party at the ensuing election when it was defeated by the Reform Party led by Huggins, who was well known in Salisbury but little known, at that time, in Bulawayo. The defeat of the Rhodesia Party came as no surprise to me. The impression I had gained of the party at the congress was that of an ultra-conservative, unimaginative body. A. R. Welsh was in the chair and ruled the proceedings with a heavy hand.

Huggins's Parliamentary following was a motley band which included some difficult people, among them Sir Hugh Williams, Bt., a mining man with a perpetual feud against the B.S.A. Company, whose mineral rights Moffat's Government had recently purchased. Huggins was not the man to knuckle down under threats from his extremist followers and he discarded some of the wild men and formed an alliance with the Rhodesia Party, out of which arose the United Party, of which I became a foundation member in the company of Tredgold and Beadle. The Rhodesia Party did not dissolve but went into moth balls for the time being, largely at the insistence of Welsh who had no particular love for Huggins and suspected that the United Party would not hold together for long. To consolidate his position, Huggins called for a general election, which took place in 1934. The United Party faced opposition on two fronts, the recalcitrant members of the Reform Party under Williams and the Labour Party under H. H. Davies. The United Party carried the day. Tredgold was elected for Shabani, and to facilitate his parliamentary duties he transferred his practice to Salisbury and took silk.

It was at this election, as previously stated, that I had my first taste of electioneering, on behalf of Hugh Beadle. After the first flush of victory, members of the Rhodesia Party wing of the United Party had a disappointment, and some felt deep resentment because Huggins took only one of their number, Sir Percy Fynn, into his Cabinet. There were murmurings which led Moffat to attempt a comeback to the political scene. Tredgold who was Moffat's nephew, however, held firmly to the United Party. A congress of the Rhodesia Party was called and a majority led by Col. Lucas Guest and Tredgold resolved to get rid of the skeleton in the cupboard by dissolving the party. Moffat and a few supporters, however, "seized the typewriter" and carried on as a rump which at a by-election, during the war years, managed to secure the election of Leggate to whom I have already referred. In the meantime, Welsh who was not enamoured of either Huggins or Moffat accepted the post of Speaker.

Hugh Beadle and I continued to play an active rôle in the United Party organisation. It soon became apparent to us that Huggins had a mastery of constitutional principles and a sound grasp of the essentials of practical politics. Guest and Tredgold were taken into the Cabinet at a later stage, and the Government went ahead with an energetic programme of development of roads and electricity supplies. The party policy included amalgamation with Northern Rhodesia and the acquisition of a West Coast port. The latter of these topics was a regular subject of debate and there were sponsors of Walvis Bay or Tiger Bay near the mouth of the Cunene River. No one at that time seemed to bother about the indeterminate status of South West Africa. Huggins, however, concentrated on the removal of restrictive clauses in the Constitution conferred by Letters Patent in 1923 rather than on the matters of a port, and paid periodical visits to London in this connection. From 1935 onwards he was invited to attend the Imperial Conference and did so in the company of the Prime Ministers of the United Kingdom, Canada, Australia, New Zealand and South Africa. Writers on constitutional law began to refer to Southern Rhodesia as a quasi dominion. In 1944, for the first time, India was represented at these gatherings though not yet by a Prime Minister.

Huggins took the opportunity of overseas visits to press the matter of amalgamation with Northern Rhodesia. Eventually, in 1938, the Bledisloe Commission was sent out by the British Government to report on this question. Its report was a disappointment for amalgamationists. Although the commission agreed that amalgamation was sound in principle they said that the time was not ripe, but they recommended setting up an inter-territorial council to deal with common services. The outbreak of war in September, 1939 put a stop to any progress until 1945 when the Central African Council was established for this purpose.

In April, 1939 Huggins, realising that war was imminent, called a general election and the United Party was returned with 23 Members to the Labour Party's seven. Hugh Beadle won the Bulawayo North seat. The new Parliament also included Edgar Whitehead who had been at University College, Oxford, though two or three years before me. On the outbreak of war, Huggins invited H. H. Davies and Keller to join his Cabinet, which they agreed to do. Tredgold became Minister of Defence and no time was lost getting Rhodesian forces into the field. An Air Squadron went north before the declaration of war and very soon afterwards a large contingent of men was sent to West Africa to become Officers and N.C.O.s in African Battalions. Among them was Hugh Beadle; later Whitehead also went to West Africa to join Lord Swinton's staff, and several other M.P.s joined the colours.

The inclusion of Davies and Keller in the Cabinet caused jealousies in the Labour Party who were in any case becoming divided on the issue of the participation of blacks in politics. The party split in two, one section under Macintyre favoured the formation of separate branches for blacks in the Labour Party. The section under Davies would have no truck with this. It is of interest that one of Macintyre's followers at this time was Miss Joan Lestor, who has since then for many years been a critic of "white settlers", from Labour Party platforms in the United Kingdom. During 1940, Hugh Beadle was recalled from West Africa to become Parliamentary Private Secretary to the Prime Minister.

The United Party's domestic policy took second place to the war effort but congresses were still held annually. In November 1941, Huggins made an important pronouncement on native policy. Incidentally, his speech was made when he opened the new school buildings at the David Livingstone Mission. It is probable that his thinking had been influenced by developments which had taken place in the Union of South Africa under the United Party Government of Generals Hertzog and Smuts. They had removed blacks from the common voters roll in the Cape Province and substituted a form of special representation for them in Parliament by Europeans. In his speech, Huggins said that the voting rights enjoyed by blacks on the common voters roll were not of much practical use to them in regard to representation in Parliament. He proposed that they should cease to be eligible for the common voters roll but that an alternative method of direct representation should be introduced. He pointed to the fact that in the northern protectorates blacks did not enjoy the vote in Legislative Council elections.

On reference to my own file of speeches, I find that in August, 1942 I spoke to the Left Club on the same subject. I was not a member of that club which was composed of a few intellectuals whose enthusiasm had received a boost from Russia's entry into the war. I supported the views of Huggins in his 1941 speech, indeed my address followed the lines of a "bill" which P. B. (Ben) Fletcher had introduced in the Parliamentary Debating Society in 1937 or 1938. Following this talk, I had a letter from an old U.C.T. friend, Julius Lewin, now a distinguished professor, in which he said "I doubt whether there is any subject more worthwhile pressing at the moment than this . . . the successful working of our (i.e. the South African) Native Representation Act should provide a good example to the British Colonies . . . However, I think it is important that the members should be elected and not nominated . . . and that it should be made clear that special representation is not necessarily an alternative to the common franchise but a supplement to it until such time as it becomes effective." He referred to the fact that the Southern Rhodesia voters roll at that date included 48 blacks. The subject of Parliamentary representation of blacks was also engaging the attention of the Federation of African Welfare Societies.

In 1943, Tredgold was appointed to a vacancy on the Bench and became resident judge at Bulawayo. His replacement in the justice portfolio was H. Bertin, K.C. who, in his day, had been an able advocate, but whose mental powers were in decline. Wartime restrictions were beginning to have an effect on the electorate who were becoming restive. Within the United Party there was increasing lethargy. Hugh Beadle worked hard to keep interest alive in Matabeleland but elsewhere little was done by M.P.s. Friends of mine in Bulawayo were expressing dissatisfaction with Huggins's *laissez-faire* attitude to the country's domestic problems. It was felt that with the end of the war in sight a more dynamic government was needed. My views were sought about the current political ills. I attended a meeting of a small group who wanted to ginger up the Government. Some were toying with the idea of a new party but ran into the difficulty, which has always bedevilled Rhodesian politics, of finding a leader of any quality. My advice was that, owing to apathy in the United Party organisation, it would be easy for a determined group to infiltrate the party, capture its machinery, infuse new ideas into it and use it to achieve the purposes they desired. This advice was not immediately accepted.

The group, now called the Action Group, decided that before rushing into the political arena they should produce a detailed policy; they set about doing so and for months members debated papers on various aspects of social and economic questions. Some of the group were convinced that an ideal policy could be produced such that on publication the electorate would spontaneously hail it as a proper blueprint for post-war society and entrust its authors with the task of implementing it. I realised that this was naive but it was refreshing to find some other men of my own age-group who were prepared to give time and thought to politics so I stayed with the group while these exercises continued.

The first paper to be discussed concerned the difficulties confronting a would-be Member of Parliament who was in the prime of life. The thesis was that the poor showing of past and present parliaments was due to a lack of a leisured and affluent class who could devote the necessary time to national affairs. Our parliaments, so the argument ran, had been largely composed of two kinds of people: retired men with their future behind them, or self-made, monied merchants or farmers who had accumulated their pile because they were selfish, and *ex-hypothesi* were not the kind to serve their fellow citizens. Up-and-coming younger men with an unselfish urge to serve their fellows could not afford to jeopardise their careers for the risks and poor rewards of a political life. At this time, if memory serves, M.P.s were paid, with allowances, only £350 per annum. The group wanted safeguards for defeated candidates and better salaries for the victorious.

As time went on and slow progress was made in shaping the Utopian policy I urged the group to cut short its academic studies and to embark on active politics thus giving credibility to the name Action Group. In May, 1944 my advice was followed but a substantial minority broke away. The purified group met Huggins to discuss the security/pay issue. He conceded that there was a certain validity in the arguments but thought that there were corresponding dangers, summing up by saying that he would give the scheme his blessing but would not go to the cross over it. The group was satisfied with this modest progress in the pursuit of the ideal and publicly announced its accession to the United Party. Members then set about joining their local branches and from there several secured election to the party executive and nomination as delegates to the ensuing congresses. In fact, things worked out much as I had predicted except that the group's influence was limited to the Bulawayo area. An attempt to form a similar group in Salisbury had a limited success, and it died away after about two years.

By 1945, Huggins had fallen out with Smit, the Minister of Finance, who for want of anyone else with political experience (backed by some finance) became the leader of a considerable band of political malcontents. They formed a new party under the singularly ill-chosen name of the Liberal Party. Smit's principal attribute as Minister of Finance had been the capacity to say "no", and his leadership was hardly inspiring, but the party had a number of energetic supporters.

Their battle cry was "Time for a change", and when their election manifesto appeared the main point of difference from the United Party was in the sphere of "native policy" where they propounded somewhat nebulous proposals known as the "two pyramid scheme". They never managed to field a complete team of 30 candidates despite strenuous attempts at sheep stealing from the United Party.

20

General Elections—1946 and 1948

B^Y 1945 a general election was overdue but it was postponed to enable returning soldiers to vote. I was hoping to be nominated for Bulawayo East but failed to get the nomination. The Action Group fielded two candidates. E. T. Hepburn, a nephew of "Hep" who is mentioned earlier in this book, was one of them and he was nominated for Hillside. He had to resign his post with the Rhodesia Railways in order to stand. He put up a very good fight against H. H. Davies, the veteran Labour leader, but was defeated and he subsequently encountered the very difficulties to which the Action Group had called attention. I believe that his effort did much to soften up the position for me when, in September, 1948, I stood for the same seat.

The outcome of the 1946 election was a near-disaster for the United Party though Huggins fared better than did his illustrious wartime contemporary, Winston Churchill, in 1945. When the results were declared the United Party had only 13 seats, Liberals 12 and Labour 5. Fortunately, an election petition gave one more seat to the United Party at the expense of the Liberals, and Huggins carried on the Government by the grace of one or other of the two Labour parties. Whitehead had been earmarked for the finance portfolio but was defeated, and a place had to be found for him by means of a by-election. Hugh Beadle became Minister of Justice and had three other portfolios, namely Internal Affairs, Education and Health. A newcomer to the Parliament was R. S. Garfield Todd, representing Shabani. He had come from New Zealand in 1934 as a missionary in charge of the Dadaya Mission.

It seemed that the country would face a period of political instability and moves were made to reconcile the Liberals and the United Party. I attended a meeting of representatives of both parties. The Liberals refused to accept the leadership of Huggins but would have settled for Guest, but he would not desert his leader. With the failure of these fusion talks, the parties began to gird up their loins for a general election which could not be very long delayed. The Action Group had enjoyed the 1946 election battles and its members continued to work with enthusiasm for the United Party. Macintyre decided to join the United Party and claimed to give it a blood transfusion. Meanwhile, in May, 1948, the whole of Southern Africa was profoundly shaken by the defeat of General Smuts and the transfer of power to the National Party under Dr. D. F. Malan's leadership.

The 1948 general election came in September on a seemingly trivial issue, concerned with the building of a Reserve Bank, but a principle was involved as this was to be part of the common services for the two Rhodesias and Nyasaland under the umbrella of the Central African Council.

The constituency of Hillside covered a considerable area and included Bellevue and other peri-urban suburbs. Petrol rationing was still in force so I acquired a motor cycle on which to do my canvassing. I prevailed on Garfield Todd, who was a most eloquent speaker, to appear with me at some meetings. He also used a motor cycle and had a nasty fall on his return to Shabani at night. I had a three-cornered fight against H. H. Davies and Dr. Olive Robertson (later Senator Robertson) who was the Liberal candidate. I won with less than half the votes. The United Party had a landslide victory taking 24 seats. The Liberals had five and Jack Keller was the only Labour Party survivor. Smit lost his seat and R. O. Stockil (now Sir Raymond) became Leader of the Opposition. His team included the youngest member of the House, Ian D. Smith. Newcomers in the United Party ranks included the Hon. Humphrey Gibbs, who years later became the last Governor of Rhodesia. The electorate which was worried by the political uncertainty of the 1946-1948 years gave a sigh of relief at the prospect of five years of stable government under a trusted leader whose team included a strong infusion of younger men.

After 15 years of dabbling in party politics outside Parliament, I was looking forward to the real thing inside. The complacency of the newly-elected United Party members soon received a severe jolt. At an early meeting of the caucus, Whitehead informed us that the financial resources of the Government were in a precarious state and that it would be necessary to make a raid upon tobacco-growers. Some of these were members of the caucus and reacted immediately. I had known Whitehead for a few years, had formed a good opinion of his ability, and greatly admired his capacity for lucid exposition of economic and financial questions, and in company with some of the other newcomers to the fold I allowed myself to be persuaded that his proposals were vitally necessary; we supported the Government and he got his way. When his proposals were divulged in Parliament the storm broke and rocked the party, despite its numerical strength in the House. Eventually, Whitehead was compelled to climb down, and substitute a forced loan for a tax. From this time on, I always had reservations about Whitehead's political judgment. Apart from this, 1949 was for me politically uneventful.

During that same year, Beadle piloted a Citizenship Bill through Parliament, thus bringing the territory into line with Australia, New Zealand and South Africa which had followed Canada's lead in enacting their own nationality laws.

In 1950, he embarked on a more controversial subject, legislation to curb subversive activities. In its original form, his Bill went to lengths which I thought were unnecessary and I became its principal critic in caucus. Meanwhile, Tredgold asked me to see him, and informed me that he was very disturbed by the proposals, so much so that if they were not watered down considerably he might resign from the Bench and, as he put it "carry the fiery cross through the land". I was able to tell him that I had already taken up the cudgels, and expected to secure some alterations to the Bill. I have always found that Hugh Beadle is amenable to persuasion if one has a sound case, and in this instance I was not disappointed, and Tredgold did not resign.

During 1949, there had been some Press speculation that I might be appointed to the portfolio of Native Affairs of which the Prime Minister wished to relieve himself. Some people thought that my long association with the United Party behind the scenes, coupled with my activities in the Federation of African Welfare Societies, made me a likely candidate for the post. Although it seemed to me to be a possibility I thought that Garfield Todd, who had longer parliamentary experience, had an equal if not better chance of the appointment. I happened to meet Sir Ernest Guest who dropped a hint that the post would go to a man with much longer parliamentary experience than Todd. Soon after this, W. A. E. Winterton, who up to that time had not, as far as I am aware, displayed any particular interest in the black section of the population, was chosen. Subsequently, in a reshuffle he became Minister of Trade, while P. B. Fletcher took Native Affairs.

As 1950 progressed, I was beginning to feel the impact on my practice of lengthy absences in Salisbury. My difficulties were not eased by the fact that, in 1949, Hugh Beadle had insisted that I should take silk. In May, 1950, an event occurred causing a chain reaction which had a profound effect in my life. Vernon Lewis, the Chief Justice, died suddenly. Tredgold became Chief Justice in his place, and Beadle took the vacant seat on the Bench as resident judge in Bulawayo. Huggins announced the appointment on 30th June, and offered me two of Beadle's four portfolios, namely Internal Affairs and Justice. It was with a sense of relief that I accepted. I was sworn in on 20th July, and almost my first assignment in my new capacity as Leader of the Bar, was to make one of the welcoming speeches when Hugh Beadle was sworn in at the High Court on the following day. His removal from the political scene deprived Rhodesia of one of its ablest administrators and legislators, and deprived the United Party of one of its most active and assiduous workers. His capacity for work and the quickness of his thinking are phenomenal, as his subsequent career on the Bench has amply demonstrated. Hugh Beadle has his detractors but I have always found him a staunch and loyal friend, and one who put service to his country first and foremost and laboured unceasingly on what he believed to be its true interests.* My Cabinet colleagues delegated to me the task of finding a candidate for the parliamentary vacancy in Bulawayo North; I persuaded Cyril Hatty to stand, and he was duly elected.

---

*It is unfortunate that Lord Blake quotes a disparaging remark made about him by a biased witness, namely Sir Harold Wilson, without mentioning that Wilson, on another occasion, credited Beadle with the courage of a lion.

21

The Electoral Franchise and Dominion Status

IN ITS 1946 election manifesto the United Party had stated as part of its objectives "The attainment of Dominion Status by the progressive removal of all restrictions in the Constitution; amalgamation with Northern Rhodesia and Nyasaland subject to a referendum." Under the heading of "Political representation" it promised that blacks would be given a form of representation on the electoral college system, the foundation of which would be councils in the rural areas and advisory boards in the urban areas. The manifesto went on: "In the meantime, in order to prevent the exploitation of immature voters, legislation will be introduced immediately to prevent the enrolment of black voters without removing those already there, and to provide temporarily for the appointment to the Legislative Assembly of special European Representatives of (black) interests on a basis to be agreed if possible with other parties."

As the election did not give the United Party a simple majority, let alone two-thirds needed for constitutional changes, no progress was made during the sixth Parliament, but the 1948 manifesto repeated the 1946 proposals. In 1949, with the election safely behind him Huggins, accompanied by Whitehead, held discussions at the Victoria Falls with Roy Welensky and other representatives of the northern territories, under the chairmanship of Sir Miles Thomas of B.O.A.C., on the subject of closer association between the two Rhodesias and Nyasaland, and in the same year Beadle was sent on a mission to London for discussions with the Commonwealth Relations Office.

In 1950, Stockil stole a march on Huggins by proposing the appointment of a select committee to consider the basis on which the country could hope to go forward to "dominion status". In view of its election manifesto, the Government had no alternative but to accept the motion. I was put on the committee while still on the back benches and remained on it after becoming a Minister until it reported in 1951. The details of the report are now only of academic interest. The main recommendation was to create a second chamber in which provision would be made for representation of blacks, on the assumption that on this basis the British Government might be prepared to cut away the apron strings and grant the country independence. It has often been asserted that if the Federation of Rhodesia and Nyasaland had not been formed, Southern Rhodesia would have got dominion status during the 'fifties. I myself, when writing in 1959 about the future of the Federation, said something to this effect. Further experience of dealings with the British Government has led me to doubt whether I was correct. I think that during the relevant period and subsequently, British Ministers, whether Labour or Conservative, were of the opinion that a mistake had been made in 1910 when the Union of South Africa was created without securing political rights for the indigenous and coloured population. They were determined, I believe, not to repeat this fundamental error, as they saw it, in the case of Rhodesia. The coming to power of the National Party in South Africa in 1948, and the introduction of the apartheid policy there, reinforced their views. What I am now inclined to believe is that Dominion Status would have been conceded to Southern Rhodesia only on terms equivalent to those which were rejected by the Rhodesian Front Government shortly before U.D.I. It is possible that such terms might have been acceptable to the electorate of Southern Rhodesia in the 'fifties, but who can tell?

The recommendations of Stockil's Select Committee were overtaken by other events. During 1950, Huggins suggested to the British Government that closer association should be discussed by a committee of civil servants representing the four Governments involved. On the 8th

November, 1950, James Griffiths, then Colonial Secretary, announced in the House of Commons his Government's acceptance of this suggestion and the appointment of a committee to be chaired by G. H. Baxter of the C.R.O. The Deputy Secretary for Internal Affairs at this time was A. D. Evans (now Sir Athol). He and I had been closely associated in the work of the Russell Commission in 1937-8 and had frequently appeared on opposite sides in criminal cases when he was a Crown Counsel. We knew each other intimately and I saw to it that he was made a member of the Southern Rhodesia team in the Baxter enquiry. He was a strong advocate of federation and I am sure that his warm personality did much to bring about the positive recommendations in favour of Federation which emerged when the committee's report appeared in June, 1951.

Before I go on to deal with the Baxter Report and its effect on Stockil's Select Committee Report I must take up the subject of the electoral franchise. During 1950, Huggins advised a congress of the United Party that it would be unwise to proceed with the 1948 election manifesto proposals because of the possible adverse effects on the climate of world opinion. It was not without difficulty that he got his way. He himself was always prepared to change his mind if circumstances dictated the need to do so and he disliked having his hands tied by party resolutions. He always felt able to take in his stride criticism that a departure from an election manifesto would be a breach of faith with the electorate.

It was the sort of dilemma which often faces politicians but Huggins believed that the Government's overriding duty was to do whatever was in the national interest in the circumstances of the day. He was impatient of suggestions that his freedom to manoeuvre should be hampered by party political resolutions taken when the circumstances were different. Some members of the party disagreed strongly. Congress temporised and decided that instead of proceeding with separate representation for blacks, the common voters roll should be retained in the meantime, but the qualifications required for getting on to the roll should be stiffened up so as to put a brake on black involvement and thus lessen the fears of those who were worried that white voters might eventually be swamped by large numbers of immature blacks.

It fell to me when Parliament resumed in February, 1951 to introduce the Electoral Amendment Bill to give effect to the congress decision. As the new minister facing Parliament in that capacity for the first time, it was not an easy task, so I took the precaution of showing the outlines of my speech to Huggins. He received me courteously but appeared to be rather unconcerned with the arguments I proposed to use to justify the proposals themselves and their departure from the party manifesto. The Bill provided for a change in the educational qualification for voters who had to be able to satisfy the registering officer that they had an adequate knowledge of English. It also provided for a substantial increase in the property or alternative income qualifications. It would be boring to repeat here my arguments which are in Hansard. Suffice to say that the Opposition let me down more lightly than did some of the United Party members who were angry at what they regarded as a breach of faith with the electorate. The Bill was accepted, but I was later taken to task by Sir Ernest Guest, one of my predecessors as Minister of Internal Affairs, who objected to the somewhat blunt manner in which I had introduced the Bill. However, the important point is that the common voters roll was retained and later on it was carried over into the Federal sphere. It was eventually eliminated by the Rhodesian Front Government headed by Ian Smith when they enacted the 1969 Constitution.

22

The Baxter Report and The Victoria Falls Conference—1951

THE BAXTER REPORT was not published until 13th June, 1951 when James Griffiths informed the House of Commons that it was a constructive approach to the problems of Central Africa, and announced that he and Patrick Gordon Walker, Secretary of State for Commonwealth Relations, would go there for discussions with whites and blacks, and then attend a conference with Southern Rhodesian Ministers and representatives of Governments, and the people in Northern Rhodesia and Nyasaland at the Victoria Falls. Baxter had recommended that the three territories should be associated in a federal form of government, with the territorial Governments retaining control of those matters most closely related to the life and ways of the black inhabitants. There should be an African Affairs Board outside Parliament to examine proposed federal legislation which would be reserved for the approval of the British Government in the event of an adverse report. There should also be a Minister for African Affairs to be appointed by the Governor-General in his discretion. The Federal Parliament was to include three persons from each territory nominated to represent African interests, and 26 other members. One of the most important statements in the report concerned partnership between the races. "The conference believes strongly that economic and political partnership between Europeans and Africans is the only policy which can succeed in the conditions of Central Africa."

I was less than enthusiastic at the terms of the report and thought that our Government would have the greatest difficulty in persuading our electorate to embark on federation on any such basis. However, the proposals were a basis for discussion and it seemed to me that efforts should now be made, using the report as a springboard, to negotiate better terms. I was, however, very concerned that the whole matter should be handled with care in case opposition to the proposals should get out of hand. I knew that Huggins considered the report to be a breakthrough, and I wondered how he would proceed to deal with it. It seemed probable that the Opposition, who now called themselves the Rhodesia Party, would be antagonistic, as the effect of the report would clearly be to cut right across Stockil's carefully nurtured scheme for dominion status. Accordingly, I went to see Huggins, and in the course of our discussions it transpired that he visualised federation being brought about by agreement among the four Governments without the necessity of a referendum in Southern Rhodesia. When I drew his attention to our election manifesto in which a principle was "Amalgamation subject to a referendum" he expressed the opinion that the party was not bound to have a referendum for federation because this was different from amalgamation. I impressed on him that if a referendum was necessary for amalgamation it was even more necessary for federation which for all of us was second best. In the course of discussion on the Baxter Report in Parliament on 20th June, 1951, Huggins referred in his own inimitable way to this discussion with me, and committed the Government to a referendum. In future negotiations with the United Kingdom Government, we made considerable use of the argument that whatever point we were objecting to would militate against the success of the referendum. We thus had a counter to the U.K. and Northern Governments when they argued that things we wanted would be objectionable to black. opinion.

The Baxter Report aroused immense public interest, and in United Party circles there was a demand for discussion. Before Gordon Walker arrived, it was arranged that Huggins and I should meet the central executive of the United Party at meetings in Bulawayo on 16th July, and at Salisbury later. We planned it on the basis that I would deal with all

the gloomy side of the proposals and then Huggins would
follow and "cheer the people up". These meetings proved
very successful.

Gordon Walker visited Southern Rhodesia in September
while Griffiths went north. The former was obviously quite
keen on promoting federation. Griffiths on the other hand
seems to have concentrated on listening to black objectors in
the north without making much effort to persuade them of
the merits of federation.

Huggins's team for the Falls Conference included Whitehead, Fletcher and myself, and the opposition were represented by Stockil, Keller and Eastwood. From the Northern
Territories came their Governors and leading officials, while
Roy Welensky and Malcolm Barrow headed the unofficials.
Two blacks from Northern Rhodesia attended and expressed
opposition to federation, but blacks from Nyasaland refused
to attend. The chair was taken by Sir John Kennedy,
Governor of Southern Rhodesia, but as no agenda had been
prepared the proceedings took the form of a series of
speeches.

Griffiths took the line that when calling the conference
he had made it clear that there was no intention of reaching
decisions which would bind any government. He therefore
declined to take the proposals in the Baxter Report as a
starting point for further discussion. However, he broke
his own rule by insisting that certain pronouncements should
be made to allay the fears of blacks in the northern territories.
Consequently, the final communique said that in any further
conference two points would be regarded as settled: namely,
that in the northern territories the protectorate status would
be preserved, and land, land settlement and political advancement of the people, both in local and in territorial government,
must remain a territorial responsibility. Griffiths reaffirmed
that his Government welcomed the Baxter pronouncement
on partnership. In the course of doing so he said that blacks
in Northern Rhodesia had accepted a vital change from paramountcy to partnership. Blacks in Nyasaland, however, had
not yet accepted that change of policy. Sir Gilbert Rennie,

Governor of Northern Rhodesia, also said that the policy of partnership had been accepted in that territory.* Patrick Gordon Walker played a minor rôle in the proceedings while Griffiths went out of his way to make a fuss of the black representatives from Northern Rhodesia.

The conference came to an abrupt end because British Ministers had news of an impending general election and were anxious to get home. It was intimated that the conference would reassemble about the middle of 1952. By the time Huggins met his own Parliament in November, 1951, Winston Churchill had been restored to office in the United Kingdom at the head of a Conservative Government. Huggins felt able, in forthright terms, to voice his disapproval of Griffiths and the way he had handled the Victoria Falls Conference. For my part, I kept in close touch with the Action Group in Bulawayo and with the United Party organisation there.

---

*The policy of partnership had been enunciated by Lord Listowel, Minister of State for Colonial Affairs on 30th November, 1949 when he said in the House of Lords: "What we want is a partnership between all who have made their homes in these territories."

23

Political Partnership

———◆———

WHEN the Federation of Rhodesia and Nyasaland was created nearly two years after the Victoria Falls conference, one of the fundamental principles was that there should be a partnership between the races, that is to say between white and black. Up to the time of that conference, as far as my memory serves, I had never given any thought to partnership as a political concept. Certainly, the term was not in use in the political circles among which I moved. The attitude both of those in power and those I knew who were aspiring to power, was one of paternalism towards the black section of the population. Their political advancement was thought of as a long-range affair. They would have to try their hand at local government in their residential areas adjacent to the cities, or in their tribal districts, and their participation in the central government seemed so remote that no serious thought was given to it. There was some concern that the common voters roll might have dangers in allowing blacks to influence elections before they were ready to exercise this responsibility. There was some anxiety that the British Government might embarrass us by over-hasty political advancement of blacks in Northern Rhodesia. Past pronouncements about paramountcy of black interests in the north were unwelcome in the south.

When, therefore, Griffiths had made it clear that the policy of paramountcy had been dropped and that partnership had been substituted, this represented to my mind a gain, but I began to see that if we in the south were to form political links with the north we, too, should have to accept political partnership as a policy for the whole. For myself this was not difficult, but I foresaw that it would be difficult to persuade a large section of the Southern Rhodesian electorate that this policy was right. It must be remembered that at this time there were no black professional men in either of the Rhodesias, if one excepts the clergy and the school-teachers. There was not a single black lawyer, doctor, dentist, engineer, accountant, architect or surveyor in any of the three territories although, of course, Hastings Kamuzu Banda had qualified as a medical doctor and was practising in London. There were probably fewer than ten blacks with university degrees. They held no senior posts in government service except as court interpreters and teachers. Relatively few outside these callings had any facility in speaking English. The white electorate was slow to grasp the speed with which changes would come as the result of the opening of secondary schools for blacks and the founding of the University of Rhodesia.

The first occasion on which I recollect Huggins referring to partnership as a political concept was on 19th November, 1951. He was speaking in a debate on a motion introduced in Parliament by Stockil on dominion status. Huggins then attempted a broad definition of partnership, though it was not perhaps as well expressed as one could wish. He said: "It means that you are working for a common purpose, and that you are not equal and . . . that there must be junior and senior partners, and as a junior in this case the native gradually works himself up in the business. He becomes a senior but it also has another implication. Having become a senior it stops. There can be no domination by either partner, and no racial superiority comes in at any stage."

It was at the insistence of the British Government that the reference to partnership was written into the preamble to the Federal Constitution in 1953. The term was never defined. Our political opponents from time to time demanded that we should define the term. During the referendum campaign, and subsequently on many occasions, I was challenged to define it. Generally, I would stress that, as in commercial partnerships, the essence of the matter was engaging in a common enterprise with a view to sharing the benefits. I also expressed the belief that a great political concept like partnership should not be put in the strait jacket of a definition.

It was most unfortunate that Huggins, in an unguarded moment, referred to partnership in terms which did immense harm to the cause of Federation, by referring to the partnership between the horse and its rider.*   Our enemies never ceased to quote this comparison, and never quoted what Huggins said in Parliament on the occasion I have referred to above.   I think it can fairly be said that we in the Federal Government throughout its ten-year life made an honest and sustained effort to implement the policy of political partnership.   It was the British Government which went back on this policy and substituted the principle of "majority rule" in the full realisation that this would mean the end of any political power-sharing by whites in the two northern territories, and the substitution of domination by blacks in those territories.

From the time when Iain Mcleod and Duncan Sandys became respectively Colonial and Commonwealth Relations Secretaries of State, the term "partnership" was discontinued from the pronouncements of British ministers though I frequently reminded Sandys that this was the policy we were pledged to follow.   Since the break-up of the Federation in 1963 successive British Governments have done their utmost to hasten the day of majority rule in Rhodesia south of the Zambezi though they must realise that here too the whites will be excluded from any share in the government.

---

*The circumstances in which he made this comparison are related by Gann and Gelfand in *Huggins of Rhodesia — The Man and His Country,* London, George Allen and Unwin, 1964, p.270.

24

Immigrants

———◆———

DURING the period that I was Minister of Internal Affairs, immigration was one of my principal responsibilities. In the immediate post-war years Whitehead and Beadle had done their best to take advantage of the chance to gain white immigrants whose skills could help Rhodesia to develop its potential as part of the Commonwealth. By 1950, the tide of immigrants was so strong that Beadle had to impose some curbs. The majority were coming from South Africa, some of them having been disturbed by the advent to power of the National Party with its policy of apartheid. With Rhodes' advice in mind they looked north, thinking that they would be happier in a British Colony which seemed to be on the threshold of development.

There were many others whose sentiments were not notably pro-British. However, an association in Rhodesia called the Sons of England became a thorn in my side. They were obsessed with the idea that Afrikanerdom was making a take-over bid, starting by infiltrating the country with Afrikaners much in the way that Hitler manoeuvered things in Czechoslovakia.

In this thinking they were in the good company of the Colonial Secretary, James Griffiths and his successor, Oliver Lyttelton. The minutes of the 1951 Victoria Falls conference record Griffiths thus: "Second, there were political reasons (for closer association); chiefly the need to create a strong British Central Africa which, looking for its guidance and inspiration to Britain and the Commonwealth, would be in a position to resist the Afrikaner challenge." He referred to the fact that during the last six years it was estimated that

174 persons had immigrated to Northern Rhodesia from the Union of South Africa for every 100 persons from Britain and said that if this trend were allowed to continue the Afrikaner danger would have disastrous results. Gordon Walker touched on the same theme.

Oliver Lyttelton, Viscount Chandos, discussing the reasons for establishing federation, says in his Memoirs:* "Another political reason, now conveniently forgotten, has to be added. Afrikaner elements had begun to penetrate deeply into Southern and, to a lesser extent, into Northern Rhodesia. The Broederbond was the active instrument of this invasion. It was calculated that Afrikaners would certainly hold political power in Southern Rhodesia within a decade and might, within that time, force a federation of Southern Rhodesia with the Union."

To what extent Huggins really shared these views I was never very certain. Though he had been a Unionist in 1922 he was inclined to be contemptuous of Afrikaners and sometimes made reference to them in terms which acutely embarrassed United Party candidates at elections where the voters rolls undoubtedly showed a large number of people with Afrikaans names. At the Victoria Falls conference he is recorded thus, "In Southern Rhodesia it was realised that union with Northern Rhodesia and Nyasaland was essential if Rhodesia was to retain its independence. The expansionist policy — Krugerism — of the Union of South Africa was a very real threat to Southern Rhodesia and there was also danger in the present spread of Afrikanerism in Northern Rhodesia. The position had become critical and Southern Rhodesia and Northern Rhodesia might well find themselves eventually engulfed if nothing were done now."

My distinct impression is that Huggins, who was well aware of Griffiths' views, played up to them, regarding the alleged Afrikaner menace as the point most likely to influence a decision to federate. I often wondered why the Colonial Office, holding the views they did, were unable themselves

---

The Memoirs of Lord Chandos by Oliver Lyttelton, Viscount Chandos. London, Bodley Head, 1962, p.387.

to control the tides of immigration in Northern Rhodesia, and
looked to a federal government to pull the chestnuts out of
the fire.   For myself, I had no evidence of Broederbond
activity, and the idea that it might wish to force a federation
between the Union and the Rhodesias, or Southern Rhodesia
seemed unlikely.   What I think may have been in the mind
of the Broederbond was that the presence of large numbers
of Afrikaners in Rhodesia would be likely to influence the
electorate in such a way as to prevent a slide to majority
rule.   But this is speculation.

Returning to my own problem, our social services,
especially in the realm of education, were under severe strain
and the immigration tide had to be curbed.   Curbs of any
kind were unpopular with certain pressure groups who wanted
to build up the proportion of white to black in the population
by the immigration of millions of whites.   They were completely unrealistic in the comparisons they kept pressing on
me with Australia.   The Sons of England wanted curbs on
Afrikaners.   Strangely enough, many of their number were
South Africans who had belonged to the parent body in
South Africa.   Quite apart from the fact that as a South
African-born Scot I was not very sympathetic to this brand
of jingoism, it was obviously politically inexpedient to risk a
quarrel with South Africa which pursued a good neighbourly
policy and on whom we very largely depended for university
places for our students (both white and black), for our Court
of Appeal in civil cases, and for a multitude of other things.
Even if one wished to curb the inflow of Afrikaners as distinct
from English-speaking South Africans, which I did not, there
was no easy means of distinguishing them as names are
certainly not an infallible guide.

However, the pressures on me continued and I bowed
to them to the extent of setting up a quota system coupled
with provision for incentives to immigrants from overseas.
I justified this differentiation in treatment on the basis that
we wanted people who were likely to settle permanently and
this was more likely in the case of overseas immigrants who
had a long way to go back, than with South Africans who
could come and go quite easily.   At all events, the South
African Government did not appear to take umbrage and the

quota system operated in a satisfactory way.   Our selection board was somewhat choosy, and on the whole only people of a good standard were allowed to come in.

25

The London Conference of 1952

DURING the debate in November, 1951, already referred
to, Stockil was fighting a rear-guard battle to save his
dominion status report. I had been involved in the report
as a member of the select committee and, as the Government's principal spokesman on constitutional questions, apart
from the Prime Minister, my position was somewhat invidious.
I endeavoured to make the point that it would be futile to
press on with the proposal for a Senate for Southern Rhodesia while the prospect of federation with the Northern
Territories remained open. I pointed out that the proposed
federation was a constitutional freak in that it involved an
association between territories at different stages of constitutional advancement, and I went on to say that if Southern
Rhodesia took unto itself a second chamber it would make
the association even more lopsided. Inevitably, it would
mean that the Federal Assembly would also have to be
bicameral. I added that dominion status in itself would solve
no problems. The purpose of the senate, in the Stockil
Committee's Report, was to take the place of the Secretary
of State in regard to discriminatory legislation. In the past,
no insuperable difficulty had been encountered in dealing
with the Secretary of State, but the senate might prove to be
a more difficult horse to ride.

One might carry the simile of horses and riders further
by comparing a Rhodesian Prime Minister in the days of
Federation with a circus performer endeavouring to ride two
horses at the same time — one being the Rhodesian electorate
and the other the U.K. Parliament. Inevitably, there would
be occasions when remarks made in order to woo voters in
Rhodesia would cause consternation in the House of

Commons. Vice versa, British Ministers would make pronouncements for home consumption which antagonised the electorate in Rhodesia and made the task of its Prime Minister very difficult.

On 22nd November, 1951, shortly before Parliament adjourned, Huggins sent a letter to each M.P. asking for his views on the Baxter Report so that he could have these views collated before going to London in January, 1952 to discuss Federation with the U.K. Government. His own Ministers received the same letter, and I replied in some detail. I listed four main objections, namely the failure to recommend amalgamation in place of federation, the provision of 13 nominated members in a legislature of 35, the proposal for a Minister of African Affairs to be nominated by the Governor-General, and the proposal for an African Affairs Board extraneous to Parliament. It had already become clear that the last two of these objections unless removed would prove fatal to the success of the referendum.

The Prime Minister was accompanied to London only by Whitehead and a few officials. Between 22nd January and 4th February, 1952, he had a series of nine meetings with the two new Secretaries of State and the two Northern Governors; Lord Ismay, Secretary of State for Commonwealth Relations presided. Both he and Mr. Oliver Lyttelton showed themselves determined from the start to push the cause of federation. Agreement was reached on several important points. Amalgamation was ruled out but so was the Minister of African Affairs who had become known as the cuckoo in the nest. It was made clear to Huggins that the U.K. Government would be prepared to override black opposition if need be. Finally, it was agreed that draftsmen should prepare in outline a federal scheme for discussion at a conference to be held in London in April. This result was a notable achievement for Huggins and Whitehead. The communique at the end of their talks was discreetly silent about the points I have referred to above.

The promised conference assembled at Lancaster House, London, on 23rd April, 1952. P. B. Fletcher and I flew over together, and when our plane landed in Kano in Nigeria we were given an opportunity of a quick tour of that fascinating city. It was my first visit to London since 1935 but there was little time for relaxation, as the Conference settled in to hard detailed work. Lord Ismay's place at the Commonwealth Office had been taken by Lord Salisbury who presided at the Conference, alternating with Oliver Lyttelton. They were accompanied by their Ministers of State, J. G. Foster, Q.C., and Alan Lennox-Boyd respectively. Roy Welensky headed the Northern Rhodesia unofficials and Malcolm Barrow those from Nyasaland. John Moffat was among the Northern Rhodesians to represent black views. The Southern Rhodesian contingent included Stockil and Eastwood from opposition parties, and Messrs. Jasper Savanhu and Joshua Nkomo, whom Huggins had included so as to be able to put the black viewpoint. Blacks from Northern Rhodesia and Nyasaland had boycotted the conference. Several committees were established and I took part chiefly in the Legal committee chaired by Foster, and the Civil Service committee. Foster was a charming and delightful personality. As a barrister with a leading practice in commercial matters of an international character, he was capable of making up his own mind without undue reliance on civil servants. He had a complete grasp of the constitutional issues involved and was much less concerned with the repercussions of the proposals in U.K. political circles than with their intrinsic merits.

The conference worked to an agenda prepared by a steering committee, which included Whitehead who was very much of an Englishman with a public school and Oxford background and able to hold his own in any company. The Rhodesian delegation was, in my view, severely handicapped by Huggins' apparently casual approach. He seldom made any effort to discuss tactics with his colleagues, let alone with Stockil and Eastwood. He was not easily accessible at any time, and less so in London than in Salisbury where at least he could occasionally be pinned down in his office. One had largely to rely on his private secretary as a go-between. I usually found him receptive of ideas and suggestions, but the difficulty was to get to him to discuss points that arose from time to time.

Our team included Athol Evans and Victor Robinson, Q.C. who were first-class advisers and in no way inferior to the English civil servants present, but they were very hard pressed. A marked feature of the conference was the influence exerted by the British civil servants, especially those from the Colonial Office. Often we won a point in open conference only to find that next day the civil servants had managed to persuade their Ministers to go back on the decision. Nevertheless, progress was made.

Savanhu made a considerable impact on the conference. The thinking of British Ministers was that subjects affecting blacks should be left to the territorial governments. Savanhu took them by surprise by seeking to have black education and other matters put on the Federal list because he believed that the Federal Government and Parliament would have more financial resources than the territorial governments and that with the special provisions for black representation in the Federal Parliament, which had no counterpart in the Southern Rhodesian Parliament, blacks were likely to get a better deal from the Federal Government. Although he made a deep impression on this point, British Ministers clung to their formula that matters affecting the daily life of blacks must be dealt with by territorial governments. They thus allowed a position to arise in which white and coloured education was put on the Federal list, while black education was on the Territorial list, and never the twain could meet except at the university level. It is fair to say, however, that when Savanhu was making his point the rest of the Rhodesian team maintained silence because we realised that if black and white education appeared together on the Federal slate the anti-federationists would have been given a trump card for use at the referendum.

Subsequent events in Southern Rhodesia's general election of 1962, when Whitehead was not very careful about the question of school integration, go, I think, to prove my point. The Rhodesian Front at that election made immense play with the suggestion that Whitehead intended to force integration in the schools. It is not only in Southern Rhodesia that this is a delicate issue, as events in Boston, Massachusetts, will show.

The conference ratified the various points that Huggins had gained in his January discussions with the Secretaries of State, and it also accepted a scheme which the Southern Rhodesia team had prepared for the election of the three persons for Southern Rhodesia who were to represent black interests.   We were opposed on principle to nominated Members of Parliament, as they would not fit into the party political system and might form a sort of Irish party holding the balance of power.   We proposed that the three representatives of black interests in Southern Rhodesia should be elected, using for this purpose the common voters roll, one of them would be white and two would be black.   Each would require to have his nomination paper signed by at least 25 African voters.   The white man would be elected by the entire electorate of Southern Rhodesia treating the whole country as a single constituency.   The two blacks would represent Mashonaland and Matabeleland respectively, and the electoral districts in these provinces would be grouped together to form two constituencies.   Thus every person on the voters roll would have three votes, to choose : (1) the member for his constituency, (2) the white man to represent black interests, and (3) the black man for Mashonaland or Matabeleland, as the case might be, to represent black interests.

I was surprised to find that the rest of the conference seemed supremely unconcerned with the method we suggested for choosing these representatives and our scheme was passed without any comment.   Nobody suggested that it was unfair to put the election of these representatives under the control of a predominantly white electorate.   Had anyone done so we would have pointed out the advantages of involving white voters in the election of blacks which I shall refer to later.   In each of the northern territories, the white man to represent black interests was to be nominated by the Governor while the two blacks were to be chosen by African Representative Councils, no white person having any voice in their election.

The final communique issued on 5th May, 1952 stated that agreement had been reached on a draft constitutional scheme and that Fiscal, Judicial and Public Service Commissions would be set up to fill in the details of certain parts. When their reports were available, a final conference would be held to put the draft into finished form.

Before leaving the Lancaster House conference of 1952, mention may be made of the remarks of Joshua Nkomo in one of the closing speeches. He said that he and Savanhu considered themselves fortunate in having attended and that much of their suspicion regarding the proposals for federation had been dispelled, and it was now their duty to try to persuade blacks in Southern Rhodesia to support federation. This would not be an easy task. It would help if some of the discriminatory laws in Southern Rhodesia could be repealed. Even more important were the day-to-day relations between whites and blacks. I may add that considerable pressures were exerted, in London, on Messrs. Savanhu and Nkomo to boycott the conference but they stuck it out to the end.

After our return from London, Huggins initiated a debate on 23rd June, on the White Paper which contained the proposals, though as yet they were incomplete because the three commissions had not done their work. In a long and forthright speech he prophesied a poor future for Rhodesia if federation did not come about and if the European section of the population did not take steps to bring the black population into partnership. He stressed the need for a strong British bloc in south-central Africa and said, "We should have the courage of our convictions and attempt to set a pattern for Africa. The Empire was not founded by people who were ashamed of their traditions, or lacking in a belief of their fitness to govern, or afraid to take risks in pursuance of what they believed to be right." He spoke of the undesirability of giving the vote to people who were not yet fitted for it, but said that blacks who qualified by education and civilisation must be accepted as voters. He quoted Chief Awolowo of Nigeria as saying, "The articulate minority are destined to rule the country . . . it is they who must be trained in the art of Government so as to enable them to take over complete control of the affairs of their country . . . they will always remain in the minority." He went on, "We must unhesitatingly reject a doctrine that our supremacy at present rests on colour of skin . . . the only supremacy there should be in this country is the supremacy of civilised people."

Quoting Lord Bryce the eminent Victorian, he said, "Do not give to a people institutions for which it is unripe, in the simple faith that the tool will give skill to the workman's hand. Respect facts. Man is in each country not what we may wish him to be but what nature and history have made him." Referring to the Gold Coast (now Ghana), he said, "In this part of Africa we are at a turning point. In the northern territories there are signs of a conflict. The increasing white population is seeking a greater degree of autonomy while the natives there, encouraged by the Colonial Office experiment in the Gold Coast, are mistakenly thinking that that has set a pattern which they can follow. They are carrying on much agitation to this effect despite the fact that successive British Governments constantly assured them that conditions in Central Africa are totally unlike those of West Africa and that there can never be domination of one race by another."

Stockil came out strongly against federation. He conceded that Huggins's notion of using Southern Rhodesia "as a braking power on the Gold Coast idea developing in the Northern Territories" was a laudable aim but wondered whether it was not too late. He alleged that federation meant a virtual loss of self-government because of "Colonial Office" control of the federal legislature in which Southern Rhodesia would have less than half the members. Subsequent events proved that Stockil had justification for his doubts on the first score, as I shall show later, when I deal with the way the Macmillan Government, in a great betrayal, went back on all the assurances and pledges which their predecessors had given to Southern Rhodesia when federation was inaugurated. As regards Colonial Office control of the Federal legislature, Stockil was clearly wrong, as I pointed out in the debate by saying that to the extent that the northern territories surrendered powers to the Federal Government (and it was a considerable extent) they were escaping from the bondage of the Colonial Office; a point which Whitehead also reinforced. Huggins in his trenchant reply to the debate referred to Southern Rhodesia as the nut squeezed between the nutcrackers of the highly-conflicting "Gold Coast policy" and the policy of apartheid which obtained in South Africa.

Parliament adjourned on 10th July, and did not resume until 3rd February, 1953 by which time the second London conference was over. In the intervening period I was kept busy with preparatory work for the conference on top of my departmental duties. Interest in the federal scheme was mounting, and a body called the United Central Africa Association was set up to promote federation. The London wing was a very effective body.

As the Government's principal legal spokesman, the burden of explaining the constitutional issues and the intricacies of the federal scheme fell predominantly on me, and I addressed numerous meetings of the Action Group, the United Party and the Rhodesian wing of the U.C.A.A. I was myself at this stage not convinced that federation on the terms so far proposed was desirable, and in the explanations I gave I tried to be as impartial as possible. As time went on, it appeared to me distinctly possible that federation would be achieved, so in my capacity as Minister of Internal Affairs I gave thought and attention to the mechanics of getting it into operation.

With a Federal Cabinet and legislature additional to the Southern Rhodesia Cabinet and legislature there would have to be two Prime Ministers instead of one, and 45 Members of Parliament would have to be found in Southern Rhodesia instead of 30, plus the two black Members. The Federal Government and Parliament could not just spring from the waves like Venus; there must be an interim government topped by a Governor-General and a Ministry. Little initiative seemed to come from the Prime Minister's Office, so with the assistance of Athol Evans I prepared a memorandum for the Prime Minister to consider and which he accepted with very minor comments.

26

The London Conference of 1953

WHEN IT came near the end of 1952 it was with relief that I boarded a plane for London to get away from it all. After Christmas at Edinburgh with relatives I was back in London for the conference at Carlton House Terrace opening on New Year's Day which was not observed as a holiday south of the border.

The conference and its committees ran smoothly. Lord Swinton was now Commonwealth Secretary but Lord Salisbury also graced the proceedings until he succumbed to the 'flu which assailed many delegates including myself. The work was hard and unremitting, but fascinating. Oliver Lyttelton and Swinton had a mastery of their briefs and put their points across with many a well-turned phrase. Some of the humour was a little near the bone. When one of the conference delegates was a little difficult to follow Swinton was heard in a stage whisper to say, "How can I tell what I think, till I hear what I say?" One of his sallies was a reference to the Congo Basin Treaty as "that nauseating receptacle". Huggins with his mischievous streak was in no way behindhand. It was noticeable that senior civil servants from the Colonial Office occasionally butted in. I have referred before to the earlier conference when they sometimes overnight undid the good work of the preceding day. Lord Chandos, in his book, refers to one of them, Gorell Barnes, later Sir William, in these terms: "Possessed of good intellectual equipment, a transparent character and deep devotion to the cause of Africa, . . . I became and remain much attached to him. His gifts of negotiation are not, in my jaundiced opinion, outstanding, and he used to pass threatening notes to me when I was conducting a particularly delicate negotiation such as, 'You should surely get the agreement of the two African members before giving the concession which you mentioned and which I can support', to which I generally replied, 'O.L. born 1893'." G.B., as we called him, had much more scope and influence on the committees than in open conference; he kept us on our toes but while Evans and I often fumed and inwardly cursed at the obstacles he put in our way, at the end of the series of conferences we had acquired a sneaking regard for him. We were to encounter Colonial Office men in the future; we would have cheerfully swopped for G.B.

The Southern Rhodesian delegation made a final assault on the African Affairs Board, which succeeded to the extent that it was converted from an extra-parliamentary body to a Standing Committee in Parliament, of six members, three white and three black. British Ministers persuaded themselves that this was not merely the removal of an obstacle to the safe passage of the referendum but an improvement of the scheme.

Another issue was federalisation of the police. I waged a somewhat lonely battle on this cause, Huggins though sympathetic was lukewarm in his support, probably because he knew from the inner workings of the steering committee how far he could usefully go. I did get some help from Colonel Wilson, one of the Northern Rhodesia unofficials, and in the end the scheme provided on a purely permissive basis for a federal force on the model of the Canadian North-West Mounted Police. It could never be started without the co-operation of the territories, and this was never forthcoming. It was interesting subsequently to find that Nigeria achieved a federal police force in its 1960 Constitution, and I have little doubt that this was a help in keeping that federation together.

There was an interesting short debate on who should act for the Governor-General in the event of his death or absence on leave. Experience in Southern Rhodesia has shown the inconvenience caused when the Chief Justice had to be detached from his court to act. I pressed hard for some other arrangement but the matter was not satisfactorily resolved. The discussion on the subject is interesting in the light of what occurred when Lord Llewellin died in 1957 as I shall relate in its place.

My colleague, J. M. Caldicott who was attending as Minister of Agriculture, achieved a notable success in getting European agriculture on to the federal list.

The concessions we had won over the African Affairs Board were paid for later by changes made at the insistence of Moffat (later Sir John). These related to the power of the Federal legislature to amend the lists of functions by adding some to the federal list. The outcome of a lengthy debate was a decision that federal powers could not be extended within a certain period. We had no serious objection to this because we realised that for the first decade the Federal Government would have enough hay on its fork without taking on new subjects. Unfortunately, in the discussions there arose a proposal for a review of the Federal Constitution after a period of not less than seven and not more than nine years from the inception of federation. This was to prove an Achilles heel.

Earlier, in both conferences, Stockil and Eastwood had pressed for a secession clause as an escape route for Southern Rhodesia. Swinton vehemently opposed this, pointing out that with such a clause the Federation could not borrow a penny on the London market. He used also the analogy of the officiating minister at a marriage ceremony drawing the attention of the bridal pair to facilities for divorce. Later, when the subject of the review came up, Eastwood raised the question whether this could not be construed as providing a means of voluntary liquidation of the federation, thus jeopardising its loan-raising capacity. In the ensuing discussion Lyttelton said, "Nothing can liquidate the Constitution unless all four Governments are agreed to it."

Whitehead had lingering doubts on the financial impact of the clause which prompted Lyttelton to say, "We must have an assurance from the lawyers that anything that is put in this thing does not abrogate what I consider to be the present position which is, I think, that without the unanimous consent of the four Governments in fact, the constitution could not be liquidated and therefore you can borrow your

next 25 millions." After certain further exchanges Whitehead said, "If you are satisfied, and the legal people are
satisfied, we are quite happy." Lyttelton then said, "I think
the position is that you cannot upset the constitution without
agreement, can you?"

At this stage, bearing in mind that none of the several
lawyers present had spoken, and that Lyttelton had spoken
about four governments whereas a fifth Government, namely
the U.K., was also involved, I said, "You could not do so
(i.e. upset the constitution) constitutionally without the
intervention of Her Majesty's Government here." Lord
Swinton immediately said, "That is a risk you always run,
in a sense it would be possible, I suppose, for Her Majesty's
Government, if they could persuade Parliament to do so, to
pass an Act of Parliament tomorrow morning to take away
the whole of responsible government from Southern Rhodesia,
and the whole of the functions which would be given to the
Federation. You cannot legislate against the U.K. Parliament
going off its head." Lyttelton chipped in, "That is Mr.
Greenfield's point. It is the other way round. He means that
as long as it requires the intervention of Her Majesty's
Government the lender is safe. Nobody is safe from the
sovereign government repudiating its obligations. In this
case there would have to be four people to do it." I then
said, "In this case it is 'The Lord giveth and the Lord taketh
away," meaning, of course, that the fifth government had the
final control. Sir Kenneth Roberts-Wray, the Colonial Office
constitutional expert began to suggest a re-wording to read,
"When reviewing the working of the Constitution and considering any alterations of detail . . ." Lyttelton cut him
short, "That is right off the point, there are no details in a
constitution. I am afraid that will not do at all. We are
proposing to leave the words as they are. All we are asking
the lawyers for is an assurance that, with the concurrence of
each and all of the governments concerned, major alterations
could take place in the Constitution."

There was no follow up of this point. From the way
Lyttelton posed the question for the lawyers there could be
no doubt of the answer, and the silence of the lawyers meant

that we all agreed that with the consent of all the Governments concerned major changes could be made.

My statement that "Constitutionally the federal constitution could not be broken up without the intervention of Her Majesty's Government" was never challenged, nor could it be because it was clearly correct in accordance with British constitutional theory. I never for one moment implied that it would be right for the U.K. to take any such action unilaterally or against the wishes of any of the other four Governments. When Lyttelton said, "Nobody is safe from the sovereign government repudiating its obligations," I imagine that he never expected a *Conservative* Government to do so, which is precisely what it did in 1962 and 1963.

During the London conferences, ministers were the guests of Her Majesty's Government who paid our hotel bills and provided us with cars enabling us to get an occasional day in the country at the week-end. The only other entertainment I recall was a dinner at which Lord Swinton presided, in the course of which he made an impassioned and emotional appeal to those who were lukewarm in the federal cause, and especially Stockil, to give it their full support. The conference wound up on Thursday, 28th January and I see from Hansard that on Tuesday, 3rd February I introduced the Federal Poll Bill to enable the referendum to be held.

27

The Federal Poll Bill and the Referendum

————

WHILE we had been in London a political storm had blown up in Bulawayo over the price of Wankie coal. Davenport, who was acting as Huggins's deputy, found it difficult to handle the critics, and even Huggins on his return seemed to be at a loss. He let the storm blow around him, knowing no doubt that it would blow itself out. For several days, Parliament's time was taken up by a motion of censure. During the debate, a dramatic and tragic incident occurred. R. A. Ballantyne, a much loved Member, was speaking in the debate. He was a fluent and able speaker, every word of his speech was completely coherent when suddenly he slumped over and died. Years later I witnessed a similar incident in which a man's last words were also accurately recorded. I was then on the Bench trying a case concerned with a motor-car accident, when the plaintiff, who was giving evidence, keeled over and died.

To return to the Federal Poll Bill, its object was simply to fix the terms of the question put to the voters and the date of the referendum — April, 1953. I was not so naive as to expect this simple measure to pass quickly in our small Parliament where every member had ample opportunity of getting to his feet, and where the flogging of hobby horses was a pastime with some. I did not, however, anticipate that the Bill would have such a long and wearisome passage. The opportunity was seized by J. R. Dendy Young, Q.C. to debate the terms of the White Paper on Federation.

Young was an able advocate practising in Salisbury with whom, fortunately, I had a good personal relationship. We had often appeared on opposite sides in court, and had also served together on the Russell Commission on the Statutes. At that time I discovered that he was very much of an individualist, as on innumerable occasions he dissented from the views of the other four commissioners. He was not a great admirer of the Prime Minister, who, indeed, seemed to show scant respect for Young's views, and I am inclined to think dealt with him on several occasions less than tactfully. In principle, Young was a federationist but the scheme gave scope for innumerable points on which a skilful lawyer could be difficult. Huggins had little sympathy with lawyers, and less with those he considered to be legalistic. At all events, Young seized every opportunity to question myself and Huggins on various points especially relating to the powers of the African Affairs Board. He made much of the fact that the referendum was to take place on a White Paper not yet translated into the precise terms of the constitution. I had some sympathy with his objections on this score, and of course ideally the precise constitution should have been before the electors. However, practical politics where other governments were also involved made this course impracticable. After the referendum, when the Constitution appeared in print, Young returned to the charge and initiated a debate in September which gave me an immense amount of trouble.

Although it is not of chronological sequence I shall deal briefly with the course of that debate here.

Article 29 (7) of the Constitution provided,

> *"Nothing in this Constitution shall affect any power to make laws for the Federation or any of the Territories conferred on Her Majesty by any Act of the Parliament of the United Kingdom."*

This point had not been included in the White Paper. In the course of drafting the Constitution, Elliston, the U.K. Parliamentary draftsman, visited Salisbury and his draft was gone through with a fine toothcomb by our own law officers who certified that there was no departure from the terms of the White Paper. If my memory is correct, the point came to my own notice and I was satisfied with the explanation given, which was of a highly technical nature. In any event, it did not seem to me at the time to be a point of importance because I accepted the constitutional theory of the sovereignty of the British Parliament. I had already, as related before, referred to such sovereignty at the final conference in London.

N. H. Wilson, who edited a political paper called *The New Rhodesia*, picked up this point, among others, and Young became interested. In May, he asked a parliamentary question, my answer to which laid the foundation for the debate in September. Young was not satisfied with my explanations and was most persistent in pursuing the various points, but eventually he signified that if I could procure an exchange of despatches between ourselves and the British Government confirming my interpretation he would be satisfied. Stockil said that he was satisfied with my explanation; Ian Smith agreed, and also went further, saying that it was a pity that the motion had been brought forward at all because it served only to create unnecessary suspicion. I will relate in due course the sequels to this incident in relation to the Unilateral Declaration of Independence in 1965.

In the course of the debate, Lord Malvern who had ceased to be Prime Minister of Southern Rhodesia but retained his seat in its Parliament, became very irritated with Young, and the exchanges between them were acrimonious and embarrassing. I was inclined to feel that Young emerged from the debate with more dignity than his illustrious opponent. Young had campaigned against Federation on the terms that were offered, and I expect that Lord Malvern's regard for him, if any, had diminished before ever the debate began. At this time, too, it was clear that Young would become leader of a new party in opposition to Lord Malvern in the Federal sphere.

The Poll Bill eventually passed its third reading on 20th February and Parliament was prorogued till 14th April, soon after the referendum which accepted Federation by a majority of just under 63 per cent.

During the campaign, my services were much in demand to explain the intricacies of the scheme. I had never been an enthusiast for federation because it was to me a second best to amalgamation and, moreover, the Colonial Office, which I thoroughly distrusted, retained a number of vital functions in the North. As I saw it, Southern Rhodesia had missed the boat by rejecting Union in 1922, and unlike Griffiths and Lyttelton I saw no prospect of a subsequent liaison with the South. It seemed to me that Southern Rhodesia would soon find itself in an impossible position if it stood alone — the nut in the nutcrackers, as Huggins would say. It was obvious that if federation were rejected the Colonial Office would accelerate the pace of the northern territories towards a Gold Coast type of government with majority rule, and this would generate pressures inside Southern Rhodesia which might jeopardise the continuance of civilised rule. Events which have happened since the Federation was broken up, have only served to confirm that opinion. Thus I became a reluctant advocate of the federal cause, and perhaps because of the dispassionate way in which I put the case I may have been one of its more effective campaigners.

I had some interesting experiences in the course of the campaign. Ian Smith was considered to be in favour of federation, unlike the rest of his Parliamentary colleagues. It was arranged that I should speak at Selukwe, spending the night at his farm, and go on from there to Shabani, Garfield Todd's constituency, to speak at Filabusi and, I think, Balla Balla. If I was not a keen enthusiast for federation I formed the opinion that Smith was tepid, but I have no idea whether he warmed up after the Selukwe meeting. I had a very pleasant short stay with the Smiths and next day went on to Dadaya Mission to link up with Garfield Todd.

We had no sooner begun our talks when he had a summons to attend to an African woman who was giving birth. On the strength of, I think, one year or so at the Witwatersrand Medical School in the early 'thirties, Garfield had acquired a considerable reputation in the Shabani area as a deliverer of babies, and a healer of diseases. At all events, we lost no time in making for the *locus in quo* which was a pole-and-dagha hut reached by a very poor track over mealie lands and other obstacles. Not having assisted at events of this kind, I remained outside for about twenty minutes after which Garfield emerged from the hut carrying a babe with a very

misshapen looking head.   He applied mouth to mouth
respiration, and soon the baby showed signs of life and was
handed to its grandmother who was instructed by Garfield
how to knead the head into shape.   We returned to the
mission and it was evident to me that this was a very minor
incident in his life; probably he has long since forgotten it.
I thought of James Griffiths and his melancholy tales about
the Africans in their unlighted huts for whom the wicked
white settlers cared nothing.

Prior to the referendum campaign, I went with the
Governor as minister in attendance to two "indabas" at
which an attempt was made by Sir John Kennedy to explain
to blacks that federation was likely to come about.   He
spoke through an interpreter and I was interested to find
that at the Mashonaland meeting the best the interpreter
could do was refer to "Lo Federation" while in Matabeleland
the interpreter spoke of *hlangana* which I would freely
translate as "get together".

28

"Annus Mirabilis" and the Rise of Todd

PARLIAMENT was opened by Sir John Kennedy on 14th April, 1953 in a speech which was considerably brighter than the usual dull affair one had got accustomed to. It referred to three matters concerned with royalty: the death of the Dowager Queen Mary, the impending coronation of Queen Elizabeth the Second, and a prospective visit to Rhodesia of the Queen Mother and Princess Margaret. It went on to refer to the Rhodes Centenary celebrations, and the acceptance of federation at the referendum. These events, in conjunction with the inauguration of the new order, gave 1953 the promise of an *annus mirabilis*. Aside from the Parliamentary programme, it was obvious that there would have to be a great deal of party political activity to arrange the political infrastructure where four governments were now involved, instead of one.

The April meeting of Parliament provided an opportunity for the Prime Minister to discuss with his U.P. caucus the party structure and dispositions required for the new era, to sort out among the M.P.s who would 'go federal' and who would stay territorial, and to settle the succession to the Prime Ministership in the territorial arena. The first question was whether to extend the United Party's activities into the federal sphere. If it were to operate in two fields there would be complications as support for federation had cut across party lines, for example Ian Smith paired off with Dendy Young. Caucus was much influenced by Whitehead who claimed that Menzies in Australia held that Federal and State politics should not mix. I discussed the point with the Action Group who saw disadvantages either way. Huggins had already determined on the name "Federal Party" which he hoped would attract a cross-section of political thinking, and that is the way it went. I soon found myself charged with the task of drawing up its constitution and helping to formulate its policy, and, later on, steering these documents through the initial congress. Innumerable meetings were held to lay the foundations for the new Federal Party, leading eventually to the initial congress on 7th August when Huggins was elected Leader.

The new party inevitably became a band-wagon, even Stockil became a member though he soon betook himself to the territorial section. Competition was keen among the 30 Southern Rhodesian M.P.s for the 14 Federal Assembly seats, and ultimately 12 of them were elected leaving only two posts to be filled by new blood. As regards the question of who was to take over the leadership of the United Party and become the Prime Minister of Southern Rhodesia, at no time did Huggins make any move that I was aware of. Whitehead who would have been the most likely successor was not available as his eyesight was failing and his doctors ordered him back to the land. Davenport had blotted his copybook in the eyes of some by his weak handling of the Wankie coal episode. Caldicott and I, who were respectively Mashonaland and Matabeleland vice-presidents, both wanted to go Federal. Neither Fletcher nor Winterton appeared to have any substantial following. Macintyre who had the lengthiest parliamentary experience of the rest was earmarked as the future Federal Minister of Finance.

It seemed to me that the succession should not be left to chance. My own assessment was that Garfield Todd had the greatest potential of those who might be available. During April I discussed the matter with Caldicott who agreed with my assessment but was not particularly enthusiastic. We arranged that I should see Huggins. In turn, he appeared to accept my assessment but offered no suggestion about further progress. I then asked for and got his agreement to take soundings in the Party, which Caldicott and I undertook, going our separate ways about it. I see from a minute of the Action Group dated 1st May, 1953 that I discussed the question with them at Bulawayo and put Todd's name forward. My recollection is that there was mild surprise but considerable interest in the idea. There was some discussion about one or other of the existing Cabinet Ministers taking the leadership on a temporary footing while Todd was "groomed", but this found little support. At some stage, I cannot be sure of the date, I spoke to Todd and found that he was very attracted to the idea of being territorial leader. At this period we were on terms of close friendship such that he often stayed with me at Northward, my ministerial house in Salisbury, during parliamentary sessions. We arranged that he should meet the Action Group in Bulawayo.

Meanwhile, as time went on, Caldicott and I had formed the opinion that Todd's nomination would be likely to split the party. Pressure was brought to bear on me to accept nomination at the congress scheduled to meet in Bulawayo on 14th August. I reluctantly decided to let my name go forward. Quite apart from doubts of my own suitability to lead a government I was convinced that in the initial stages of the Federation my presence was necessary on the federal side. It was already obvious to me that although Huggins would be flanked in a triumvirate by Welensky and Barrow, the spade work of attending to the electoral arrangements, and a host of other matters would depend for its political direction largely on myself. The only available machinery and personnel was under the Southern Rhodesian Government. Some minister had to remain there who could work quietly behind the scenes maintaining the closest touch with Lord Malvern and his colleagues, and that Minister should be one who was thoroughly versed in the negotiations that had preceded federation. Added to that was the burden of getting the Federal Party safely launched in an ocean that embraced the northern territories which, in Northern Rhodesia, had virtually no party political structure, and in Nyasaland none at all.

A day or two before the United Party congress, Todd met the Action Group. I abstained from attendance at this meeting and did not advise the Group or any of the members of my decision to let my name go forward at the congress. When the time came, Todd and I and Davenport were all nominated, but Davenport withdrew. I could see that the

Action Group were well represented but it appeared to me that they were taken by surprise at my accepting nomination. The ballot resulted in a tie, and the chairman adjourned the proceedings for lunch which I had with Garfield at his invitation. After lunch, I told congress that as I wanted to go Federal and Todd did not I would withdraw. The voting had satisfied me that Todd would have enough support within the party because I felt sure that many who had voted for me would find him acceptable.

I was reproached at the time, and on subsequent occasions by some friends and many acquaintances. In 1957 and 1958, when Todd was the focus of a political storm, many of these people harked back to the 1953 congress and blamed me for failing in my duty then. It is idle to speculate on what might have been. What remains certain is that there was an immense job for me to do on the Federal side which I believed myself better qualified to do than any of the possible alternatives. Whether I was right and how well I succeeded is not for me to judge.

Now that Huggins was installed as Federal Prime Minister and the succession in Southern Rhodesia was settled, events began to move fast. I decided to hand over Northward, my official residence, to the new Prime Minister; my wife and family returned to Bulawayo before going overseas on a holiday, and the Todds very kindly invited me to be their guest until I could arrange for other accommodation.

Todd asked me to join his new Cabinet as Minister of Justice and Internal Affairs on the understanding that I would carry on these portfolios until the Federal election when I expected to be appointed in a similar capacity in the Federal Cabinet.

At the outset of his new career, Todd's position was a little insecure, as there were talks of fusion with the Rhodesia Party which might throw the leadership into the melting pot. Todd though well known in Parliamentary circles and in his own constituency, had yet to make his mark on the country as a whole. He was at some disadvantage in leading a Cabinet which included experienced Ministers while he had never previously held office and had not attended any of the conferences leading up to Federation. He lost no time getting about the country and impressing people with his magnetic personality, quickly grasped the techniques of administration and soon found his feet. The fusion talks failed and Todd formed the United Rhodesia Party while the former Rhodesia Party changed its name to the Dominion Party.

I served in Todd's Cabinet for about six months during which time I was also living under his roof. Our relationship was cordial and it was interesting to watch his developing confidence. During this period, Todd's Cabinet was largely preoccupied with arrangements for the transfer of functions and civil servants to the new Federal Government. I had a foot in two camps and in effect performed the function of a Federal Minister in regard to the arrangements for the Federal election to be held in mid-December, 1953, while at the same time performing similar functions in regard to the Southern Rhodesia election which followed in February, 1954. The connecting link was Athol Evans, now seconded to the embryo Federal civil service, who kept me completely informed of arrangements being made on the Federal side.

One matter of considerable concern at this time was a threatened influx of Asians into the northern territories in an effort to beat an embargo which they knew the Federal Government would impose. The Governor-General, Lord Llewellin, had interim discretionary powers and these were used to make regulations which stemmed the flood, until a Federal Immigration Act was passed.

One of my main preoccupations was the arrangements for the election to the Federal Assembly of the special representatives of black interests. Our one-man-three-votes system was without precedent and a great deal had to be done to inform the electorate of their opportunities. The newly formed Federal Party, to my disappointment, showed a hesitant approach, and at first refused to allow the candidates for the special seats to stand under the party banner. The furthermost they would go was to "sponsor" them. In practice, this became a distinction without a difference and Percy Ibbotson, Jasper Savanhu and Mike Hove, when elected, were at once admitted to the Federal Party caucus.

There was very keen competition for the seat that Ibbotson won. Several disappointed candidates for the ordinary constituencies tried to get the nomination, notwithstanding lack of any previous concern for the affairs of black people. Many of the voters were shocked at the idea of casting a vote for a black man, but large numbers surprised themselves by attending political meetings addressed by Savanhu and Hove, coming away wiser and, one hopes, better for the experience. In Northern Rhodesia, party political organisation was virtually non-existent, and I found myself much involved in creating an organisation there to fight the Federal election during the campaign.

The Federal Party gained an overwhelming majority throughout the Federation, winning all but two of the seats available for open election, these two being taken by Dendy Young, leader of the Confederate Party, and Dr. Scott of Lusaka, an independent. I won the Umgusa seat which covered my former constituency of Hillside, but stayed on in Todd's Cabinet until his election was over in February when I joined Lord Malvern's Cabinet as Minister of Home Affairs and Education. I settled down to the problems of "federalising" the statute laws of the territories in subjects on the federal list, and creating the Federal Public Service. Fortunately, I was blessed from the start by the secondment to the federal sphere of men of outstanding ability, such as Athol Evans, Victor Robinson and Thomas Chegwidden (all of whom were later knighted).

Todd with his newly-formed United Rhodesia Party had a runaway victory in the Southern Rhodesia election, winning 26 of the 30 seats.

When the Federal Parliament assembled, Dendy Young constituted the main opposition and kept me and other Ministers on our toes. He turned out to be champion of the liberty of the subject, even though the "subject" was a would-be Asian immigrant; his views and actions in this regard would have horrified most of his supporters in the Confederate camp but they were chiefly rustics who did not frequent Parliament. I was not unhappy when Young became a High

Court Judge and left the political scene about the end of 1955. Some years later in a speech at a Bar dinner I heard him say "I loved the Federal Assembly". There was more than a tinge of regret in his voice.

29

The Federal Supreme Court

———◆———

ONE OF my early responsibilities was to set up the Federal
Supreme Court whose principal function was to hear
appeals from the High Courts of the three Territories. The
two northern territories used English law whereas Southern
Rhodesia followed the Roman-Dutch legal system, which it
had inherited from the old Cape Colony. The difference
in legal systems made it desirable, if not essential, to have
at least two judges who were fully versed in both English
and Roman-Dutch law.

One such person with an obvious claim to appointment
was Sir Robert Tredgold, then Chief Justice of Southern
Rhodesia. Some years earlier he had held an acting appointment in Northern Rhodesia and nobody could challenge his
capacity in both legal systems. I was also able to secure the
services of an eminent South African judge, H. J. Clayden,
who had qualifications in both English and Roman-Dutch
law.

The third appointment presented more difficulty. The
Colonial Office judges with whom I had come into contact,
with one or two exceptions, had not impressed me as being
of appeal court stature. I thought it would be right to try
to get someone of the appropriate calibre from England, and
to this end I applied to Lord Kilmuir, Lord High Chancellor,
for help. Eventually, he proposed that we should invite a
Scottish advocate who was Dean of Faculty of Advocates
in Edinburgh and was incidentally also an English barrister.
I replied to Kilmuir that although his proposal was very
attractive we would prefer to have someone whose practice
was at the English Bar. His answer was that the Scot was

quite the best man available and that we would be foolish to lose the opportunity to take him. Meanwhile, I had kept in touch with Tredgold who agreed that Kilmuir's advice should be followed but thought that before clinching the matter we should consult the two northern Governors. A meeting was arranged at which Lord Llewellin presided. The northern Governors expressed themselves as strongly opposed to this appointment. Within a few days I received news that the Scot had accepted a much more remunerative post in the world of international finance or commerce.

I was left with no alternative but to select one of the northern judges, and chose Sir Arthur Lewey. He was a dedicated believer in the Federation, and a most charming and pleasant man but the reports of the Federal Supreme Court show that he seldom wrote any of the judgments and usually contented himself by concurring with his brothers.

In 1956, Sir Arthur Benson, the Governor of Northern Rhodesia, wrote a despatch to his superiors, a copy of which fell into the hands of Welensky. It was a lengthy attack on the Federal Government for all sorts of iniquities, including a charge against me of attempting to pack the Federal Supreme Court with judges versed in the Roman-Dutch system. Scots law is founded on Roman law and has analogies with Roman-Dutch law, which was the very reason I had begged Kilmuir to find us a man from the English Bench or Bar.

The Federal Supreme Court was inaugurated with considerable pomp and ceremony on 1st July, 1955 at a swearing in of the judges in the Federal Assembly. The occasion was graced by the Lord High Chancellor of Britain who flew out with his purse-bearer; the Chief Justice of South Africa, A. van der S. Centlivres, and the South African Minister of Justice, C. R. Swart, later the first State President of the Republic of South Africa. The two latter were invited because the South African Court of Appeal which had served Southern Rhodesia from 1910 would now cease to entertain appeals from that territory.

During the eight years that followed, the Federal Court enjoyed an excellent reputation, and I never heard any criticism from the North about its decisions. Lewey, F. J. retired within a few years and I was fortunate in securing as a replacement a judge from the East African Court of Appeal, F. Briggs, later Sir Francis, and when he regrettably had to resign for health reasons we again raided the East African Appeal Court and appointed Sir Alistair Forbes. Tredgold, C. J. did not stay the course; in 1960, he became gravely disturbed at the turn events were taking in Southern Rhodesia. R. Knight, the Minister of Justice, had introduced a somewhat drastic piece of security legislation. I was myself somewhat concerned at the terms of the Bill and made representations to Whitehead which resulted in modifications to it. Before this happened Tredgold sent for me to voice his objections to the Bill. I was able to tell him that I had already interviewed Whitehead and expected to see some changes. Not very long afterwards Welensky sent for me to say that he had just had an interview with Tredgold who had informed him that he considered that Whitehead should resign and make way for a new government in Southern Rhodesia which he, Tredgold, would head. Welensky was to approach Whitehead and ask him to step down. Welensky told Tredgold that he would inform Whitehead of the proposal but could hold out no assurance that he would comply. It came to our knowledge that Tredgold had been persuaded by a group of men in Bulawayo to take the extraordinary course I have related.

Whitehead declined to resign, and within a few days Tredgold himself did so, informing me himself beforehand. He issued a Press statement intimating his intention of entering into active politics. No general election was pending, and there was no split in Whitehead's Cabinet, so the public was mystified as to Tredgold's plans. Apparently there was no plan, or no practicable one, because no action followed, and the movement fizzled out. Unfortunately, the resignation of the Federal Chief Justice was naturally construed outside the Federation, and by enemies within, as reflecting a quarrel with the Federal Government, whereas the quarrel was with the Southern Rhodesia Government.

Sir John Clayden became Chief Justice and V. E. Quenet, now Sir Vincent, filled the vacancy in the court. When the Federation was wound up at the end of December, 1963 the Federal Supreme Court remained in being for several months. R. A. Butler at the Victoria Falls conference made a feeble effort to persuade Kaunda to consider a common court of appeal for the Rhodesias but he would have none of it.

30

Three Prime Ministers

IN THE latter part of 1954, after a wearisome session of the Federal Assembly, I had a pleasant break of a fortnight in South Africa. The Commonwealth Parliamentary Association had met in Nairobi and some of them went on to do a tour of South Africa which I joined. The party was led by Harold Holt, who subsequently succeeded Menzies as Prime Minister of Australia, and Edward Heath was also among us. At a lunch in Cape Town I was called on to make a "Thank you" speech, and referred to the fact that 1954 marked 100 years of Parliament in the Cape, (an event which the Union Parliament ignored). I also pointed out that Rhodesia was a Colony not of the United Kingdom, but of the Old Cape Colony, whose illustrious Prime Minister of the 'nineties had been our founder.

The impact of Federation on the Southern Rhodesian Parliament in 1954 was somewhat traumatic. Most of the members were newcomers, and all of them seemed rather bewildered as to the rôle they had to play now that so many of the territory's functions were "going federal". In an early debate on a motion to exchange the word "State" for "Colony" in the territory's designation, Todd revealed his own preference for a unitary state rather than a federation and seemed to be under the impression that, as time went on, a closer union between the three territories than federation might be possible. Federations generate rivalries and sometimes petty jealousies between the territorial and federal parliaments and ours was no exception. Several members of the Federal Assembly were indiscreetly talking of themselves belonging to the "Upper House" or the "First Team". As time went on, one sensed a distinct coolness among some of the Southern Rhodesian Parliament towards their Federal counterparts. The separation of the United Rhodesia Party from the Federal Party also tended to a lack of understanding between the two sets of members. In this situation a close working relationship between the two Prime Ministers was desirable. On the other hand, it might create friction with the two northern governors if Malvern and Todd were seen to be always putting their heads together.

In 1954, I was present at two heads of government meetings in Salisbury attended by both Prime Ministers and one or both of the northern Governors. These were connected chiefly with security matters. I do not recall any further such meetings until near the end of 1956. During 1954, Todd ran into industrial troubles, first at Wankie Colliery and later on the Railways. He dealt very firmly with the strikes and on the first occasion called up the defence forces. He was able to do this without the consent of the Federal Government as defence had not yet gone Federal. (He very probably consulted with Lord Malvern but of this I have no knowledge). The electorate on the whole was considerably impressed by the way Todd had dealt with the strikers, and his stock stood very high until some time in 1955 when his relationship with Lord Malvern came under strain. There was, of course, a "generation gap" between the two Prime Ministers, but it had always been assumed by their mutual friends that they were on good terms; it was generally believed that Huggins had originally persuaded Todd to stand for Parliament in 1946 having encountered him as a heckler at a political meeting in Shabani before that date. When the United Party had chosen Todd as territorial Prime Minister in 1953, Huggins had been entirely neutral and certainly revealed no opposition.

It was therefore a considerable shock to many members both of the Federal Party and the United Rhodesia Party when at a congress of the latter party at Umtali Todd launched an attack on Lord Malvern who happened to be away from Rhodesia at the time. Some months later he made a further attack. I cannot now remember what it was all about, but Todd revealed a growing impatience with the older man and a desire to see him hand over the reins of government to a younger one. It was well known that Welensky would be Malvern's successor when the time came. As far as I was aware, Todd and Welensky were not particularly well known to each other but Todd may have hoped that he could develop a closer relationship with Welensky than he had been able to establish with Malvern.

I was very disturbed by Todd's two outbursts; I thought that he had shown very bad political judgment because inevitably he would do a lot of harm to himself. Malvern was immensely respected throughout Rhodesia, his supporters were also mostly supporters of Todd, thus attacks on Malvern would cause resentment among the very people whose support Todd himself needed. In any event, the attacks were counter-productive and caused Malvern to delay his retirement which in turn must have resulted in a certain amount of frustration on Welensky's part. Eventually, in October, 1956 Welensky was sworn in as Malvern's successor. I retained my portfolios of Law and Education, but in addition became Leader of the House. Welensky also asked me to maintain a close connection with the Federal Party organisation. I was to have responsibility for framing the legislation to deal with Federal elections, constitutional changes and Federal citizenship.

Welensky's methods and style were completely different from those of Lord Malvern who had always held himself somewhat aloof from his ministers. He maintained a close and warm relationship with all of us. He was keenly interested in everything his colleagues were doing and kept us in close touch with his own plans. Caucus meetings too seemed to be better directed. During the seven years that followed I was in almost daily touch with the Prime Minister as his closest adviser on difficult constitutional and electoral problems, from which we were never absent until the Federation was dissolved.

31

Citizens and Elections

IN THE first two years after Welensky became Prime Minister my main preoccupation was with the threefold subjects of citizenship, electoral laws and constitutional amendments to enlarge the Federal Assembly. Temporary arrangements had been made for the first federal election at the end of 1953, based as far as possible on the existing electoral laws of the three territories which differed widely It was necessary to have a new Federal Electoral Act for the next general election which had to be held at latest in 1959. Meanwhile, in Southern Rhodesia, Todd was grappling with the problem of electoral law reform which had been shelved in 1951. In territorial political circles some people thought that federal elections should be based on the territorial electoral laws. They overlooked the facts that Nyasaland had no electoral law at that time, and that the Federal Assembly had peculiar features in that three seats were reserved for whites who were to represent black interests, six were reserved for blacks while the other 26 were unreserved.

Todd decided to appoint a judicial commission to advise his government what to do. He appointed to his commission the Federal Chief Justice, Sir Robert Tredgold, the Southern Rhodesian Chief Justice, Sir John Murray, and a retired Sudan Chief Justice, Sir Charles Cumings. Both Todd and Tredgold would have liked the scope of this inquiry to cover Federal elections but we did not think that this would be wise for several reasons. Nevertheless, when the commission reported we studied its recommendations closely and we went as far as we could to bring the Federal electoral voting qualifications into line with those recommended in the report.

The subject of voting qualifications is one on which most members of Parliament regard themselves as experts but few are able to agree. Our first difficulty was to get agreement among the members of the U.F.P. caucus. I was the most difficult member because I favoured a single common voters roll system but I was the only one who did so. The Prime Minister and all the others favoured a dual roll on which voters with lower qualifications would only vote for the representatives of black interests, while the voters with higher qualifications would have, in addition, the right to vote for candidates of unspecified race. As I did not want to be like little Johnny, the only man in step, I gave way.

The Tredgold Commission recommended a single common voters roll for Southern Rhodesia. On closer examination of the report it appeared that it contained elements of a dual roll scheme because it provided for two categories of voters: those with high and those with low qualifications, and it recommended that in certain defined circumstances the lower category would have the value of their votes reduced. The Southern Rhodesia Government did not accept this recommendation as it stood but varied it so that when the numbers of the lower category of voter reached a certain percentage of the total electorate the enrolment of further lowly qualified voters would cease.

The amendments to the constitution to enlarge the Federal Assembly were required because we had found in practice that its membership was much too small. In the first place the size of most of the rural and even peri-urban constituencies was far too large for a member to be able to cope with. In the second place, taking account of the fact that nine members out of 35 had been chosen to represent black interests, and six of them were involved in special functions in regard to the African Affairs Board, the Prime Minister's choice of persons for his Cabinet was too restricted, especially in view of the fact that he had to ensure that the Cabinet was properly representative of all three territories. A stage might have been reached when there would be as many Cabinet Ministers as backbenchers in the governing party.

In order to enlarge the Federal Assembly we had to get the approval of the legislatures of all three territories by means of resolutions passed in these bodies. Our Electoral Bill theoretically did not require approval by the territorial legislatures, but it was obvious that if any territorial government strongly disapproved of our electoral franchise proposals it could show this by blocking our constitutional amendments. Arrangements were therefore made to have discussions between the heads of the four governments to try to reach an overall agreement. We had originally decided to double the membership of the Federal Assembly, but we also wished to provide that the additional special black representative from the two northern territories should be elected in the same way as the blacks from Southern Rhodesia. The Governor of Northern Rhodesia, Sir Arthur Benson, disagreed with our proposals and at one time it seemed likely that a deadlock would occur. However, we arrived at a compromise under which the number of special black representatives was doubled but the overall membership was increased only by two-thirds. At one stage it seemed likely that Todd would block the scheme because of his dislike of our dual roll but eventually he decided to let it pass. The Nyasaland Government preferred our dual roll proposals and gave us no problem. It was a tremendous relief to me when eventually the three territorial legislatures passed the necessary resolutions. We had still to get the approval of the British Government, which was obtained in April, 1957 when Welensky and I saw Lord Home and Lennox-Boyd in London.

The Citizenship Bill presented almost intractable problems. Southern Rhodesia was the only territory which had its own Citizenship Act. This was keyed into the British citizenship and nationality laws in such a way that S.R. citizens were automatically British subjects, which status at that time was prized. The indigenous population was included in the scope of the S.R. Act. In the northern territories, people who had been born there were automatically British protected persons, a status not desired by whites but one to which we were told the blacks preferred to cling rather than become British subjects. It was obviously desirable to have a Federal citizenship law which would draw the loyalty of most of the population. The S.R. citizenship law would have to be superseded, since we did not want a competing loyalty. The difficulty which we never managed to overcome was in regard to the blacks in the north who did not want to become British subjects. It might have been overcome if the British Government had agreed to make certain modifications in the U.K. citizenship laws but they declined to do so. We were thus forced to have a Federal citizenship law which was all-embracing in Southern Rhodesia but did not automatically embrace blacks in the north unless they individually chose to apply for citizenship.

In both Rhodesias there were links between the electoral laws and the laws relating to citizenship or nationality. To vote in Southern Rhodesia one had to be a citizen, and to vote in Northern Rhodesia one had to be a British subject. This requirement had excluded the great mass of the indigenous population in Northern Rhodesia from voting. Their representatives in the Legislative Council were chosen by a sort of electoral college. In our Federal Electoral Act we gave voting rights to British protected persons as well as Federal citizens. Thus it came about that blacks in Nyasaland and Northern Rhodesia became entitled to vote in Federal elections before they gained that right in territorial elections. Our critics in the U.K. and elsewhere gave us no credit for this.

Once our set of three Bills had been agreed with the other governments concerned, I began the task of explaining their complicated provisions at innumerable meetings. Then came the job of piloting them through the Federal Assembly. Moffat, chairman of the African Affairs Board, was strongly opposed to the Electoral Bill and the Constitution Amendment Bill, and persuaded the African Affairs Board (by a majority) to declare them to be differentiating measures. This entailed the Bills having to go through a special procedure in the U.K. Parliament and provided all those British M.P.s who were hostile to the Federation with a platform to air their views.

The Board contended that the Bill differentiated because the election of the four additional African Members for the northern territories would be put under the control of the general body of voters now to be enfranchised. Thus the proportion of African members whose election would be controlled exclusively by Africans would be reduced from four out of 35 to four out of 59. Lord Blake* points this out but does not give the Federal government's reasons for rejecting this contention. Shortly, these were: first, the objection lost sight of the fact that the number of seats to be reserved for Africans would be increased by 100 per cent whereas the number of unreserved seats would be increased by only 67 per cent; secondly, participation of the whole body of the electorate in the election of Africans in the north would advance the cause of political partnership. It would tend to divide Parliament on party lines rather than on ethnic lines. Moreover, the involvement of white voters with black candidates and Members of Parliament would be beneficial to both.

The U.K. Parliament by a fairly good majority eventually approved the Bills, thus overruling the objections of the African Affairs Board. As I look back now over a distance of nearly twenty years, I still marvel that in spite of all the obstacles that confronted us we were able to get these three complex Acts into the statute book.

Our Electoral Act worked very well in the ensuing Federal general election towards the end of 1958. All the political parties, except the African nationalist parties in the north, fielded teams which included both white and black candidates. The U.F.P. won a large majority. Its Parliamentary caucus included 7 blacks, while Winston Field's Dominion Party also won one of the reserved black seats. We thus had a Parliament in which it could be claimed that for the most part divisions were on party political lines and not on racial lines. Political partnership began to operate. Welensky included two blacks as Parliamentary Secretaries in his new government, not merely one as Blake implies.†

---

*A History of Rhodesia by Robert Blake, London, Eyre Methuen. 1977, p.299.
†Ibid, p.290.

While the Tredgold Commission was still at work, I had an interview with the chairman, who, among other questions, asked my opinion about the value of the special representation of blacks in the Federal Assembly. It seemed to be in his mind that consideration should be given to making a similar provision in the Southern Rhodesian Parliament. Indeed, it seemed altogether anomalous that the Federal Assembly, which was not primarily concerned with aspects of administration affecting the indigenous populations, should have special black representatives while the Southern Rhodesia Parliament, which was charged with responsibility for the affairs of black people generally, did not include such provision. Theoretically, blacks could be elected in any constituency in Southern Rhodesia but in practice they did not stand for Parliament and none were elected.

I told Tredgold that the federal scheme had worked reasonably well and that I believed an even stronger case could be made for having similar provision for black representation in the S.R. Parliament. I probably mentioned the anomaly of a black M.P. in the Federal Assembly having the right to discuss and vote on questions relating to white education, whereas in the Southern Rhodesia Parliament there were no black M.P.s available to speak on the education of blacks, the cost of which was one of the largest items in the S.R. Budget. As it turned out, the Tredgold Commission's report made no mention of this subject, and when the S.R. Electoral Bill emerged it made no provision for reservation of seats for blacks. In the ensuing Southern Rhodesian general election none of the three political parties put forward black candidates although it would have been open for them to do so.

Early in 1957, while Tredgold was still engaged on the Commission's inquiries at Bulawayo the Governor-General, Lord Llewellin, died. Welensky rang me in the early hours of the morning to give me the news and instructed me to prepare for a meeting with Tredgold for whom he had sent a plane. He warned me that Tredgold was strongly opposed to stepping into the breach as Acting Governor-General, because he did not wish to interrupt the commission's work. Later in the morning, I was present when Tredgold met the

Prime Minister to discuss the situation. He very firmly held to his opinion that the constitutional instruments did not require him to step into the breach. I held the opposite opinion in which I was fortified by the views of the Federal Attorney-General. The deadlock had to be resolved by a telephone call to Lord Home who supported my view. At one stage Tredgold affirmed that he regarded the commission as the most important assignment of his life and that rather than give it up he would resign from the Bench. Fortunately, Welensky was able to arrange that after only a fortnight Tredgold would be relieved by Sir William Murphy who had formerly been a governor in another part of the Commonwealth, so Tredgold was able to return to his assignment. It will be recalled that in 1953 I had unsuccessfully tried to get the London conference to make arrangements for a Deputy Governor-General without involving the judiciary.

Some time after the Tredgold Commission reported, rumours began to reach us that Todd was having difficulty in getting his caucus to agree on the proposed Electoral Bill. Then we heard that he had told his caucus that if they did not accept his plan he and Tredgold would resign their respective offices and join forces in the political field. I do not know what truth there was in this, but the suggestion that Tredgold might consider resignation caused me no surprise. Sir Harold Wilson has some pertinent remarks on the folly of a Prime Minister threatening his Cabinet or his parliamentary following with a dissolution.* At all events, Todd and his caucus apparently composed their differences, if they existed, at least for a few months, and the Minister of Internal Affairs, A. R. W. Stumbles, skilfully piloted the Electoral Bill through Parliament, basing it on the Tredgold report with the modifications I have mentioned. The Act made provision also for the use of the single transferable voting system and, as it later turned out, this saved the day for Whitehead at the territorial elections in 1958.

---

*The Governance of Britain by Sir Harold Wilson. London, Weidenfeld and Nicolson, and Michael Joseph, 1976, p.40.

32

April, 1957 in England

————◆————

WHEN Welensky and I met the two Secretaries of State in London in April, 1957 our discussions ranged wider than the field of citizenship and electoral laws. Among other subjects we wanted to get the earliest possible date fixed for the Federal review, and to clear up the question about the operation of Article 29 (7) of the Federal Constitution about which Dendy Young had said so much in 1954. Macmillan was now Prime Minister following the Suez debacle. When he entertained us to lunch at No. 10 both of us were impressed by his confident air of assurance and appearance of unflappability for which he was to become famous. Lord Home had succeeded Lord Swinton at the Dominions Office while Lennox-Boyd had moved to the top position in the Colonial Office. Both were well disposed to the Federation and sympathetic to our proposals. Nevertheless, the concessions we gained in talks spread over a fortnight did not come easily. Welensky wanted the British Government to set up a single department to deal with the affairs of the Federation and its territorial governments thus by-passing the Colonial Office. In this we failed to persuade them. At the end of the talks an agreed statement was issued. It said that the review conference would be held in 1960 and,

> *the purpose of this conference is to review the constitution in the light of experience gained since the inception of the Federation and in addition to agree on the constitutional advances which may be made. In this latter context the conference will consider a programme for the attainment of such a status as would enable the Federation to become eligible for full membership of the Commonwealth.*

In regard to Article 29 (7) the agreed statement said:

> *U.K. Ministers made it clear that the U.K. Government recognises the existence of a convention applicable to the present stage of the constitutional evolution of the Federation whereby the U.K. Government in practice does not initiate any legislation to amend or to repeal, any Federal Act, or to deal with any matter included in the competence of the Federal legislature except at the request of the Federal Government.*

The British Ministers also made a strong affirmation of faith in the Federation.

The April, 1957 declarations were well received in the Federation and we felt distinctly encouraged. Our relations with the British Government had reached the highest point they were ever to attain, and the bogey raised by Dendy Young had been scotched.

While we were in England, Neville Barrett, Federal M.P. for Mtoko, died suddenly and in the resultant by-election Winston Field, the new leader of the Dominion Party in the Federal sphere, won the seat. When Van Eeden defected to that party its membership increased to three. It probably did not occur to anyone at this time, least of all to Field, that five years later he would be Prime Minister of Southern Rhodesia with the sands running out for the Federation.

Field was a successful farmer who in the early nineteen fifties had an obsessive plan for settling Italians on small farms in Rhodesia. This was based on a scheme which had been introduced in Israel by Weizmann. Field's idea was to bring in Italian farmers with large families. Initially, they would be tenant farmers, on small acreages, which they could develop using the labour of their older children and dispensing with local black labour. As Minister responsible for immigration I was firmly opposed to Field's ideas, but he had powerful allies in the farming world, pressures mounted, and eventually I decided that the best way to deal with the matter was to let Field begin with a pilot scheme. I had little doubt that it would fail. He was allowed to bring in four families, the term "family" being used in an extended sense. The Government had to provide a school for the immigrants' children, and this could not conform to the normal school calendar as the children were required to do farm work at times when ordinary schools were in session. I believe that some of the families improved their own lot but they soon found that they could do better for themselves in other ways. At all events, Field's enthusiasm waned within a year or two, the school was closed and we heard no more about the idea.

My first few meetings with Field were concerned with this venture. I found him to be somewhat impulsive and opinionated but entirely straight-forward. After he entered political life we began to have a mutual regard, although we disagreed on many subjects. Field had been an opponent of Federation. He was by no means a racialist, and he had managed to strike up a sort of friendship with Dr. Banda, presumably based on their mutual objection to Federation. Initially, however, he entered the Federal Assembly with the intention of accepting the Federation and helping to make it work. After the Devlin Report in 1959, he and his party believed that the Federation would fail and they drew up an outline plan called the Central African Alliance which in essence was a scheme to amalgamate Southern Rhodesia with the so-called "line of rail" areas of Northern Rhodesia including, of course, the Copperbelt. Perhaps Dr. Banda might have supported the scheme but Kenneth Kaunda would never have done so.

33

Fusion and Confusion

EARLIER I referred briefly to Todd's attacks on Lord
Malvern in 1955 and 1956. It should have been obvious
that very close co-operation between the two Prime Ministers,
and indeed between them and the northern Governors, was
desirable, especially in the early years of the Federation. On
the party political level the Governors were not involved.
The Federal Party was now constituted so as to operate not
only in the federal sphere but also in the territorial spheres
in the northern territories, because the white populations were
not large enough to sustain two sets of political parties. Even
in Southern Rhodesia it was clear that there would be
advantages in merging the U.R.P. into the Federal Party
structure. As I was so much involved in the party political
side of affairs I began to press for fusion, pointing out that
membership of the two parties was virtually identical. There
was considerable overlapping in meetings from branch level
upwards and useful economies in manpower and money
could be effected. Moreover, fusion would enable policy
matters to be better co-ordinated. At the 1956 congress of
the Federal Party I proposed a resolution for fusion and this
was accepted in principle, Ian Smith being one of two or
three who voted against it. Then followed a series of protracted negotiations which wore on for over a year. Todd,
I think, was never enthusiastic, while Welensky saw the
advantages but left me to do the pushing. Agreement was
reached with the U.R.P. in time for the Federal Party to
deal with the matter at its 1957 Federal congress at Ndola,
when it converted itself to the United Federal Party and
made the necessary amendments to its constitution. It

remained for the U.R.P. to dissolve itself and merge into the U.F.P. and this was done a little later.

No sooner were we back in Salisbury from Ndola on 23rd November, 1957, than news reached me from an unimpeachable source that Todd had fallen out with most of his Cabinet and that the issue between them was about to come to a head. Rumours began to spread. The news was most unwelcome and caused Welensky great concern. Although Todd and Welensky had not seen eye to eye on the electoral franchise for the Federal Assembly, Todd had agreed not to block our legislation for which we were grateful. In any case, the split between Todd and his ministers could do nothing but harm to the cause of maintaining the Federation. The last thing we wanted at this juncture was political instability of any kind.

However, Todd issued a public statement within a few days in which he categorically denied that he was about to resign or had been asked to do so. He emphasised that he had been seeing the Federal Prime Minister and other ministers and that relations were cordial. He also said, "Now that the U.F.P. has been formed, the whole position of the moderate political forces in Southern Rhodesia has been strengthened and the new party dominates the political arena . . . My Ministers and I are not only fully united in our policies but also in our confidence in one another . . ."

I did not believe that Todd and his Ministers were united, but on the surface things appeared to have settled down, and Todd went off to South Africa for a short holiday over Christmas. On his return to Salisbury on 14th January, 1958, he was met at the airport by P. B. Fletcher who told him that most of the Cabinet were demanding his resignation. *The Rhodesia Herald* published a photograph of the two men which made it apparent that there was a quarrel. The upshot was the resignation of Fletcher and all the other Ministers except Davenport. Todd was able to find another set of Ministers from the ranks of the U.R.P. and thus to carry on, although it began to appear that he could not count on a majority in his caucus so that he would be in a precarious position as soon as Parliament met.

He decided to put his leadership to the test at the ensuing meeting of the territorial congress of the newly formed U.F.P. which was due to meet on 8th February, 1958. The congress was to consist of delegates from the branches of the former U.R.P. and also from those of the former Federal Party's territorial wing. A difficulty arose as to who should chair this congress. Todd and Fletcher could not reach agreement despite efforts on the part of neutral Federal Ministers to mediate. Eventually, it was left to Welensky to chair the meeting but he had second thoughts about the propriety of doing so and saddled me with the task. I was most reluctant to accept this invidious rôle but no one else could be found. Information began to reach me that strenuous efforts were being made in various parts of the country to revive moribund branches, and it was soon evident that the credentials of a number of delegates would be challenged. On the eve of the congress, I called on Todd to let him know that this was likely to occur so that he should be forewarned. At the outset of the congress I proposed the appointment of a legal sub-committee to deal with the challenges, of which there were about seven. The unfortunate members of this committee had to get into a huddle while congress proceeded, and so they missed most of the drama that ensued. When they eventually reported most of the challenges were upheld.

Fletcher opened the attack on Todd. Although in his day Fletcher could make a very able speech, and in fact was something of an orator, on this occasion he was not on form and made a poor showing. The other renegade ministers followed. Todd made a brilliant speech in reply though to my mind it did not seem to dispose of the points made against him. Eventually, congress proceeded to the election of a leader. Fletcher and Todd were nominated and a third candidate also, namely, Edgar Whitehead who at that very moment was celebrating his birthday in Washington D.C. where he had gone as the diplomatic representative of the Federal Government.

Todd won the first round with Whitehead second and Fletcher third. On the run off, with Fletcher eliminated, Whitehead was elected. The meeting closed at about midnight, and Whitehead's supporters cabled him. I met him at the airport a few days later. Todd resigned in his favour, but accepted a post as Minister of Labour in his Cabinet. A seat had to be found in Parliament for Whitehead, and a by-election was held in Hillside, the constituency I formerly represented. I had no part in the selection of the constituency and had I been consulted I would have advised that it was by no means a safe seat. It was a golden opportunity for the opposition who led Whitehead into a trap by challenging him to bring Todd to speak on his platform which he agreed to do. Todd made the speech of the evening but it did not win any votes for Whitehead. I waited for polling day before going off by car to South Africa on holiday immediately after casting my vote. I was intercepted at Pretoria by a message from Welensky informing me that Whitehead had been defeated, and recalling me to Salisbury.

When I got back I found everything in confusion. Whitehead's only way out was to hold a general election for which the newly formed U.F.P. was in no way prepared. Meanwhile, a rift had developed between Whitehead and Todd who was expelled from the Cabinet and proceeded to gather his supporters into a new party called the Central African Party or C.A.P. The United Federal Party had to take immediate steps to field a full muster of candidates for the 30 constituencies, as several of the sitting members had gone over with Todd and others did not seek re-election. Once again I found myself involved in the task of persuading candidates to come forward, and with considerable difficulty the U.F.P. was able to muster a full team. Todd's C.A.P. was less successful. The electorate was thoroughly confused by the turn events had taken and things seemed to be running strongly in favour of the Dominion Party led by Stockil. Fortunately, the latter made a gaffe by demanding that the Governor should suspend the constitution on the ground that the new electoral laws should not be allowed to operate. This gave the U.F.P. a much needed weapon against the Dominion Party.

When the results of the poll were declared the U.F.P. had won by the slender majority of 17 to 13, and its victory had been won by virtue of the preferential voting system

which had just been introduced. Todd and his entire following were eliminated. His departure from the political scene
also had the effect of bringing to a close more than ten
years of my own political association with him which, until
1958, had been a very happy one.

In my time, I have seen all eight of Rhodesia's Prime
Ministers, I have known six of them, and worked at close
quarters with most of these. For me, Garfield Todd was the
most unforgettable character of them all. It is a tragedy
that his great potential did not come to full fruition. The
fault, I believe, lay not in his stars but partly in his friends,
and mainly in his enemies among whom he must himself
be numbered as the worst. Tredgold in his autobiographical
work blamed the U.F.P. leaders for ousting Todd but this
is quite incorrect. Todd's fall was due entirely to his failure
to carry the support of his first Cabinet and, more important,
the support of his parliamentary party. None of the Federal
Ministers was involved in the disputes between Todd and his
colleagues.

34

Northern Rhodesia under Benson
and Lennox-Boyd

BEFORE Federation, Northern Rhodesia had an Executive Council presided over by the Governor (Sir Gilbert Rennie) in which there was a mixture of civil servants holding office as Ministers of the Crown, and unofficial members, the leading personality among these being Roy Welensky who did not hold a portfolio but had an enormous influence in the council. To a person such as myself who was accustomed to Cabinet government, the idea of a civil servant being at the same time a Minister is rather strange. Welensky seems also to have thought it peculiar because he sometimes quipped about government by the civil servant for the civil servant, and remarked that while the unofficials in the council went home every night the civil servants went "home" every two years.

The Legislative Council consisted of 12 elected unofficials all of whom were white, four blacks chosen by an electoral college, two whites nominated by the Governor and eight civil servants. The voters roll for the election of the 12 unofficials was based on income and property qualifications and was confined to British subjects. It thus excluded all the indigenous population, who were classified as British protected persons, except eleven who had been naturalised.

It had been intended that when Welensky joined the Federal Government his mantle in Northern Rhodesia would fall on his friend and colleague Geoff Beckett but in the 1954 election Beckett failed to get nomination due to some slip. Leadership of the Federal Party went to John Roberts, a successful farmer but a man lacking political experience. Following the election, Roberts and two other Federal Party men were given portfolios in the Executive, as were also John Moffat and Harry Franklin, a retired civil servant, both of whom were nominated members of the Legislative Council. Franklin in his book* glories in his opposition to Federation, and tells us that he worked closely with Moffat. The latter alternated for some years between the Federal Assembly and the Northern Rhodesian Government.

Roberts was somewhat younger than Welensky and me. I got to know him well as we were constantly meeting to discuss constitutional questions; our relationship was always cordial and I formed a high opinion of his ability. He had an unenviable and difficult rôle to play in the years from 1960 onwards which he did with great dignity.

While the Federal and Southern Rhodesian Governments were working at their plans for the electoral franchise, Benson, the Northern Rhodesia Governor, was doing the same with a view to a new dispensation to be made in time for a general election in 1959. Roberts kept us informed of what was afoot and eventually we got a draft of Benson's scheme which was presented to the Northern Rhodesia Legislative Council in March, 1958. Welensky in *4 000 Days*† has referred to this scheme; its proposals were, as he says, very complex. There were to be two voters rolls, the qualifications for which were set at levels based on the Tredgold Commission's recommendations. Benson accepted the Tredgold "devaluation" proposal although the Southern Rhodesia Government had discarded it.

Despite Welensky's criticism I thought that there were considerable merits in Benson's scheme, the avowed object of which was to bring about a government conducted by members of all races working in partnership. The provisions of the scheme were such that a political party, if it wished

---

Unholy Wedlock. The Failure of the Central African Federation by Harry Franklin. London, George Allen and Unwin, 1963.

†*Welensky's 4 000 Days. The Life and Death of the Federation of Rhodesia and Nyasaland* by Sir Roy Welensky, London, Collins, 1964.

its candidates to succeed, must seek the support of voters of all races. As I had myself consistently advocated the same thing I had no quarrel with Benson in this respect. Unfortunately, he introduced a novel idea that candidates for six rural constituencies, in order to secure nomination, should have to get certificates of approval from two-thirds of the chiefs in the constituency. Some of these rural constituencies covered areas as large as England or Scotland, but were not as well served as those countries with roads or railways. One of them had 34 chiefs within its bounds.

We objected in principle to this requirement which would in effect give the chiefs a veto on the candidates of a political party of which they happened to disapprove. We also had strong objections on practical grounds, as the actual mechanics of obtaining a large number of certificates would prove most difficult in the time available to the candidate. These six rural seats were designed for the return of black members, and we were anxious that the U.F.P. should be able to field a full team of black and white candidates, in keeping with our ideas of a political partnership. Benson obstinately refused to modify this part of the plan. We appealed to the U.K. Ministers, Lord Home and Lennox-Boyd, and discussions were held in London during 1958 at which we sought changes in this and other respects. Certain minor changes were agreed to but the British Ministers were just as obstinate as Benson. We pointed out to them the enormous difficulties that would surround the candidates for some of these six constituencies. We were not seeking an advantage simply for the U.F.P. Our representations fell on deaf ears. We subsequently listened to a debate in the House of Commons when we had the mortification of hearing James Callaghan from the Labour front bench attacking the chiefs' veto, but he too failed to make any impression on the Government.

In the election that followed, which occurred during a heavy rainy season, in one of the constituencies no candidate was able to surmount the hurdles of the chiefs' veto, while in other constituencies one or more candidates failed. One U.F.P. candidate, in the constituency where there were 34 chiefs, failed by one certificate after journeys to which justice could only be done by the pen of an R. M. Ballantyne. The U.F.P. were therefore deprived of the opportunity of having a full muster of black candidates which was a keen disappointment; three of its six candidates were eliminated by the veto. Other political parties suffered in the same way.

The outcome of the election was a considerable success for Roberts whose U.F.P. candidates won 11 of the 12 seats designed for whites and two of those designed for blacks. Four U.F.P. members including one black, Mr. Musumbulwa, were given portfolios in an executive council now consisting of ten, but still including Moffat who had formed an alliance with Todd and his C.A.P., and Franklin.

Benson when he introduced his constitutional scheme had said among other things :

> *In order to inject stability certain provisions of the scheme would be entrenched in the constitutional instruments so that the main lines of constitutional advance would be settled for some time ahead and the confidence of the people would not be continually jeopardised by the prospect of drastic changes every few years.*

Lennox-Boyd said much the same in his dispatch of September, 1958. "Entrenchment" in the strict constitutional sense was hardly compatible with a constitution such as Northern Rhodesia had at this stage which fell far short of responsible self-government, and was under the thumb of the British Government. Nevertheless, the point Benson attempted to make was both clear and sound. His scheme needed only to be shorn of the chiefs' veto to provide a workable basis for at least one more general election after that of 1959.

What we in the U.F.P. were anxious to see mapped out in 1960 was an advance towards a Cabinet system of government, not the drastic alteration in the electoral franchise arrangements which was made in 1962. The "entrenchments" referred to by Benson and Lennox-Boyd were then brushed aside despite the Federal Government's objections.

35

Nyasaland under Armitage and Lennox-Boyd

BEFORE Federation, Nyasaland, now Malawi, had very few links with the Rhodesias. From about 1940 it participated in a joint Court of Appeal called the Rhodesia and Nyasaland Court of Appeal. When the Central African Council was formed after the end of Hitler's War further contacts were made at the political and civil service levels. For the great majority of white Rhodesians, however, their only link with Nyasaland was through the employment of blacks from that territory in domestic or farming occupations.

I had never been in Nyasaland before Federation but heard a good deal about it from my father who had made a missionary journey there and was much impressed by the cheapness of food such as chickens, fish, pineapples and the like. It appeared that visitors to Nyasaland would be well advised to take plenty of small change with them. My father's missionary flock in Matabeleland included many Nyasaland Africans and I got to know several teachers and evangelists who spoke English with a heavy Scottish accent. I have already mentioned Wellington Manoah Chirwa as one of these teachers.

Up to 1951, when the conferences concerned with Federation began, there was no political demand in Southern Rhodesia for linkage with Nyasaland. At the Victoria Falls conference that year our delegation had in mind a scheme to exclude Nyasaland and link the two Rhodesias together under a unitary government plus a subsidiary government exclusively for Northern Rhodesia to deal with subjects which intimately concerned the black population. Griffiths insisted that the Nyasaland delegation must continue and we had to drop the scheme. Later, when the Conservative Government came to power, Huggins again tried to have Nyasaland excluded but, as he put it, the Secretary of State thumped the table and insisted that it was all or nothing. It was obvious that this territory was a Cinderella of which the U.K. wanted to be rid. In the event, Nyasaland became a kind of keystone in the federal arch comprising itself and the two Rhodesias.

Soon after I became a Federal Minister in 1954, I paid my first visit to Nyasaland where I was very hospitably received by the Governor, Sir Geoffrey Colby, at Government House, Zomba. The Colonial civil servants I met were also very friendly and co-operative, far more so than their counterparts in Northern Rhodesia. Even on a short visit it was apparent that the territory had been very badly neglected. Facilities and services to the public were primitive by Rhodesian standards. As Minister of Education I had no responsibility for African education but I was concerned with the provision of schools for Nyasaland's white community and its much larger Asian community. Before Federation the Nyasaland Government had provided three primary schools for whites, but had left the Asians to fend for themselves. There were several lamentable establishments housed in ramshackle premises, presided over by teachers with minimal educational attainments, the language medium being Gujerati. The leaders of the white community soon demanded improvements and in particular the establishment of a secondary school. The Asians were also clamouring for better facilities. By the end of Federation we had transformed the educational scene, and the same can be said for other departments such as health and the post office.

Lord Malvern's description of Britain's neglect of Nyasaland before Federation, written in 1959, is worth quoting :

In 1890 when a protectorate was declared over Nyasaland to deal with the slave-trade something positive was done but since that, regardless of what party was in power at Westminster, the country was left neglected until Federation came to pass. (An exception to this general neglect was when the inhabitants were encouraged to grow tung trees for oil production, but unfortunately when the oil was produced the U.K. bought their tung oil from China).

Nyasaland was ruled by a Governor with a nominated executive council. There was also a legislative council but its membership did not spring from democratic institutions. The first elections ever to be held were those to choose members of the Federal Assembly. A few years later the constitution was amended to allow non-blacks to elect five or six members of the Legislative Council but black members were still chosen by indirect means through the African Representative Council.

In 1955, Macintyre had produced a Budget resulting in customs duties being imposed on some items which had hitherto escaped taxation in Nyasaland owing to the Congo Basin Treaty of which Lord Swinton had spoken in such derogatory terms. As a result, Federal Party members of the Federal Assembly representing Nyasaland constituencies became mutinous and voted against the government. Apart from Barrow who was in the Cabinet, only Brereton voted with the Government, and the Nyasaland division of the party promptly sent him to Coventry. It was against this background that the third congress of the Federal Party met in Blantyre in 1955. The breach had by then not quite been healed and there was still much bitterness. Lord Malvern in his presidential speech referred to the matter saying that the Nyasaland members of the party had not yet been house-trained. This sally went down very well and did not appear to reopen the wounds.

The white members of the Legislative Council were a small clique with whom I found it most difficult to get co-operation. Though nominally members of the U.F.P. their allegiance to the party was rather thin. My relations with them over several years were uneasy and on some occasions severely strained. Eventually, we reached a certain degree of mutual respect, especially as we began to find common ground in our opposition to the policies of Iain McLeod. Michael Blackwood, a Blantyre solicitor, was much the ablest of them. When the Federation was finally dissolved, Dr. Banda who had come to recognise Blackwood's fearlessness and ability persuaded him to remain a member of the Legislative Council, where his rôle as a constructive critic could be useful to the doctor.

Welensky in *4 000 Days* has recounted some of the events in 1959 that led to Dr. Banda's detention with his principal lieutenants and several hundred of the lesser lights. I was involved in these affairs because of my responsibility for the federal prisons. In the course of quelling the riots that occurred in March and April, 1959 some 51 people had been shot and 79 injured by gunfire. Macmillan appointed the Devlin Commission of Inquiry. Meanwhile, the Press in the U.K. made sure that most of the odium relating to the killings and preventive detention should attach to the Federal Government where, of course, it did not belong. Welensky and I were in London when the Devlin Report first became available to the British Government; Lennox-Boyd gave us copies hot from the press and asked me as a matter of urgency to give him my views about the report which was to be the subject of an early debate in the House of Commons. I sat late into the night before flying back to Salisbury preparing my comments.

The terms of the report were a considerable shock to the U.K. Government and to Lennox-Boyd in particular. He had very recently had the misfortune to be the Minister responsible in connection with a most unpleasant affair in Kenya known as the Hola Camp incident in which 11 Mau Mau detainees had been beaten and assaulted to death following a refusal to work. Lennox-Boyd, needless to say, had no personal involvement and was thoroughly distressed by this unhappy event but he had to bear the brunt of a difficult debate in the Commons which ended in the small hours of a very long parliamentary night, 27th and 28th July, 1959. Incidentally, Enoch Powell, not then in the Conservative Government, made a memorable speech attacking those responsible. In the afternoon of 28th July the debate on the Devlin Report began, on a motion by the Attorney-General, Sir Reginald Manningham-Buller, the effect of the motion being that the Government adopted only part of the findings of the Commission and in general supported the actions of the Governor, Sir Robert Armitage, which the Devlin Commission had criticised. The Attorney-General was highly critical of some of the Commission's findings. The Labour Party spokesmen, of course, took full advantage of some of the many openings given to them by the report. Finally, Lennox-Boyd wound up the debate at 10 p.m. after what must have been for him a particularly gruelling two days.

The Government won the debate by a substantial majority but they had received a severe mauling in the two unrelated debates. The Attorney-General dealt with a number of the points which I had covered in my comments to Lennox-Boyd. As I saw it the Devlin Report was a disaster. It used quite unjustifiable expressions like "police state" to describe the territory. Inevitably, much of this description continued to stick, while Dr. Banda was whitewashed. It is interesting that shortly after the Devlin Report was published, Mr. Justice Beadle (later Chief Justice of Rhodesia), and two assessors who formed a tribunal to deal with matters connected with certain detainees in Southern Rhodesia had Dr. Banda before them as a witness. They took a different view from that of the Devlin Commissioners as to his credibility and in their report of 10th August, 1959* gave detailed reasons for doing so.

Arising out of complaints brought to notice by Mr. Dingle Foot I appointed a commission of inquiry into the treatment of detainees at Kanjedza. The chairman was Advocate Fieldsend, later a judge; his report fully exonerated the Federal Government, but never attracted any publicity for us in the U.K.

Despite the setbacks in Kenya over Hola, and the Devlin enquiry, Macmillan led the Conservatives to victory in the Autumn of 1959 with the slogan, "You've never had it so good", ringing in the voters' ears. In the aftermath of the election, Lennox-Boyd took a peerage and Iain Macleod took over at the Colonial Office. Lord Home remained at the

---

*(C.S.R. 27/59), 10th August, 1959.

Commonwealth Relations Office until nearly the end of July, 1960 when he became Foreign Secretary and Duncan Sandys replaced him at the Commonwealth Relations Office. This was the man Macmillan had earlier selected as Minister of Defence to cut up historic British regiments and join some of the pieces together in different combinations.

36

Monckton's Hopeless Report

———————

THE EVENTS in Nyasaland in the period covered by the Devlin Commission profoundly shocked the British Government; they were highlighted by the Press and the report was meat and drink to the opponents of Federation, including the Church of Scotland. Welensky has given an accurate account of the events leading up to Macmillan's decision to set up the Monckton Commission to prepare the way for the 1960 review. I saw all the exchanges of messages passing between the two Prime Ministers and I prepared drafts of all those that Welensky sent. It was exacting and frustrating work trying to pin Macmillan down and we never quite succeeded in doing so as he made equivocal statements in the House of Commons as to whether secession on the part of any territory fell within the Commission's terms of reference while trying to assure us in the next breath that it was not.

Lord Home in *The Way the Wind Blows,** categorically says that the British Government gave an assurance that the break-up of the Federation would not be in the terms of reference. This is difficult to reconcile with his further statement that the commission did not breach its terms of reference, as the right to secede, which the commission ulti- mately recommended, clearly paved the way for the break-up. Lord Home has acknowledged that the commission was his own brainchild. He envisaged it doing what he says Federal politicians had failed to do, that is tell a success story about their achievement in development. He thought that if an

———————

The Way the Wind Blows. An autobiography by Sir Alec Douglas- Home. London, Collins, 1976.

impartial commission did this there was a chance that Africans could thereby be convinced that the Federal structure could serve the people of the Federation better than any other. Of course, he underestimated the thirst for power of people like Dr. Banda.

Lord Home's argument about the success story entirely failed to convince us at the time he used it. The Devlin Report had killed any faith we might have had in Commissions appointed by the British Government. The reason why we submitted to the setting up of the commission was that Lord Home told us politely but firmly that if we did not agree the U.K. would hold an inquiry directed to the situation in the two northern territories, in which we would have no voice. This we thought would be just as dangerous if not more so than the wider inquiry Lord Home was asking us to agree to.

When the commission was first mooted we envisaged a relatively small body but this snowballed into a circus of about 25 members some of whom were accompanied by their wives. Having regard to Macmillan's repeated assurances that the terms of reference would not be extended to cover secession we did not fully appreciate at the outset that the Commission would become obsessed with the views of African witnesses fanned up by nationalist propagandists, while evidence favourable to the Federation was largely excluded because of intimidation so skilfully used by Banda's Malawi Congress Party (M.C.P.) and Kaunda's United National Independence Party (U.N.I.P.). In the light of this experience, the outcome of the Pearce Commission in 1971, dealing with acceptability of a new constitution for Rhodesia, was entirely predictable. There was intimidation on a massive scale which killed any chance of acceptance by blacks.

R. A. Butler in *The Art of the Possible** tells us that although under collective Cabinet responsibility he was a party to the appointment of the Monckton Commission, he had not been in favour of this course of action, and did not

---

The Art of the Possible: The *Memoirs of Lord Butler.* London, Hamish Hamilton, 1971.

believe that it would achieve the aims that Macmillan had in mind, particularly that of getting the Labour Party committed. No more did we in the Federal Government believe that it would be beneficial.

In July, 1959, I accompanied Welensky to London for talks with Macmillan and Home about these matters. I quote from a letter to my wife written on 7th July :

> *We met at Alec Home's office before lunch and with Macmillan at No. 10 at 4 p.m. He had decided that we should talk informally in the garden. He was sitting under a tree on a cane chair with other chairs around him in a circle. Roy was invited to sit on one of these and was on the point of doing so when it was noticed that the bottom had fallen out. Evidence of the decay of the Commonwealth? Talks were quite amicable but we went on later to discuss matters with Lennox-Boyd and Home, and they got near to being acrimonious. L-B is a bit on edge over Hola, I think, and also because the prospect of "Devlin" is not too good.*

At the turn of the year 1959-1960, Macmillan visited Salisbury in his "winds of change" tour of Africa. I was present at several meetings he had with Welensky, and he appeared to me to be evasive whenever we attempted to discuss our problems. We certainly derived no satisfaction from the visit.

The Monckton Commission began its sittings on 15th February, 1960. Before then we had to prepare to deal with it. There was never any question of the Federal Government as such giving evidence to the commission. It was decided to use the United Federal Party machinery for the expression of our views. Welensky put me in charge of the task of drawing up the U.F.P. document, and this was a heavy assignment. We submitted a 70-page memo under the aegis of the Federal Standing Committee. I was considerably helped by J. A. Clark, later Federal Minister of Trade, and others, but I prepared the final draft myself. Each of the territorial divisions of the U.F.P. also submitted a memo which I helped to prepare so as to co-ordinate their views with ours. The commission's report makes no mention of these documents or the witnesses who presented them so it is impossible now to say whether they made any impact. Most likely, any impact was blunted by the welter of memoranda and testimony submitted by others. The U.F.P. document has still some importance as it contains the Federal Government's case for the continuation of Federation.

On 12th May, 1960 I reported to Welensky on a visit paid to my office in Salisbury by Lord Monckton who spent an hour with me. I said among other things :

> *He hopes to get a majority if not unanimity for keeping the Federation intact, while he is looking for adjustments that may sweeten up the Federation for African consumers; he is looking at it in a most responsible way. I did not get the impression that a heavy inroad on the electoral franchise was in his mind, still less a radical redistribution of seats in the Federal Assembly. We did not, however, specifically discuss these questions . . . last, and possibly most important as an indication of Lord M's conservative approach, he asked what were the possibilities of consultation in London in June between himself and the Federal Government. I told him there was a chance that I might be in London in June. Lord M. said . . . he would welcome a discussion with me sub rosa.*

During the English summer in 1960, the commission went to London to consider their recommendations. Athol Evans accompanied them as the Federal Government's liaison officer. His reports to us showed that the Commissioners were in a state of muddle, frustration and defeatism. In July, I went to London for talks with Lord Home about the date of the Federal review. We had our meetings at his office in the House of Lords. On one occasion, before formal business began, he suddenly turned to me and apropos of nothing at all said, "Have you got a woman in *your* house?" I was a little taken aback but recovered in time to answer in the affirmative and to give the lady's name as Mrs. Muriel Rosin, M.P. for one of the Salisbury Constituencies. Mrs. Rosin had been in London about this time and I expect that Lord Home had met her.

Monckton invited me to lunch in the City at the Midland Bank of which he was chairman. The security arrangements were most impressive. I was handed from one flunkey to another through a series of corridors till at last I reached the inner sanctum where I shared a splendid repast with the great man. I voiced the fears disturbing me since seeing Evans that the commission might recommend changes that would emasculate the Federation. Monckton replied by referring to the 1914-18 War in which he had served, and compared the lot of the Federal Government with that of the men in the Flanders trenches; he assured me that he appreciated our difficulties and would do his best to see that we were not let down; his sympathies were with us. I left feeling rather more hopeful but the hopes began to wane as I recalled what Dingle Foot had said to Dr. Banda in the Gwelo Prison.* After my return to Salisbury I sent Monckton, as he had suggested I should, a memo on the points about which the Federal Government felt most strongly. He acknowledged receipt, but his failure to make any comment increased my fears that no good would come of his report.

When the document finally emerged, Welensky was on holiday at the Cape. I flew in a military aircraft to the Transvaal and boarded the train at Johannesburg so that Welensky could look at the report on the journey from there to Pretoria. It made dismal reading. We dined that evening with Dr. and Mrs. Verwoerd at their State residence. This was my first and only meeting with South Africa's sixth Prime Minister. Like myself, he was a son of the manse and during the Kaiser's war had attended Milton High School in Bulawayo where his father was minister of the Dutch Reformed Church. I saw him in London in 1961 at the Guildhall lunch for the Commonwealth Prime Ministers, a few days before he took the fateful step of withdrawing South Africa from the Commonwealth. I noticed that he got his full share of the applause that marked the entry of each Prime Minister.

Little purpose would now be served by going into the Monckton Commission's recommendations in any detail

---

*Welensky's 4 000 Days, p.175.

Twenty-three members agreed up to a point, but with varia-
tions, on some broad recommendations. They recommended
the continuance of the Federation in an emasculated form
with rights of secession which would kill all hope of its
continuance for the reasons given by Lord Swinton in 1953.
They wanted parity of representation between whites and
blacks in the Federal Assembly, but gave only superficial consideration to the question how stable government could
emerge or be maintained in these circumstances. In the
northern legislatures, black majorities were to be hastened on
and electoral franchise standards lowered to a point which
made it virtually certain that Southern Rhodesia would be
the first territory to secede.

Welensky, on 11th October, broadcast a statement
denouncing the commission's proposals for secession, pointing out that, being aware of the Federal Government's views
that secession was outside the terms of reference, the commission should at least have invited us to make representations as to the effects of recommending a secession clause.
Lord Home's view, in his book, that the terms of reference
had not been breached is not supported by any argument.

When Macmillan discussed the report in Parliament, he
tried to make the best of it, relying on its wishywashy recommendation for the continuance of Federation in a watered-
down form. In paragraph 71, the report of the majority
said :

> *To break it up at this crucial stage in the history of
> Africa would, we believe, amount to an admission that
> there is no hope of survival for any multiracial society
> on the African Continent and that the differences of
> race and colour are irreconcilable. We cannot agree
> to such a conclusion. We believe rather that our object
> should be to preserve the benefits of Federation by
> recasting the structure of the present association in a
> form more acceptable to its inhabitants.*

The belief expressed in the final sentence was mere
wishful thinking having regard to the recommendations for
secession, which made it a certainty that if the commission's
recommendations were implemented the Federation would

disintegrate.   Macmillan must have realised this because neither he nor Sandys at any stage attempted to persuade Welensky to change his mind and accept the commission's recommendations.

37

U.K. and Federal Consultations
1958-1963
Principles and Motives

WHEN Federation was inaugurated in 1953, all concerned realised that the three territorial constitutions would not remain static. If the Federation was to advance to independence so also must the territories progress to full self-government. Southern Rhodesia had nearly reached this goal and we thought that the northern territories would also eventually have Prime Ministers and Cabinets of their own choosing. We who came from the south hoped that the dead hand of the Colonial Office would gradually release its grip on the north.

Federation was founded on the concept of partnership between the races as appears from the preamble to its constitution. As early as 1951, James Griffiths had stated that in the northern territories paramountcy had given place to partnership. The Federal Government was entitled to assume that changes in the constitutions of the territories would be so devised that partnership could continue in all spheres. The White Paper* made it clear that while the British Government had control of the territorial constitutions, the Federal Government had the right to be consulted. This was essential because changes in the territorial constitutions could undermine the Federation unless care were taken to keep them in tune with the principles on which the Federation was founded.

---

*Cmnd. 8753.

From 1957 to 1963, I was intimately involved in these consultations between our Government and the British Government. Much of what follows is an account of them as seen from my viewpoint. From 1961 onwards, bitter quarrels arose between the two Governments. The fundamental difference between us was that the British Government had begun to turn its back on the policy of partnership and was now giving way to black nationalist demands for majority rule, which, if conceded, would spell black domination and the end of racial harmony and the policy of political partnership. Neither Macmillan nor any of his ministers ever told us this, on the contrary, they paid lip-service to partnership though on a diminishing scale. While doing so they kept subtly hinting that the Federal and S.R. Governments were not doing enough to make a reality of partnership. Everyone knows that Rome was not built in a day, but our critics did not seem to realise that a political partnership between people culturally as far apart as whites and blacks in the Rhodesias and Nyasaland could not be built in as short a period as seven years, especially when we were subjected to outside interference. Nevertheless, despite the difficulties, after the Federal general election of 1958 and the Northern Rhodesia general election of 1959 political partnership had made a good beginning. In the Federal Assembly the U.F.P. caucus included several blacks, two of whom were appointed as junior Ministers, while Winston Field's Dominion Party caucus also included one black member. Political divisions were beginning to be on party rather than racial lines. In Northern Rhodesia, Roberts' U.F.P. caucus included some blacks, one of whom was appointed on his recommendation as Minister of Education.

This is not the place to expand on the way in which we were developing the policy of partnership, but it is important to have an understanding of the motives of the Federal and British Governments during this period. We were trying to build on the basis of partnership; they were undermining the foundation by substituting black domination. It should also be remembered that the British Government held the whip hand. A succession of British Ministers, Iain Macleod,

Duncan Sandys, Reginald Maudling and R. A. Butler wielded the whip under the direction of Harold Macmillan, and beat the life out of the Federation which their predecessors had been mainly responsible for creating.

In the chapters that follow, rather than pursue a completely chronological sequence I have divided the events into territorial and Federal compartments. Readers, I hope, will appreciate that when the events were occurring their results could not always be confined within these compartments. We kept pointing this out to British ministers but sometimes they could not, or would not, visualise the repercussions of decisions taken in one northern territory or the other, or on Southern Rhodesia, or indeed on the Federal centre.

38

Nyasaland under Jones and Macleod

ON 26th January, 1960 Macmillan was in Blantyre during his "winds of change" tour of Africa. The Malawi Congress Party staged a demonstration for the benefit of the world Press who had assembled to report his luncheon speech at Ryall's Hotel. A day or two later several British and foreign papers carried lurid reports of police violence to the demonstrators. The London *Daily Herald* made comparisons with the Hola Camp scandal, said how right the Devlin Commission were to call Nyasaland a police state, and demanded an immediate impartial enquiry into the Nyasaland Police. The editor sent an impudent telegram to the Governor running on the same lines.

The British and Nyasaland Governments tamely submitted to these demands and an enquiry was held by Mr. Justice Southworth of the Nyasaland High Court. His report runs to 126 pages, that is about two-thirds the length of the Devlin Report. Southworth J. must have enjoyed himself; he had the opportunity to produce a devastating indictment of the distorted biased reporting which had been calculated to promote the cause of Dr. Banda and his Malawi Congress Party against the wicked white federationists. In a classical passage* he discussed the affair of Miss Phombeya's toe :

> *As far as can be ascertained the amount of skin lost by both police and demonstrators as a result of injuries received on this occasion would hardly cover an area of one square inch, probably no more than the area of*

*Page 113.

*a penny postage stamp, and it does not appear that the
amount of blood that was shed would be sufficient to
test the capacity of an ordinary mustard spoon. Con-
templating the measure of the injuries sustained by the
demonstrators one cannot avoid the reflection that when
the face of Helen launched a thousand ships, and
brought Agamemnon and the great Achilles to the
shores of Phrygia, it hardly achieved as much as Miss
Phombeya's toe when it brought the paladins of Fleet
Street in the aerial argosies of our day across two
continents to appear before your commissioner in the
remote highlands of Middle Africa.*

Macleod's impending visit to the Federation in March,
1960 filled federal ministers with foreboding. His shadow
had already fallen on Kenya. We had two meetings with
him, before and after his trip to Malawi, and at both he
faced a barrage of questions over his plan to release Dr.
Banda and engage him in the territorial Government. Sir
Malcolm Barrow at the outset took a particularly strong line
prophesying that Banda's release would cause serious disturbances. Macleod's assessment was different. Barrow was
unwise to make his gloomy prediction because he had
underrated Macleod's skill in preparing the ground and
Banda's intelligent appreciation that the plum of secession
would fall into his lap if he let Macleod manage it for him.
Macleod asserted to us, with what sincerity it is difficult to
say, that the U.K.'s policy was to maintain British influence
and that it continued to subscribe whole-heartedly to the
Federal scheme and to the policy of partnership. Banda was
released while Macleod was in Nyasaland. The arrangements
for this were made by D. D. O'Donovan who was my right-
hand man as Secretary for Law. Banda was of course given
a hero's welcome by his compatriots and a good deal of
attention from the Governor and Macleod, though the latter
denied to us that he had accorded Banda red-carpet treatment.
At his second meeting with us Macleod made no effort to
conceal his satisfaction that Barrow's predictions had not
been fulfilled. I told him that Banda was determined to lead
Nyasaland out of the Federation and that any hope of persuading him to pursue a minor rôle within the framework of

Federation would be in vain. Macleod agreed that I might be right but insisted that an attempt should be made to involve him in the processes of Government in the hope that the economic advantages of Federation would eventually impress themselves on his mind. There was, of course, no question of the Federal Government dictating to Macleod, all we could do was to try to dissuade him from giving way to Banda and in this we failed. We had seen Nkrumah and Makarios taken from prison to become Redeemer of Ghana and Prime Minister of Cyprus respectively. Jomo Kenyatta, gaoled for his connection with Mau Mau, was, under Macleod's auspices, clearly being earmarked for the top post in Kenya, and now it seemed likely that Banda would have a similar destiny.

In July, 1960, while the Monckton Commission was deliberating in London, I went there as previously related with the threefold object of setting the date for the Federal review conference with Lord Home, having discussions with Macleod on his Nyasaland plans, and seeing Lord Monckton. I had some constructive ideas about how the Nyasaland territorial constitution could be devised so as to ensure that political parties working on the principle of partnership between the races would have some chance of winning black support. Our talks were pleasant and Macleod seemed willing to consider my ideas but made no promises. In the event little came of them.

A conference to review the Nyasaland constitution began at the end of July; Dixon and Blackwood who represented the U.F.P. had an unhappy time and Macleod had to use various forms of persuasion to get them to see the conference out. Macleod cabled Welensky on 5th August to say that the conference had ended with full agreement. His cable mentioned "understandable (by the U.F.P.) anxiety was that what was being agreed now might be quickly torn up". He stressed that all the delegates, (Banda included) "declared that they mean to work the new constitution".

Lord Blake* refers to the U.F.P. delegates signing the agreement and infers that they would scarcely have done so

---

*A History of Rhodesia, p.331.

THE AUTHOR AND MRS. GREENFIELD WELCOMING THE SULTAN OF
ZANZIBAR TO RHODESIA IN 1953.
THE MAYOR OF SALISBURY, MR. SANDFORD, IS ON THE RIGHT.
(Photo: *The Herald*, Salisbury)

CHIEF JUSTICE SIR ROBERT TREDGOLD ADDRESSING LORD
LLEWELLIN (centre) AND (left to right): LORD KILMUIR (seated behind
Sir Robert). CHIEF JUSTICE A. VAN DER S. CENTLIVRES (South Africa),
AND CHIEF JUSTICE SIR PETER BELL (Northern Rhodesia) IN SALISBURY
IN 1955.
(Photo: Federal Information Dept.)

PHOTOGRAPHED WITH SIR ROY WELENSKY BENEATH THE FEDERAL FLAG DURING AN OFFICIAL FUNCTION IN DECEMBER, 1963.

THE AUTHOR AND MR. DUNCAN SANDYS. SECRETARY OF STATE FOR COMMONWEALTH RELATIONS. AT THE SALISBURY AIRPORT IN SEPTEMBER, 1960.

(Photo: Federal Information Dept.)

if Welensky had objected. There might have been some substance in this suggestion if Welensky had been present in London and available for consultation but of course this was not so. Welensky and his Ministers were horrified.

Blackwood on his return left us in no doubt that he and Dixon had been led into a trap. The new constitution provided that blacks would have a clear majority in the Legislative Council but it left many of the important details regarding electoral franchise and delimitation to be worked out by a committee to be set up in Nyasaland.

Meanwhile, Dr. Banda at a Press conference hailed the outcome of the conference as a triumph for himself presaging the break-up of the Federation. He spoke of the possibility of federation with the Congo and Tanzania "but with Southern Rhodesia never, never, never".

Welensky cabled Macleod protesting that Banda's utterances were incompatible with his agreement to "work the constitution", and pointing out that the new constitution was within the framework of the Federal constitution. Macleod replied,

> We must give Banda what both he and reasonable people believe is a fair chance of settling down. We are dealing with a man who is extremely voluble. We must expect him now that he has gone back to Nyasaland having achieved practically nothing of the aims which he set out to his followers when he left, to look around for some issue to conceal this failure and keep up his own position. I believe that if we accept that we have to work with him we must recognise that he must do this and ourselves strive to create a situation which will allow him gradually to move even further to the centre of things both in the political and constitutional scene. Our instrument in the handling of Banda has to be the Governor (at the moment Jones).

Jones had recently been appointed Chief Secretary but was soon to become governor and to acquire the nickname of Malawi Jones. If Macleod really did have serious thoughts of handling Banda "so as to get him to the centre of things" Jones proved to be a broken reed.

The arrangements for enrolling voters and delimiting constituencies took a lengthy period. Macleod had arranged matters so that fundamental points in the new constitution were to be dealt with by a committee; he completely by-passed the local legislature. Several things were done to which Welensky took strong objection but Macleod refused to budge.

In a memo to Welensky in January, 1961, I wrote :

The Malawi Congress Party (has taken) control in Nyasaland to a great extent. For example the Nyasaland Police have virtually handed over the control of the crowds and processions to "Malawi Police". The Malawi Congress Party has gone from strength to strength. Intimidation has become the order of the day. The Malawi Police have instituted their own pass law, the necessary pass for every one, including even a visit to the market, being a Malawi membership card or a Banda badge, issued at a price.

Under conditions such as these, it was not surprising that Dr. Banda's Malawi Congress Party swept the board at the elections in so far as black members were concerned. The U.F.P. only managed to win most of the seats for non-blacks.

39

The 1960 Review Conference

THE 1960 Federal review conference might be judged the wordiest and most futile conference in the history of Southern Africa up to that date. It is hardly surprising that Lord Blake rates its worth at only a paragraph.* Even then he repeats Macmillan's error in saying that Welensky had never met Dr. Banda before. I shall devote a little more space to the proceedings, if only to show something of the delaying tactics employed by Macmillan when dealing with problems for which he had no glimmer of a solution.

Caldicott and I travelled with most of the Federal, and some of the Southern Rhodesian, delegates in a Royal Rhodesian Air Force plane which landed us at Malta in the early hours of a winter morning. We were given a hearty welcome and breakfast in the R.A.F. Mess and had a glimpse of Valetta before taking off from the George Cross Island. When we landed at Gatwick we were welcomed by the head of the U.K. Government Hospitality Department. Guy van Eeden who was then Winston Field's constitutional adviser amused me by asking the name of the "U.K. handshaker". British Government hospitality, at any rate to the Federal delegation, was less evident than at the conferences at the beginning of the decade. Perhaps for this reason one of our number strayed one evening to a night-club. When he arrived at Lancaster House not many hours later and was asked for his security check card he produced his night-club membership card and was at once admitted.

I had hoped that, as in the case of the early conferences,

A History of Rhodesia, p.332.

there would be a steering committee but Macmillan had a different technique. He opened the conference himself on 5th December with a short speech in his best "winds of change" style but added, "Those who will come after us will rightly condemn us if we cannot rise to the level of events, particularly if we allow the promptings of immediate difficulties political or otherwise to divert us from the ultimate aim of creating in Central Africa a way of life which all races may share in friendship." Before ending he said, "We have no simple or painless solution to propose. We can offer only our goodwill and perhaps our experience. We must believe that this conference may find a happy outcome and that the men and women of the Rhodesias and Nyasaland will not look to us in vain, for they look to us to lead them forward to an assured future of peace and stability." Macmillan was as good as his word in one respect at least — he had no solution to propose. Nor did he, Sandys or R. A. Butler ever offer a solution unless one regards the final break-up of the Federation as such. The assured future of peace and stability has not yet dawned though eighteen years have passed.

After these platitudes, the conference adjourned till the following day when there began a round of lengthy speeches. Almost every delegate from Africa delivered a lengthy speech. All these are on record. They have not as far as I am aware been published, though at the time they were given only a "confidential" rating. Welensky opened the debate with a well reasoned speech. Dr. Banda, Kaunda, Nkumbula, Nkomo and Mclean, Southern Rhodesian members of the Dominion Party, and some others joined in the attack. Several African members in the U.F.P. team strongly supported Federation, and many speakers complained of the intimidation practised by the M.C.P. and U.N.I.P. Among the speakers who impressed me most were Blackwood and A. R. W. Stumbles, Minister of Justice in Southern Rhodesia. Stumbles said :

> If the U.K. Government elects to support the extreme Nationalists who have been lionised, televised and feted ad nauseam to the exclusion of all moderate elements then indeed the consequences will be grave.

He went on :

> *The special favouritism that has been shown by the*
> *U.K. to the extreme merchants in the past fortnight has*
> *caused us to have grave doubts whether they still believe*
> *in the policy of non-racial partnership.*

He issued a warning that Southern Rhodesia might have to consider very seriously its future relations with the U.K. Government.

A very fine speech was made by Mr. R. C. Bucquet, a long-standing resident of Nyasaland and a Federal M.P., who spoke in eloquent terms of the iniquitous intimidation practised by the nationalist parties.

During Whitehead's well-reasoned and able speech, Dr. Banda and his team began rude and noisy interruptions and staged a walk-out which of course gained them the desired publicity. Earlier, he himself had delivered a tub-thumping harangue. When Welensky wound up the debate he challenged the U.K. Government to say where they stood. He asked :

> *Are they going to back those who have loyally carried*
> *out the work of building up the Federation which the*
> *U.K. Government founded or are they backing those*
> *who wish to tear it down? In the issue between racial*
> *nationalism and partnership one would have expected*
> *the U.K. to be unequivocally on our side . . . I think*
> *the other four governments have the right to know and*
> *to know soon. The U.K. Government can no longer*
> *sit on the fence.*

(Welensky underestimated their capacity to do so).

Duncan Sandys then proceeded to sum up the debate. He evaded the challenge but gave a pointer in the direction of backing those who wanted to tear the Federation down when he said :

> *If the Federation is to win the confidence and support*
> *of the African population we believe that Africans must*
> *be allowed to play a bigger part in running the country.*

We had drawn the attention of the British Government to certain events in Nyasaland, which induced Sandys to say :

> *I am sure we have all read with horror of the attacks which have been made upon the homes and families of some of our fellow delegates sitting around this table* (these were U.F.P. delegates) *and we express to them our profound sympathy. Whatever differences there may be among us I sincerely trust that we are, all of us, united in firmly condemning violence and intimidation as a method of securing political ends. I do hope, when I say that, I speak for every member of this conference.*

Not a voice was raised to contradict these pious hopes but many of us felt nausea knowing as we did that among those present there were people who, so far from condemning violence, constantly used it as a method of securing political ends. They continued to do so in the years that followed. The Martin Wray Report, giving an account of disturbances in Northern Rhodesia from July to October, 1961 spells it all out in 77 pages, and firmly attributes the disorders there to U.N.I.P. The outcome of these disturbances was that the U.K. Government made concessions which assisted the party to win the election in 1962 as related elsewhere. But, to return to the 1960 conference, Macmillan pronounced the benediction, endorsing what Sandys had said, and adding several more ifs and buts of his own. Here is a typical passage in which, on behalf of the British Government, he washed his hands of the problems :

> *The British Government have a duty towards all the people of all the races in the Federation but the British Government can only discharge that duty if they — all the races, all the peoples — will co-operate with one another in developing a truly non-racial society. If we accept the principle of partnership, the rest falls into its place.*

This was another way of saying, "We have a duty to the whites but if the blacks won't co-operate we cannot discharge our duty to the whites". The conference adjourned on 17th December, never to meet again.

On our way back to Salisbury, our R.R.A.F. plane refuelled in Libya where the R.A.F. still had a base, and at Khartoum where a black colonel representing the Sudan Government met us and kindly gave us an excellent breakfast, that is Caldicott, Savanhu and myself. Caldicott and I were somewhat uneasy when Savanhu asked the colonel why the Sudanese had found it necessary to have the coup which had fairly recently occurred. However, the colonel answered with the greatest of good humour that when the British Government had relinquished control of the Sudan five years before they had left behind a very fine civil service but unfortunately the politicians had not proved to be of the same high standard. (These were, as I remember vividly, almost his exact words). We all laughed merrily.

At the airport I bought the *Sudan Daily* which under the heading "News from Wau" carried a report of a "major court trial". The judge the report said, "completed the trial of the case of a Catholic priest and three Rumbek secondary school students who were accused of publishing a provocative leaflet against the Government last March with a view to distributing it among the citizens. The four accused were found guilty under Section 4 (1 A 2) and 4 (I.E) of the Defence of the Sudan Act 1958 and were sentenced accordingly." "Accordingly" was 12 years imprisonment for the priest and 10 years each for the students. The unkindest cut of all was that the typewriter and Gestetner machines were confiscated. The paper also reported that at Bulawayo a petrol bomb had been thrown by a black into a car belonging to Joshua Nkomo who was at the time attending the Southern Rhodesia constitutional talks in London.

Very soon after my return from London, I passed through Johannesburg on 30th December on my way to a conference organised by the International Commission of Jurists on the Rule of Law in Africa, held at Lagos. *The Star* carried this report date-lined Blantyre 29th December:

A member of the Congress Liberation Party in Nyasaland has been stabbed to death at Nkata Bay area according to a telegram received at party headquarters in Limbe today.

The telegram described the situation as "tense" and said that two houses were burnt down by Malawi youths in addition to the killing.   According to reports from Nkata Bay, the man died after a fight when he refused to produce a Malawi Congress Party membership card.   The two houses were burnt down after the occupants had refused to join the party.

40

The Law of Lagos

WELENSKY was on friendly terms with the Prime Minister of Nigeria, Sir Abubakar Tafewa Balewa, and persuaded him to allow the Rhodesia and Nyasaland Federation to be represented at Lagos by a High Commissioner. Mr. M. H. Hove, a black Federal M.P. for Matabeleland, was appointed to the post in 1960 and supplied us with very interesting reports. He also managed to persuade the Nigerians to send a party of their own Members of Parliament to tour the Federation.

When I received an invitation from the International Commission of Jurists to a Conference on the Rule of Law in Africa to be held in January, 1961 at Lagos, together with an air ticket and coupons for hotel accommodation, all at the expense of the Ford Foundation and the Nigerian Government, it was an opportunity I welcomed. It was to be my first experience of an international conference and would give me a chance of a few glimpses of West Africa. All the Ministers of Justice, and many of the judges and legal practitioners of every country in Africa had been invited, with the exception of the Ministers of Justice in South Africa and the Portuguese Colonies. In a stop-over at Accra, the U.K. High Commissioner for Ghana entertained me in a most hospitable way, and enabled me to see around the city. Nigeria had very recently celebrated its independence and Lagos was humming with activity among the diplomatic corps; the 50 new Chevrolets presented by the U.S.A. to mark independence were very busy transporting chief justices, law lords and lesser legal luminaries. Hove managed to arrange for me to have a five-minutes meeting with Sir Abubakar before he opened the conference.

Most of the delegates had submitted, in advance, papers
on aspects of the rule of law in their Territories. A glance
through some of the mass of documents awaiting me showed
that Southern Rhodesia would be one of the main targets.
When the conference split into three committees I chose
the one which seemed likely to sift the charges brought against
Southern Rhodesia. It was soon apparent that the notions
about "the rule of law" I had learnt from Dicey, Maitland,
Anson and others were outmoded; the fundamental rule was
majority rule. Without this the rule of law was non-existent.
After two or three days' discussions when the committee was
in the process of formulating a report to the main conference
an Indian solicitor from Blantyre sprang upon the committee
a resolution denouncing the administration of justice in the
Federation of Rhodesia and Nyasaland and demanding an
investigation by the Commission of Jurists into the rule of
law there. The chairman accepted the resolution, stating that
it did not call for debate, and that it should be adopted
forthwith. When I protested I was noisily shouted down,
but managed to grab a microphone and to say that I thought
the rule of law ought to begin to operate in our committee.
One of the Nigerian delegates supported me, not because he
opposed the resolution but because of the discourtesy shown
to a visitor to his country (most of which stemmed from
Ghanaians). Thanks to the Nigerian I was allowed a hearing.
In the final event the conference did not single out the
Federation for special treatment.

The conference was well stage-managed so as to produce on the final day, as if by magic, a series of high-flown
resolutions with alliterative titles all of which were adopted
with acclamation. The only slip was when the Chief Justice
of Liberia, the Hon. A. Dash Wilson was included among
those to make short valedictory talks. He seized the opportunity to offload on the conference, now wearying for tea,
the speech he had intended for the opening ceremonies which
had not been squeezed in at that time. After half an hour
the chairman adjourned for the now cooling tea, after which
the learned C.J. returned like the proverbial giant refreshed
to give us the other half. The last two or three pages made
reference to biased and destructive criticism of the courts

and judges of Liberia, the effect of which was probably lost on the audience now becoming comatose.

But there was a sequel to the conference which gave a clue to the Chief Justice's persistence in reading his speech. In June, 1961, the International Commission of Jurists circulated a report under the caption, "Liberia. The strange case of a lawyer". This reported that upon return from the Lagos conference, Counsellor C. A. Cassell was indicted before the Supreme Court of Liberia for contempt of court allegedly committed through critical comments on some aspects of the Liberian administration of justice in a paper prepared for and submitted to the third committee of the conference. Judgment was pronounced in April, 1961 after a hearing by the full court which included Dash Wilson, C.J. and Cassell was disbarred. The circular indicated the disapproval of the Commission of Jurists about certain disparaging remarks made in the judgment of the court about "new fangled ideas under the supposed rule of law".

41

Northern Rhodesia under Hone
and Macleod

AFTER the autumn general election in the U.K. in 1959, but before the Monckton Commission got into its stride, Iain Macleod took over from Lennox-Boyd at the Colonial Office. On 21st May, 1960 he told Kenneth Kaunda and his U.N.I.P. that there would be no change in the territorial constitution that year, nor would the matter even be considered until after the Monckton Commission had reported. However, in October Hone, the new Governor, began talks with Roberts. The U.F.P. in its evidence to Monckton had urged the need to advance the status of Northern Rhodesia in the direction of Cabinet government. We did so on the assumption that no radical changes would be made in regard to electoral franchise and delimitation of constituencies settled by the Lennox-Boyd Constitution of 1959. Following on the abortive Federal review conference, Macleod called a conference at the end of January, 1961 to deal with the Northern Rhodesia constitution. It had become apparent that he was determined to make radical changes so as to increase black representation, but was not considering any advances towards a Cabinet system. We, in the Federal wing of the U.F.P., were very concerned at the line Macleod was taking and our concern was shared by Roberts and Whitehead. The latter, in particular, realised that if black nationalists were put in a position to dominate the political scene in both the Northern Territories there was little hope for the survival of the Federation.

In pursuance of the Federal Government's right to be consulted about changes in territorial constitutions, Welensky

sent me to London in February while the N.R. constitutional
talks were in progress. These talks soon ran into difficulties
as, owing to Macleod's attitude, Roberts, with Welensky's
approval, decided to withdraw his team from the conference.
My task was an extremely exacting and exasperating one. I
was kept pretty fully informed of the progress, or rather the
lack of progress, of the conference and tried to keep in touch
with Welensky by telephone. Early in February, Macleod
invited me and Roberts to a "working dinner" at his Eaton
Square flat attended by the Governor, Hone. Mrs. Macleod
was our hostess throughout the dinner, but took no part
in the deliberations. As Welensky mentions in his book, I
described the occasion to him as a fantastic Mad Hatter's
Dinner Party. Macleod put forward a plan which Roberts
and I found unacceptable and he was not at all pleased.
A day or two later I was Macmillan's guest at dinner at
Admiralty House (No. 10 Downing Street being then under
reconstruction). He had invited me to come an hour before
the other guests assembled so that we could have an undis-
turbed talk. It was a new experience for me to have a tête-
à-tête with him. He made a very obvious attempt to gain
my goodwill by flattery, and extended an invitation to a
week-end at Chequers so that we could continue our discussions there. He asked me to give him an outline of the
Federal Government's thinking and philosophy, keeping
himself to the rôle of listener. When the other guests arrived,
including the Lord Chancellor, Kilmuir, and Lords Home
and Hailsham, the conversation became general and as far
as I was concerned not particularly notable. At the ensuing
week-end at Chequers, I arrived in the late afternoon
on Saturday, and Macmillan and I had another tête-
à-tête. Dinner followed at which Lord Home was present.
As I wrote to my wife :

> *Macmillan's technique was to outline his own picture
> of the Federation and the territories and to get me to
> fill in the gaps in his knowledge and after doing most of
> the talking to let me state my views about how the
> future political set-up should be devised. He gave me
> the impression of being impressed with some aspects*

of what I told him. Home as ever was pleasant and helpful.

What I did not mention in my letter was that Macmillan spoke of De Gaulle deciding to leave a million Frenchmen to their fate in Algeria, which left me with an uneasy feeling that Whites in Rhodesia could expect no better treatment. We were to meet next morning for a further talk before church. After breakfast in bed and a quick perusal of the deluge of Sunday papers that came with it I waited for Macmillan to appear but he only came downstairs when it was time to go to church. Alport and Lord Carrington came to lunch after which we resumed our discussion. My letter goes on :

> *Macmillan again did most of the talking, recapitulating for Alport's benefit some of the discussions of the previous day. We finished up in a fairly nebulous state but with the understanding that Alport and I would meet next day and try to work out together some alternative scheme to the one Iain Macleod has in mind.*

There was considerable Press speculation about the purpose of my visit to Chequers. Kaunda in a newspaper interview expressed his displeasure at the attention paid to me. The Press not unnaturally supposed that we were negotiating terms regarding the electoral changes in Northern Rhodesia whereas our discussions never got down to the level of constitutional plans, but were high up on a philosophical plane. To me it was then, and still remains, something of a mystery why the British Prime Minister should have gone out of his way to study at close quarters the man who was Welensky's principal adviser on constitutional matters; certainly I felt somewhat like a fly invited into the spider's parlour.

At this time Duncan Sandys who had replaced Lord Home at the C.R.O. was in Rhodesia negotiating the 1961 constitution with Whitehead. I wrote :

> *Meetings with Alport have not served much purpose as he is only No. 2. It was evident that the U.K. were waiting for Sandys to get back and hoping for something to turn up out of his visit.*

Something did turn up. Sandys, had, in the eyes of the British Press and of his colleagues, scored a notable success in reaching agreement with Whitehead, whereas Macleod was floundering at his N.R. conference. My letter continues :

I saw Sandys briefly on Wednesday (8th February, '61). He had a fantastic scheme which we argued about but he is not at all receptive of other ideas and one moves at the pace of the ox.

The effect of his new scheme was to scrap the 1959 Lennox-Boyd franchise and delimitation arrangements and substitute a plan I can best describe in rugby terms. The territory would be delimited three times over so as to elect three sets of 15 members each, the All Blacks, the All Whites and the Greys. Blacks and whites would be on separate voters rolls and would vote separately for the All Blacks and the All Whites, but vote together for the Greys. To win a seat a Grey "must obtain the same prescribed minimum percentage of the votes cast on each roll and the votes on each roll would be equalised by averaging the percentage of votes cast on each roll which is secured by each candidate." I will not attempt to explain this baffling formula. James Callaghan later expressed the hope in Parliament that Macleod would give each candidate a slide rule to work it out for himself. He did not appear to know that Sandys was the parent of the scheme but credited Macleod with it.

To me it was obvious that the only safe prediction about the Greys was that they would all turn out to be black. The scheme contained no advance in the direction of Cabinet government. We realised that it would become infinitely more difficult to operate politics on the basis of a political partnership between the races and the changes would play into the hands of racial extremists especially the U.N.I.P.

I spent a harrowing fortnight in London before Macleod presented his White Paper to Parliament, during which time I was trying to head Sandys and his colleagues off this scheme or to get it modified, all to no avail. I was constantly trying to telephone Welensky in Salisbury to explain what was happening. The line was often blocked probably because Sandys was doing the same from a different angle. Macmillan also took a hand by sending cables to Welensky, who gives a vivid account in *4 000 Days* of the way he was misled. The White Paper was finally laid on 21st February, and I realised that relations between the U.K. and Federal Governments were now at crisis point. Welensky recalled the Federal Assembly and made a trenchant attack on the U.K. Government and their proposals.*

Before I flew back to Salisbury on 22nd February I wrote to Lord Salisbury to give him an account of the discussions. He replied saying that he could not understand why Macmillan had not delayed the White Paper for a fortnight so that Welensky who was due in London for the Prime Ministers' conference in March could discuss the matter with Macmillan. On 26th February, an article by Lord Salisbury appeared in the *Sunday Express*. He described Rhodesia as a country engaged in a bitter dispute with Britain, hating the British Government as no British Government had been hated by men and women of British birth since the dispute with the American colonies 180 years before. He said that a miasma of mistrust had arisen to cloud the relations between the home Government and the British people overseas.

I accompanied Welensky when he went to London for the Commonwealth Conference though I was not present at any of its meetings. At this time there were some 90 Conservative Members of Parliament who formed a lobby of supporters for our cause, headed by Robin Turton. On Saturday, 18th March we were due to have lunch with Macmillan and Sandys, followed by discussions on certain proposals we had made for the modification of Macleod's February White Paper scheme. In the morning I had talks with two of the "lobby", one of whom was a junior Minister with a cynical outlook; he advised me that we should have a notary public with us when we saw Macmillan, a remark not calculated to inspire confidence. The lunch passed off with no worse than an angry rebuke Macmillan saw fit to administer to Welensky for something he had said to a meeting of Conservative backbenchers. We then got down to

---

*Hansard, Vol. 14, p.4175.

VISCOUNT MALVERN
(Sir Godfrey Huggins)
Federal Prime Minister, 1956

SIR EDGAR WHITEHEAD
Prime Minister of
Southern Rhodesia, 1960

MR. JOSHUA NKOMO
In the 1950s

MR. M. M. HOVE
Federal M.P., in the 1950s
(Photos: The National Archives
of Rhodesia)

THE AUTHOR
A break from building operations
in 1968
(Photo: *The Sunday Mail*,
Salisbury)

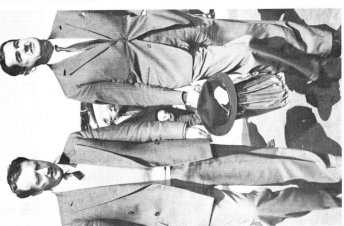

MR. WINSTON FIELD
Prime Minister of Southern Rhodesia, 1963,
with his deputy, Mr. Ian Smith (left).
(Photo: *The Herald*, Salisbury)

MR. GARFIELD TODD
Prime Minister of
Southern Rhodesia, 1950s

discussions, and just when we seemed to be getting somewhere Macmillan signified that he wished to continue the discussions with Welensky alone.   I withdrew to have some desultory talks with the Cabinet Secretary, Burke Trend (now Lord Trend).   Welensky had a final meeting with Macmillan on Monday, 20th March before flying back to Salisbury. This was largely taken up by a tearful appeal by Macmillan to Welensky not to precipitate a rupture with the U.K. at this juncture when South Africa's departure from the Commonwealth had caused such a trauma in the Conservative Party.   I personally felt that Welensky should have delayed his return to Rhodesia and insisted on finality, but he decided otherwise.   A statement issued on 20th March signified that the U.K. Government would consider "proposals within the framework and spirit of the White Paper and statements by Ministers in the House of Commons which might be put forward by political groups in N.R. (to the Governor) and of course due regard will be paid to the considerations which the Federal Government have brought to the attention of the U.K. Government."

The March visit was memorable for me because of the debate in the House of Lords in which Lord Salisbury shocked that august and normally urbane assembly by describing Macleod as "too clever by half".   I listened to the debate and to the Lord Chancellor's defence of Macleod in which he taxed Lord Salisbury with failing to produce any evidence.   I had some evidence but unfortunately had no means of producing it before their lordships.   Fate took a hand when next morning I saw the Duke of Montrose, better known as Lord Graham, come into my hotel.   Angus Graham was now a member of the opposition in the Federal Assembly, but as a brother Scot I prevailed on him to incorporate in the speech he intended to make in the Lords, some of my evidence.   He was kind enough to spend an hour or two absorbing the material, and I went to the Lords in the afternoon to hear him deliver.   He made a lengthy speech which in its own way began, I thought, quite well.   When he came to the "evidence" which related to Macleod's handling of matters in Nyasaland I noticed a lot of scurrying about among some of their Lordships.   Unfortunately,

the noble Duke did not finish his speech at this point but
rambled on into a peroration about the way in which white
Rhodesians had fought for the mother country in all the
wars, "starting if you like from the Jameson Raid which set
out from Rhodesia itself". This not altogether auspicious
reference became the focus of the speech in the minds of
most of the hearers and my "evidence" lost any of the impact
it might otherwise have made. I was interested to find later
that Sampson, in the first edition of his *Anatomy of Britain,*
singled out this item for mention as one of the oddities of
the House of Lords.

The debate was memorable for the support Lord Salisbury drew from Lord Fisher, Archbishop of Canterbury, and
for an immoderate speech by Lord Hailsham attacking the
noble marquess to an extent that was counter-productive.
The views of Members of both Houses of Parliament in the
U.K. often make strange reading for "white settlers" who
have lived their whole lives in Africa but I agreed with the
speech of Lord Milverton. Unfortunately, the views of this
man, with an admirable record of administrative experience
in Nigeria, seemed to carry no weight with the government.
Following this debate, I wrote a letter to *The Times* which
I reproduce because it gives the other side to some of the
hostile press attacks upon white Rhodesians :

> *Your leader of Saturday, 11th March speaks of the
> danger that Lord Salisbury's policy may encourage
> stubborn attitudes among African whites in blind
> resistance to change. No doubt there are some "African
> whites" who have the attitude you describe, just as there
> are "African blacks" who were blindly resistant to the
> changes which 1953 brought. In the present situation,
> the attitude of white African political leaders is of
> special importance. The U.F.P. leaders and their
> followers are not blindly resistant to change. This was
> demonstrated in relation to Nyasaland by the agreement
> reached in the conference last August. In Southern
> Rhodesia, Sir Edgar Whitehead during the short period
> of his Prime Ministership has instituted remarkable
> changes in the public service, the pass laws, land
> apportionment and African education, all designed to*

*implement the policy of partnership. More recently he
has negotiated with Mr. Duncan Sandys far-reaching
changes in the constitution. These are dependent upon
a referendum among an electorate, mistrustful, as never
before, of the intentions of the British Government
towards their future. In this situation it would be
disastrous if the voters were to be persuaded that the
British Government is determined to impose on Northern
Rhodesia, constitutional changes which are designed,
or will inevitably lead, to black African racialists gaining control of the Government of that territory. Sir
Roy Welensky, whose Government's desire is to preserve the integrity of the Federation and to promote a
true political partnership among its races, has made it
abundantly clear that within the principles enunciated
in the Lennox-Boyd despatches he is willing to see
considerable additional black African representation in
the Legislative Council of N.R. Mr. John Roberts is
also willing. But Sir Roy and his supporters, among
whom are numbered many black Africans, are determined to oppose changes which lead inevitably to the
domination of N.R.'s legislature by immature and
extreme racialists whose objective is the antithesis of
partnership.*

The one crumb of comfort derived from the March
journey was that it was left to the Governor, Sir Evelyn
Hone, to carry out discussions with political groups at which
modifications in details might be considered. During the
next three months, discussions went on in Lusaka and a great
deal of my time was taken up with advising John Roberts.
Sandys came out to Salisbury and carried on further discussions with us in his heavy-handed style, but no agreement
was reached. On 20th June, I was back in London, accompanied by Evans, in a final effort to get some modifications.
After one meeting with Sandys it became apparent that I was
no longer *persona grata* with him. Further discussions were
held on an official level in which Evans had a most difficult
time but with the skilful assistance of Sir Albert Robinson,
our High Commissioner, at last succeeded in wringing out

some changes which we thought would give us a better chance of saving the situation in the North.

On the night of Sunday, 25th June, Sandys told Robinson that Macmillan wanted a message conveyed to Welensky to the effect that the agreement that had been reached was to be the very end, and he could take no more. Macleod announced the modifications to Parliament in a White Paper* and Welensky, in a speech to the Federal Assembly the same day said that some of the weaknesses of the original scheme had been removed, and it would provide a constitution which could be made to work. A political party to succeed must appeal to and have the support of all races, he said.

Kaunda and his fellow-travellers, Moffat and Franklin, were very annoyed by the changes, and Kaunda set about implementing his so-called "master plan" to intimidate the British Government. He himself masqueraded as a man of peace but his party set about a campaign of violence on a scale that Maudling, who succeeded Macleod as Colonial Secretary, in March, 1962 described to Macmillan in my hearing as an "armed insurrection". It resulted in many murders and 2 000 other crimes of violence and sabotage. 1 753 members of U.N.I.P. were convicted of such offences. The British Government yielded to this intimidation by announcing on 13th September, 1961 that when the violence ceased a further opportunity would be given to re-examine the proposals. Macmillan had forgotten Sandys' pious denunciation of violence at the end of the Federal review. It became apparent to us that the changes we had won in June were now at risk. The announcement, of course, came after the referendum in Southern Rhodesia had accepted the Sandys-Whitehead constitutional plan, the outcome of which Macmillan did not want to be influenced by his submission to U.N.I.P. intimidation.

Welensky in a speech to the Federal Assembly on 14th September denounced the British Government's actions in strong but measured terms. He said that the S.R. electorate

---

*Cmnd, 1423, 26th June, 1961.

had been deceived. In the course of the debate Mr. H. E.
Davies (now Judge Davies) made a notable speech in which
he referred to Sir William Harcourt's aphorism, "The Tory
Party never yet took up a cause which it did not betray". A
congress of the N.R. division of the Federal Party was held
at Broken Hill (now Kabwe) on 24th September, 1961.
Welensky was unable to attend and asked me to go up north
for the meeting. I had discussions with Roberts and some
of his lieutenants the day before congress to discuss tactics.
The mood of congress was extremely bitter towards the
British Government and some rather foolish resolutions were
mooted. I reported subsequently to Welensky that I had
been drawn into the discussions, telling him "my intervention
took the form of pointing to the unwisdom of attempting
to tie the hand of the P.M. I expressed complete sympathy
with the feelings of those present, which I shared, but said
that in my opinion there were one or two constitutional cards
which had still to be played before it was necessary to consider anything unconstitutional. With some obvious
reluctance, but with a very good grace, congress accepted my
advice and the standing committee's resolution was then
passed with about 6 or 8 dissentients.

42

Northern Rhodesia under Hone
and Maudling

IN OCTOBER, 1961, Macmillan shifted Macleod from the
Colonial Office and installed Reginald Maudling there.
He was qualified for the post in the sense that most of his
predecessors in office were, namely, that he had never pre-
viously set foot in the territories comprising the Federation
and that his knowledge of these countries was derived from
Cabinet discussions in the U.K. and debates in the House of
Commons. He was to have only a short run as Colonial
Secretary.

Maudling paid his first visit to our part of the world in
December, 1961. He discussed with us various proposals for
modifying Macleod's scheme for N.R. but nothing ever came
of them. In February, 1962, Sandys paid us another visit
when we held protracted and unsatisfactory discussions in the
course of which he blurted out that Britain had lost the will
to govern in Africa. Welensky has described the occasion.
In subsequent discussions with R. A. Butler, we learned that
Sandys' colleagues had been upset at his revelations to us,
but events were to prove him right. It was on this same visit
that Sandys went to Nyasaland and, without any mandate
from his colleagues, gave Banda to understand that secession was on the way, a fact of which R. A. Butler subsequently
informed Welensky.

On Sandys' return to London, *The Times* in a leading
article of 22nd February said, "Mr. Maudling and the
Colonial Office believe that there is no alternative to adjust-
ing N.R.'s constitution so as to lead to an African majority

after the elections next winter even if it is a small majority. This means that the Colonial Secretary accepts a course of action that would almost certainly put just as anti-federal and secessionist a government in power in Lusaka as Mr. Sandys met in Nyasaland." This assessment and forecast was correct. As so often occurred, the U.K. Press were better informed of the British Government's real intentions, probably by deliberate leaks, than we were. It was no doubt part of a softening-up process by which the U.K. Government hoped to spare themselves the embarrassment of telling us directly what they had in store for us.

On 28th February, 1962, Maudling announced two changes which appeared to be minor but, in fact, tipped the scales in favour of Kaunda, and no doubt satisfied him that U.N.I.P.'s campaign of violence had yielded a good dividend.

Welensky has described the events leading up to this announcement and the visit to London which immediately followed. I was present at the discussions early in March between the two Prime Ministers and the two Secretaries of State, and it was revealing to notice the somewhat rough handling Macmillan gave his colleagues. Relations between the Commonwealth Relations Office and the Colonial Office were wearing thin, a matter of no surprise to me in the light of my own experience of Sandys' abrasive tactics. In his "no-will-to-govern" visit, Sandys had discussed with us a possible scheme for the partition of N.R., in which Barotseland might become a separate State within the Federation. The scheme had some resemblance to the Dominion Party's "Central African Alliance". In the London talks, Sandys kept reiterating that Banda would shortly be in London pressing his demand for secession, and that Welensky must put forward a plan to meet the situation. Welensky refused to fall into the trap of making proposals to break up the Federation. Sandys put up no proposals and we returned to Salisbury with nothing accomplished.

43

Barotseland

MACLEOD'S White Paper* said that the application of the new Northern Rhodesia constitution proposals to Barotseland would be the subject of discussion with the Paramount Chief, that is to say the Litunga, Sir Mwanuwina Lewanika, who was related to a U.F.P. Federal Parliamentary Secretary, Godwin Lewanika.† The Litunga had paid a visit to Salisbury and Kariba in 1959 and I had met him on that occasion. He was a courteous old gentleman but did not give the impression of any great mental powers.

Barotseland was a protectorate within the confines of the wider protectorate of N.R. In discussions with Macleod in April, 1961, the Barotse delegates had requested that Barotseland should be recognised as a State separate from N.R. During the talks, Macleod was told very firmly that the Litunga was opposed to Barotseland being placed under the heel of Kaunda and would prefer to become a fourth state within the Federation. The British Government informed us that as the outcome of their talks Macleod had given an assurance that the special position of Barotseland would not be affected by the constitutional changes for N.R. that were then under consideration.

On 18th April, Macleod wrote a letter to the Litunga in the course of which he said very specifically :

> *No constitutional change affecting Barotseland will be made without full consultation **and consent** (my emphasis) of the Paramount Chief and Council.*

*Cmd. 1301, 20th February, 1961.
†Godwin Lewanika, in fact, became Litunga a few years later.

Welensky was informed of this by Duncan Sandys. The Litunga was therefore constitutionally in a stronger position vis-a-vis the British Government than was the Federal Government. To me it was clear that constitutional changes affecting N.R. which would result in the whole of that territory being handed over to majority rule, with secession from the Federation to follow, would vitally affect Barotseland by depriving it of its special protectorate status, leaving it at the mercy of Kaunda. This was what the British Government were intending to do at the instigation of Kaunda, Moffat and Franklin. With this in mind and with the full approval of Welensky, I paid a visit to Mongu, the principal town in Barotseland, in order to see the Litunga, point out to him the dangers of his position and enlist his aid, if possible, to blocking any such changes. Godwin Lewanika had already asked for the Federal Government's help in getting a lawyer to advise the Litunga. My visit to Mongu was of a somewhat delicate character. As it happened, there was a Federal hospital there which had been the subject of hostile and lying propaganda by U.N.I.P., and there was a Federal prison. I paid official visits to these but there could be no masking from the Northern Rhodesia Government that the real purpose of my visit was to see the Litunga.

It was arranged that I should stay with the Resident Commissioner who received me most hospitably on 3rd October, and took me the same afternoon by Land-Rover to Lealui, the Litunga's summer residence. It was hardly a mere coincidence that on 2nd October Sir Evelyn Hone, the Governor, had written to Welensky about a petition he had received from the Ngambela (Prime Minister) for Barotseland to become a fourth state in the Federation. Hone said that the internal situation in Barotseland was very far from favourable to the step contemplated by the Barotseland Native Government, which he said was meeting with a formidable body of local opposition, largely because of its unrepresentative and outmoded character. Hone added that if word got around that the Native Government were seeking to become a fourth state the regime, and possibly the Litunga, might well be placed in serious jeopardy, and Barotseland might be opened to the full force of African nationalist pressure and political conflict. I pause here to remark that Hone made no suggestion that Britain would honour its treaty obligation to "protect" the Litunga and his Native Government. However, on 3rd October I was ignorant of the fact that Hone had written in these terms to Welensky. What I did become aware of, however, was that on the very day that Hone had written his letter U.N.I.P. had threatened to stage a demonstration at Mongu.

When I met the Litunga in the presence of the Resident Commissioner, we first discussed the need for improved hospital facilities at Mongu. Then the matter of the U.N.I.P. demonstration was raised and I asked the Litunga if he would be in a position to cope with a demonstration if one were to be staged at Lealui. Both the Litunga and the Ngambela said they had no police except their own "Kapassos" who were not adequately trained as policemen, and they doubted whether the police force at Mongu was sufficient for the purpose of dealing with this kind of thing. The Resident Commissioner expressed surprise and a contrary opinion. The Litunga signified that he was most concerned at the activities of U.N.I.P. and that the existing forces of law and order might have to be strengthened.

On the following day, I went out alone to Lealui to renew my discussions with the Litunga. My time was short as unfortunately the road between Mongu and Lealui, which was the worst I had ever encountered, absorbed an hour in each direction to do a mere ten miles or so. Further time was consumed in the mediaeval ceremonies which are attendant on a visit to a potentate like the Litunga. For example, each of half a dozen councillors who entered the holy of holies to join the meeting had to do so on his hands and knees, keeping, as the modern idiom has it, a low profile. The councillors to a man confirmed the desire of Barotseland to be separated from Northern Rhodesia and to become a separate state within the Federation. I pointed out that the first thing to be done was to halt the British Government's plans for altering the N.R. Constitution so as to tip the scales in favour of Kaunda and his U.N.I.P. I reminded them of the powerful position they had by virtue of Macleod's pledge, and finally I made arrangements to get legal assistance for them in their further dealings with Hone and British Ministers. The Litunga was a lethargic figure and gave me the impression of being completely supine. Although I was convinced that he and his advisers were genuinely alarmed at the prospect of being submerged in Zambia under majority rule, I had little faith that they would be able to stand up to the combined pressures of the U.K. and U.N.I.P. In the ensuing months I did my utmost to put some more fire in the Litunga's belly, but eventually he and his Native Government were hoodwinked into submission. On 7th June, 1962, Hone was able to welcome the decision of the Litunga to give his consent to the application of the new N.R. Constitution to Barotseland. The Government, he said, would soon set up a special inquiry to ensure that Barotseland's special position was preserved for the future.

Welensky, in the final pages of *4 000 Days,* has recounted the episode on 29th March, 1963 when R. A. Butler informed him of the U.K.'s decision to allow any territory in the Federation to secede. Godwin Lewanika, who was with us, asked whether Barotseland would be allowed to secede from N.R. and received an evasive reply. Welensky protested and stated that the Barotse had been sold down the river. Britain had not only lost the will to govern in Africa but the will to protect.

44

Federal General Election, 1962

ON OUR return from London in March, 1962, Welensky called the Cabinet together and told us that he intended to have a general election. The life of the Parliament was not due to expire from natural causes for more than a year, there was no internal issue, and I personally was not convinced that any good purpose would be served by the election. Welensky, however, felt that as the Federation in its present form appeared to be disintegrating he must seek a mandate to negotiate with the British Government to save what was possible from the wreck.

When Welensky announced his decision in the Federal Assembly, Ian Smith who had already crossed the floor and joined Field, made a bitter attack. The Dominion Party decided to boycott the election. They saw the Federation as doomed and decided to devote their full energies to preparing for the forthcoming territorial election in Southern Rhodesia. Smith had been among those who were opposed to the Whitehead/Sandys 1961 Constitution. Associated with him in his opposition to this constitution was Tredgold, though their objections were probably based on different considerations. Adversity, they say, makes strange bedfellows. Whitehead was by now becoming somewhat unpopular in many quarters. Field and Smith saw their opportunity to oust him and they set about forming the Rhodesian Front. They completely ignored the Federal election, in which most of the seats in Southern Rhodesia, including mine, were uncontested.

While the Federal election was in progress, Macmillan announced the appointment of R. A. Butler with the title of First Secretary of State to take over the affairs of the

Federation and its constituent territories from Sandys and Maudling. Welensky was delighted that a single British office to deal with our affairs, for which he had unsuccessfully applied in 1957, had now been conceded, and hoped, as we all did, that Butler would prove to be a more understanding person than Sandys, Maudling and Macleod had been. I am inclined to doubt whether Macmillan's decision to take this step was in any way connected with the Federal election. It had been fairly obvious on our last visit to London that there was friction between Sandys and Maudling, and we later learnt that Sandys had queered the pitch in Nyasaland by virtually giving Dr. Banda a promise that secession would be coming his way. I think that Macmillan had got thoroughly tired of the bickering between Sandys and Maudling, and that as he was probably intent on a break-up of the Federation he thought that this could be best achieved by Butler, than whom there was no more adroit politician in his Cabinet. Welensky has hinted that it suited Macmillan to cast Butler in the rôle of undertaker.

The Federal election brought some new personalities into Parliament, rid us of some tiresome people and enabled Welensky to choose two younger and able men, J. A. Clark and J. P. G. Duncan, to replace Macintyre and Eastwood in the Cabinet. The opening of the first session of the third Parliament was marked by a speech from the Throne delivered by Lord Dalhousie, who had succeeded Lord Llewellin as Governor-General, in which the British Government was roundly denounced for its treachery. It must have been an unpalatable speech for Dalhousie to read, but he never faltered.

45

The Art of the Expedient

R. A. BUTLER, now Lord Butler of Saffron Walden, began what he describes as operation "Large Elephant" in March, 1962, and we in the Federal Government were relieved to think that we should no longer be working against blunt instruments like Sandys and Maudling. The end result, however, was the same — the destruction of all we had carefully built up in more than a decade.

I had met the First Secretary of State on several occasions before he became responsible in Britain for our affairs. During a visit to London in 1961, I was included with Welensky in an invitation to lunch at Stanstead. At that time I gained the impression that he was much more sympathetic to our cause than were those of his colleagues who were actively concerned with our affairs, but as it turned out this sympathy, if it was real, did not assist us. Butler has made it clear in his book that he had not been in favour of setting in train the Monckton Commission although he accepts collective responsibility in going along with Macmillan's decision to appoint it. Butler says that he did not expect the commission to have the political results Macmillan hoped for, namely to involve the Labour Party in a bipartisan approach to the Federation. In this respect he proved to be correct. Nevertheless, it is also clear that he put the aspirations of African nationalist leaders before those of us in the Federation who sought to maintain the ideals of political partnership between the races.

In *4 000 Days,* Welensky has given his version of events during Butler's regime and I shall not attempt to cover all the ground again, except to touch upon the dispute over the constitutional conventions which Butler does not mention in *The Art of the Possible.* We maintained that although the

United Kingdom under its doctrine of Parliamentary sovereignty had the legal power to legislate the Federation out of existence, the U.K. was a party to a convention, or gentleman's agreement, which should have inhibited it from doing so. We also maintained that in 1953 British Ministers had given certain pledges in this respect. My views about the conventions are fully stated in a Federal Government White Paper* which I laid before the Federal Assembly on 19th December, 1962, the day on which Butler announced in the Commons that Nyasaland would be allowed to secede from the Federation, and on which Welensky, in turn, denounced the British Government for a breach of its pledges, and said that it had little honour left.

It so happened that earlier, on 8th May, 1962, Butler had made a statement in the House of Commons about a convention relating to Southern Rhodesia which was identical in its terms with the one relating to the Federation which we had negotiated in April, 1957. When he made this statement, Butler put an interpretation on the Southern Rhodesia convention which entirely accorded with our interpretation of the Federal convention. Subsequently, I wrote a letter to *The Times* pointing this out. During a visit Butler paid to Salisbury about this time, I showed him a copy of my letter to *The Times,* and he was obviously somewhat annoyed.

During the week preceding Butler's statement on 19th December, 1962, I had gone to London with my colleagues Barrow and Caldicott in an attempt to persuade Butler to modify his announcement in various ways. Originally, it had been the intention that I should not be of the party as the discussions were primarily concerned with financial problems relating to Nyasaland and its secession, which were matters in which my two colleagues were primarily concerned. They felt, with every justification, that my negotiations in London during the preceding two years had borne very little fruit and that my presence at these talks might not be advantageous. However, Welensky received a message that the Lord Chancellor would like me to come with my colleagues so that he could have discussions with me on the

*C.Fed. 232.

convention issue. For this reason I was included in the expedition to London.

I had met the Lord Chancellor, Lord Dilhorne at the time when he was Attorney-General (as Sir Reginald Manningham-Buller). It was he who had handled the Government's case in the House of Commons when the Devlin Report was under discussion. On another occasion, he had kindly arranged for me to have a seat at the Old Bailey during a famous spy trial in which he was prosecuting. I had a premonition that the proposed discussions with him were designed to put me in my place. The meeting was held at the Lord Chancellor's office in the House of Lords. Barrow and Butler came to see fair play. Sir John Hobson, the current Attorney-General was present when we arrived, as were various officials on both sides. The double doors leading from the office into the realms of their Lordships were flung open and the Lord Chancellor made his stately appearance, and took the head of the table. Barrow, who was somewhat unaccustomed to proceedings in courts of law, was rather startled by the ensuing "dialogue". My arguments did not impress Lord Dilhorne who laid down the law and had it dutifully confirmed by the Attorney-General. My arguments are set out in the White Paper, and Dilhorne's were repeated in the House of Lords on some occasion, and are no doubt recorded in Hansard, so that others who may be interested can judge which of us was right.

Butler in his book refers to me as a "man with a good legalistic brain". The compliment which might otherwise have been conveyed by the first adjective is a little marred by the second. When it comes to "legalism", the issue of the convention and the pledges makes an interesting study. I had always accepted that the U.K., in accordance with the British theory of the sovereignty of Parliament, did have the *legal* right to legislate so as to destroy the Federation. In fact, it was I who in the 1953 Conference pointed this out. Dilhorne and Hobson fastened on to this fact, but of course we were relying on pledges that the British Government would not exercise its legal right.

In a debate in the House of Commons on 28th February, 1963, Hobson made at least two incorrect statements, one being that "between January, 1953 and December, 1962 not one word is ever heard in public or private from Sir Roy Welensky, or Mr. Greenfield, or anyone else about the existence of these pledges, when they are paraded for the first time". I wrote to Hobson pointing out that their existence had been raised in July, 1962. He replied promising to withdraw his incorrect statement at a suitable opportunity. It took a year before he found the opportunity, but on 11th July, 1963 he referred to his incorrect statement as a "slip" and went on to say that it was not material to the argument he had been previously advancing. He did not explain why he had found it necessary when he made the "slip" to repeat it with added emphasis three times over in the space of only two columns of Hansard.

At the end of the chapter, "Large Elephant" Butler modestly concedes :

> *Politics being the art of the possible all I was able to achieve was an orderly dissolution of the Federation, the establishing of two new states in Zambia and Malawi, and the chance given to Southern Rhodesia to have a strong army and air force with the opportunity for its ruling clique to open the door to Africans if they paid any attention to world opinion.*

This "achievement" was hailed in the British Parliament by many speakers in all parties as a triumph, with glowing tributes to its author; but there were a few discordant voices, one of which said that the Federation had been foully bludgeoned to death.

In one respect at least, Butler performed a remarkable feat; he persuaded Winston Field, flanked by Ian Douglas Smith, to throw away the only card which he had which might have enabled Southern Rhodesia to emerge from the Federation as an independent state. This was the card of "No attendance at the Victoria Falls conference without a guarantee of independence". I was closely in touch with Field and his principal Constitutional adviser, his Minister of Justice, Clifford Dupont, during the Butler regime, and I helped them with the drafting of a number of messages to Butler over the subject of independence for Southern Rhodesia. I was convinced that if the Southern Rhodesian and Federal Governments stood together they could effectively block the unscrambling of the Federation or delay it to a point when the U.K. Government would have been compelled to make concessions to Field on the independence issue.

For a long time Field stood firm and refused to attend the proposed Victoria Falls conference until he got an assurance that Southern Rhodesia would get its independence. Eventually, Butler was forced to invite Field to London for talks on this subject. The U.K. insisted on conditions that Field could not agree to. He returned to Rhodesia on 6th June. Unfortunately, Field had publicly and privately taken the line that the Federation was doomed and that the quicker it was dissolved the better it would be for everyone. Lord Alport, the U.K. High Commissioner, to whom Butler pays an eloquent tribute, had the measure of Field, and I am convinced played a large part in wearing him down. At the other end, A. E. P. Robinson, our High Commissioner in London, was keeping us informed of Butler's reactions up to the time Field fell into the trap. He described to Welensky the transformation in Butler from gloom and despondency to jubilation when he received Field's message on 15th June in which he virtually agreed to go to the Victoria Falls, a decision which Field announced in Parliament on 18th June, 1963.

There can be no doubt that Butler displayed great adroitness in his "achievement", if this is the right term, of an orderly dissolution of the Federation. It was not, however, a flawless performance. On 10th July, 1962, speaking as the guest of honour at a dinner of the Rhodesia and Nyasaland Club, he had said, "We want you to understand that if you put your money into the Federation we shall be behind you." Some would rate this as another broken pledge. *The Times,* commenting on these remarks at the time, said that if they had revived the hopes of white Rhodesians they might get a jolt. It warned Butler that "verbal subtlety even for sound reasons has pitfalls in the suspicious African terrain". (One is tempted to ask whether verbal subtlety can ever be justified by sound reasons).

I have said a good deal about intimidation as my tale

has proceeded. Dr. Banda and Kaunda skilfully used this political weapon to beat their opponents. We in the Federal Government did our utmost to persuade the Colonial Governors and their British masters to combat intimidation. We had no success. Those who peruse the British Parliamentary debates on Central Africa in the Federal decade will see that friends of the Federation often brought to the notice of Parliament diabolical acts of political intimidation on the part of black nationalist politicians. Their representations made no apparent impact on the Conservative Government, still less on the Labour Opposition. I never quite got over the shock of discovering, in 1957, at a meeting that Welensky and I had with the Labour shadow Cabinet that they condoned the Mau Mau atrocities, which they obviously regarded as a legitimate means to an end.

By contrast, incidents like the Hola Camp affair or Miss Mphombeya's toe caused many Labour and some Conservative Members of Parliament to shed many a crocodile tear. I cannot refrain from applauding a certain District Officer, Mr. K. M. Chittenden, who resigned from the Colonial Service after 13 years in Northern Rhodesia. In a letter to *The Times* on 21st December, 1960, prompted no doubt by news of intimidation which occurred during the Federal review conference, he gave a detailed account of serious political intimidation on the part of Kaunda's U.N.I.P. and said that his own resignation had been prompted by the sense of personal disgrace he felt to many Africans for being able only inadequately to protect them from intimidation. His letter ended with these words :

> *Intimidation is by our rules of conduct an extremely difficult thing to combat, the more so where the local administration is susceptible to instructions from a government in Whitehall which has changed the saying, "Politics is the art of the possible" into "Politics is the art of the expedient".*

Perhaps the greatest tragedy is that Dr. Banda, Kaunda and their likes succeeded in intimidating not only their defenceless fellow-Africans but also the once great nation which in Duncan Sandys' dictum "lost the will to govern in Africa".

46

The Churches and the Federation

FROM its inception in 1953 until the end of 1963, the Federation was subjected to much hostile criticism and many biased and bitter attacks by certain missionaries and churchmen. A leading part in these was taken by certain elements of the Church of Scotland, prominent among whom was the Reverend Sir George Mcleod, now Lord Mcleod, founder of the Iona Community of which my wife happened to be a member. He had visited Salisbury in 1951, and stayed with us for a few days during a money-raising tour in aid of the community's funds. Some would later think that he was "spoiling the Egyptians".

The Church of Scotland had a considerable missionary work in Nyasaland and Northern Rhodesia dating back, in the former case, to 1874. By the time of Federation "Africanisation" had set in, and the Scottish missions had linked with those of the Dutch Reformed Church under the title of the Church of Central Africa, Presbyterian. In the first Federal Parliament, the Rev. Andrew Doig, a Church of Scotland missionary, was the white member representing the interests of blacks in Nyasaland. Although somewhat critical of the Government and its policies, his speeches were well balanced and reasonable. He declined reappointment in the Second Parliament. In 1959, I persuaded him to serve on the commission of enquiry into the Kanjedza Prison after the disturbances of that year.

Some of Doig's colleagues in the mission field were obsessed with the idea that the wicked "white settlers" of Southern Rhodesia would exert their evil influences to the detriment of the natives of Nyasaland, though how they

would do so was never really explained. My own view is
that these missionaries may have sensed that interest in true
religion in Nyasaland, as in certain other countries, was in the
descendant, whereas the substitute religion of African
nationalism was very much in the ascendant. At all events,
in some cases churches and schools became the venue for
political indoctrination by the Malawi Congress Party, and
in Northern Rhodesia by U.N.I.P. Many voices were raised
from church pulpits and school platforms in denunciation
of the Federation and Federal politicians. Seldom, if ever,
were they heard to denounce political intimidation even when
it went the length of arson, grievous bodily harm or murder.

During 1959, following the disorders in Nyasaland and
the Devlin Report, certain sections of the Church of Scotland
became increasingly hostile to the Federation. The General
Assembly of the Church of Scotland had a special committee
anent Central Africa, of which Dr. Mcleod was the convener,
which, in May, 1959, published a report and supplementary
report of a highly tendentious kind to which Sir Gilbert
Rennie, then Federal High Commissioner in London, and
himself an elder of the kirk, prepared a very able reply
called, "Why not be fair?"

Earlier that year, on 9th April, 1959, Archbishop Hughes
in his charge to the Anglican Synod in Matabeleland gave
an address which was a model of reasonableness which
ought to have been made compulsory reading in all schools
and churches. In June, 1959, Rennie made a suggestion in
a National Affairs Association address during a visit to
Salisbury, that there should be a joint meeting between the
representatives of all the churches in the Federation, and
representatives of all the governments, to discuss the work
of reconciliation and the improvement of race relations. In
the course of his speech, he referred to a recent visit of Dr.
Mcleod to Nyasaland, and a subsequent statement by that
reverend gentleman, that going from Nyasaland to Ghana
was rather like going from darkness to light. Rennie added,
"I wrote to him saying that that remark did not pay much
tribute to missionaries in Nyasaland . . . I received a courteous
acknowledgement in which it was stated that when time
permitted I would get a reply. Time has not yet permitted."

As I happened to be the only Presbyterian in the Federal Cabinet I thought that I might follow up Rennie's suggestion to the extent of paying a goodwill visit to some of the missionaries in Nyasaland. With the blessing of the Prime Minister I went on a six-day visit in October. My idea was to engage in what is nowadays commonly spoken of by journalists and politicians as "dialogue" with some of the missionaries, and to promote a better understanding among them of the philosophy of the Federal Government and the U.F.P. I got in touch with Rev. Doig who was helpful, but I felt not enthusiastic, about my plans. I met him and some others in Blantyre, attended a service in the huge cathedral there, and went on to Livingstonia near the lake. There, accompanied by the District Commissioner, I lunched with the senior minister, a black; his wife did not appear and lunch was served by his daughter of twelve. Our host was quite friendly but rather a colourless personality. After lunch, he chaired a meeting of the missionaries and school staff, but made no effort to steer the discussion into any useful channel. After I had said my piece about the reasons for my visit and my desire for a better understanding, a Scottish spinster schoolmistress said that it was useless for me to expect any sympathy from the missionary folk as I was there among them with one hand under the table clutching a dagger. As no dissentient voice was raised I withdrew at a convenient moment, dagger and all.

The same afternoon, I went on to Loudon where I met the staff at one of their houses. White and black members of the staff and their wives and children were assembled in one of the houses to meet me at tea. My main recollection is of an argument with a Clydeside mechanic whose gospel appeared to be trade unionism. The atmosphere, with a number of squalling brats milling about on the floor, was hardly conducive to reasoned discussion, but I managed to get the attention of a medical missionary who patiently listened to my views.

In their day, the buildings I saw at Livingstonia were a magnificent achievement but one could imagine that the great Dr. Laws would have been saddened at the way they were obviously mouldering into decay in 1959. From what

I saw of the secondary school there it bore no comparison with many mission and Government schools for blacks in the south.

From Loudon I went on to Fort Johnston where I stayed a night with the White Fathers and had a pleasant chat with one or two of them.

In a subsequent interview with the Press, I said that the ice had been broken, and that I felt that some of the people I had met had now a better understanding of the U.F.P. policy. I was really disappointed, though not surprised, at the chilliness of my reception among the Presbyterians. However, it was warm by comparison with that given to a distinguished Moderator of the Church of Scotland who presided over the General Assembly in Edinburgh in 1959, namely the Right Rev. Dr. R. H. W. Shepherd, of Lovedale in South Africa. Shepherd was in the chair when a resolution hostile to the Federation was passed. He himself took a neutral stance in the debate. Subsequently, he was appointed by Macmillan to the Monckton Commission and travelled with it in Nyasaland. To his grief, some of the missions of the C.C.A.P. refused to receive him. In Professor Oosthuizen's *Life of Shepherd** occurs this passage :

> *Dr. Shepherd wrote to the head of Livingstonia declaring that he had been welcomed in all the continents by people of all classes, from the Queen downwards, but he had to come to mission stations founded by the Church of Scotland to find that he was not welcome. He could not conceive of any spiritual interests suffering because he made an appearance, but the event confirmed reports that had reached him from different quarters that control in some mission stations had deteriorated.*

Shepherd, in fact, was a supporter of Federation as I know from personal discussions with him.

Rennie was succeeded as High Commissioner by Sir Albert Robinson, who, though not a Presbyterian, took a

---

Shepherd of Lovedale — A Life for Southern Africa by G. C. Oosthuizen, Johannesburg, Hugh Keartland Publishers, 1970.

considerable interest in the campaign carried on by Dr. Mcleod and his supporters. During one of my visits to London, he urged me to prepare a reply to the latest report of the General Assembly's Committee anent Central Africa, which was mainly concerned this time with events in Northern Rhodesia. I quote two passages of the document I prepared :

> *There has of course been considerable violence in the Northern Provinces of N.R. This has undoubtedly been promoted by U.N.I.P., some 1 783 of whose members have been convicted of crimes among which various sorts of sabotage predominate, including the burning of churches and schools, many of them built by the missionaries for the very people who burnt them down. It is surprising that the Church of Scotland Committee in its report has not said a word of criticism of these actions of the party responsible for them. It is to be hoped that the Commission of Assembly will not also condone the wickedness of U.N.I.P., some of whose leaders, taking a leaf out of Goebel's book, at Belgrade recently accused the British Government of genocide in N.R.*

I dealt at some length with the merits and demerits of the constitutional proposals then being considered for Northern Rhodesia, and continued :

> *Finally, the U.F.P. hopes that the Church of Scotland will not allow itself to become a pressure group in support of a revolutionary party with the evil record of U.N.I.P. The Church should consider events in Northern Rhodesia in the light of Christ's attitude to the revolutionaries of His day when He advised His followers to "go the other mile" with the Romans.*

I never heard what effect, if any, my reply had among the Assembly commission; probably it never reached them.

I often wonder whether men like the Rev. Andrew Doig think in their heart of hearts about conditions in the Malawi of Dr. H. Kamuzu Banda, and whether they believe that the cause of true religion has in any way been promoted by the break-up of the Federation.

47

The Congo and Hammarskjold

THE DECOLONISATION, in 1960, of what was called the Belgian Congo, but which is now called Zaire, happened precipitately. Under the Belgians, there had been no attempt to set up parliamentary institutions in which the indigenous people could participate. To the outside world there was little sign of change coming until Ghana attained its independence and the ideas of its "redeemer", Nkrumah, began to spread south. After this a sort of panic seemed to seize the Belgian Government which paved the way for a hand-over of power to majority rule under the leadership of Patrice Lumumba. Within hours of the independence celebrations chaos began to set in. The majority of the whites lived in Elisabethville (now Lubumbashi), in the Katanga where they worked in, or in connection with, the copper mines. This city was not far distant from the Northern Rhodesian Copperbelt towns. Belgian refugees began to stream into Kitwe and Ndola, and soon spread south to Salisbury and Bulawayo, where private citizens offered them temporary shelter till things settled down in the Katanga or till they could return to Belgium. My wife and I were among numerous people who accommodated refugees. To the whites in the Federation, it appeared that the Belgian Government had made an abject surrender of its responsibilities to its own people. The Dominion Party opposition was not slow to play upon the emotions of Rhodesian whites, suggesting that any concession to political advancement of blacks was simply a sign of weakness that would lead to a similar surrender or sell-out of whites in the Federation. When the Rhodesian Front was formed it made full use of propaganda of this sort.

Out of the Congo chaos, Tshombe emerged as the leader of a break-away movement in the Katanga where he established a regime which brought a certain amount of stability. It appeared that he was not antagonistic to whites, and, in fact, was anxious for the Belgian mineworkers to return which many of them did. To us in the Federation, it seemed that the best hope of maintaining some sort of order, security and stability was to support Tshombe and his regime. The United Kingdom, United States and United Nations lent their support to the forces working against Tshombe and his separatist movement.

At the time, it seemed to me a strange anomaly that the British Government at one and the same time, should be, trying to prevent Katanga breaking away from the Congo and giving encouragement to those who were bent on breaking up the Federation. Some would say the anomaly was two-edged as federalist Welensky was seen to be supporting break-away Tshombe. But Welensky's actions did not arise from a desire to Balkanise the Congo. He wanted desperately to prevent the Katanga, where there was a fair measure of peace, order and stability under Tshombe, dissolving into chaos like the rest of the Congo. But for the time which was bought by his support of Tshombe, racial violence would probably have erupted in the Katanga on a scale threatening to engulf the Rhodesian Copperbelt. As I saw it, Welensky handled the Katanga/Congo problems with great skill and wisdom, but his efforts gained him no friends. In the situation of turmoil that grew, Hammarskjold, the Secretary-General of the United Nations, personally intervened, and met his death in a dramatic aeroplane crash in the vicinity of Ndola airport in the Northern Rhodesian Copperbelt. The story of this event has been adequately told by Lord Alport in his book *The Sudden Assignment*. I became involved in the matter because of the obvious need to set up an inquiry into the cause of the crash, which was wrapped in mystery.

It was no surprise to me that some of the enemies of the Federation in United Nations circles should hasten to pin the blame for the crash and Hammarskjold's death on the Federal Government. Such people work on the principle, "thrice is he armed that hath his quarrel just, but four times he who gets his blow in fust". In much the same spirit, when a black doctor who belonged to the African National Congress was killed in a collision between his car and a train at a level crossing, it was given out that Welensky had driven the engine of the train. We decided that our commissioners must be of such a calibre that their integrity and impartiality should not be capable of serious challenge. Accordingly, we appointed the Federal Chief Justice, Sir John Clayden, an English High Court Judge, Sir Claude Jacob, and a British aeronautical expert. Their report, I need hardly say, fully exonerated the Federal Government.

The United Nations were not content to leave the field to the Federal commission of inquiry but decided to set up their own inquiry. Their commission included a chairman who was a judge in one of the Indian Principalities, judges from Sweden, Sierra Leone, and a South American Republic, and a legal professor from Yugoslavia. With considerable difficulty we managed to get some inklings of information about the doings of this international body, who volunteered none to us about their programme. They began their inquiries in the Congo but eventually arrived at Ndola, and we managed to arrange for a Federal lawyer to have a watching brief on the proceedings there.

In the course of its travels the commission came to Salisbury. I made diplomatic inquiries as to whether it would be proper for me to offer hospitality to the commission, and as a result the members came to my house some ten miles out of Salisbury for tea on a Sunday afternoon, followed by a visit to see some game near Lake McIlwaine. The U.N. commissioners were all very charming gentlemen. The Yugoslav professor was able to converse with my wife as both spoke French fluently. He was greatly interested in the fact that our house was situated in an isolated spot in the bush and that it was completely unguarded by either barbed-wire entanglements or police, something unimaginable in Yugoslavia. The views he expressed to my wife about the way to govern the indigenous black peoples of the Federation were illuminating, and would, I fear, not have been well received by the followers of such leaders as Comrades Machel and Neto had they been able to listen in. When the U.N.

commission's report appeared it made no direct finding as to the cause of the crash and left matters somewhat "in the air".

To return to the Katanga: the United Nations eventually intervened by sending armed forces to invade that peaceful province, causing much unnecessary bloodshed, killings and misery before they eventually settled down to a peace-keeping rôle.   Events in the Congo certainly did much harm to white morale in the Federation, while boosting the morale of the black nationalist leaders.

48

Three Chips

DURING 1963, Dr. Banda, having secured the promise of independence for his country, was demanding the right to secede from the Federation "now now". There were, however, difficulties in doing things in quite such a hurry as the doctor wanted. Nyasaland itself would suffer most from over-hasty action. For a short time that year I acted as Minister of Health and on one occasion I was asked a parliamentary question about the number of doctors in the Federal health service in Nyasaland. I gave the figures supplied by the ministry, which were correct, but the upshot was that Dr. Banda, from the shelter of his Legislative Council, called me a liar and said that I had grossly exaggerated the numbers. I assume that his motive was to give the impression that after secession Nyasaland would have no difficulty in replacing Federal doctors who elected to depart. He was, when the time came, able to get a number of Israeli doctors on short service contracts to tide him over.

When it became certain that the British Government had irrevocably decided to bow to Dr. Banda's demands, we in the Federal Government did not try to obstruct, we sought to make the transition as rapid as practicable having regard to the formidable problems involved in the unscrambling process. To this end, it was arranged that Barrow, Caldicott and I should go to Zomba to meet three of Dr. Banda's principal lieutenants, namely Messrs. Chiume, Chipembere and Chirwa (that is, Orton Chirwa a recently-fledged barrister). Chiume and Chipembere had been incarcerated with Dr. Banda in the Gwelo prison while Chirwa kept Dr. Banda's flag flying in Nyasaland. This trio, together with two brothers called Chisiza, were known in U.F.P. circles as the five Chips.

Chiume took the chair when we met in Zomba. His manner was hostile and obviously calculated to humiliate us and rub in the fact that we were vanquished enemies. Chipembere left the meeting when we had scarcely begun, telling us with obvious pride that he had been selected for an American leadership course and could not wait to go off and make his travel arrangements. Chirwa was determined to impress upon us that he knew how to deal with white civil servants. He told us that in the beginning, when he instructed the Attorney-General to produce a Bill forthwith on any given subject the A-G. would demur and stall for time. But, said Chirwa, it was wonderful how, if one insisted, the A-G. was always able to draft a Bill overnight for presentation to the Legislative Council next morning. We forbore to point out that legislation rushed together in this fashion might have its imperfections.

I doubt whether we succeeded in satisfying the Nyasa-land trio that we were not trying to be obstructive, but were trying to help in an orderly hand-over of functions. I had the feeling, when the meeting was over, that they were well pleased with the opportunity it gave them to show how clever they were. It subsequently became manifest that they had convinced Dr. Banda that they were too clever by half, because he got rid of them all. Chiume and Chipembere were banished from the country and subsequently made abortive attempts to return and overthrow Dr. Banda.

In the event, the transition of Nyasaland, as a territory within the Federation, to Malawi as an independent State with a seat on the United Nations and on the Common-wealth Prime Ministers' Conference, proceeded very smoothly. Malawi is now a state where the system of one-man one-vote has resulted in one party and one dictator. As the Press is not free it is difficult for the outsider to know what goes on in the country. Surprisingly, Dr. Banda accepted financial aid from South Africa, and has diplomatic relations with that country, thus putting himself beyond the pale in the eyes of most of the O.A.U. Moreover, of all Rhodesia's near neighbours he seemed to be the least antagonistic to the

R.F. regime. No doubt, the fortunes of some people have prospered under the new order, but the plight of others may have retrogressed. To outward appearances, the land is peaceful but Jehovah's Witnesses might be able to give testimony tending to show that too high a price has been paid for the peace. For ten years, Nyasaland was subsidised by the Federal Government at the expense of the taxpayers in the two Rhodesias. Since 1963, Malawi has been subsidised by international agencies in various forms. Whether Dr. Banda did his country a service by disrupting the Federation is, I believe, open to serious question.

49

Rise of the Rhodesian Front

THE RISE to power of the Rhodesian Front may fairly be attributed mainly to the British Government's betrayal of the Federation, which had become manifest before the fateful general election at the end of 1962. This betrayal had, among other disastrous results, the discrediting of the U.F.P. leaders and their policy of political partnership. The electorate, in effect, asked why they should sustain the policy of partnership in the south when the British Government had thrown it overboard in the north and substituted the policy of majority rule, or, in other words, black domination. The R.F. victory was, nevertheless, a disaster of the first magnitude which ranks equally with the electorate's foolish rejection of the chance to join South Africa at the 1922 referendum. Their victory led inevitably to U.D.I., which, in turn, is leading to black domination, the very thing that its authors were anxious to avoid. The United Kingdom, aided and abetted by the United States, is now on the point of thrusting greatness on black politicians who have neither the training nor the experience to administer Rhodesia's sophisticated economy which is so dependent on the white element in the population. It can be expected that the next few years will witness changes in Rhodesia which will be disastrous for many people of all races and which will play into the hands of Russia.

Caldicott and I were in London during the 1962 election campaign and we warned Sandys that the R.F. would win. He did not believe us, as he assumed that the U.F.P. victory in the referendum, which had ushered in the 1961 Sandys/Whitehead constitution, would be repeated at the election held under its provisions. Whitehead probably made the same assumption. He expected to win all the 15 B Roll seats which were designed for blacks, and enough of the 50 A Roll seats, designed in the first instance for whites, to give him a working majority. In the result, he won only 14 B Roll seats, and, by a strange coincidence, only 14 A Roll seats. The odd B Roll seat went unexpectedly to a white, Dr. A. Palley, an independent. The R.F. had put up black candidates for the B Roll seats, but concentrated on the A Roll seats, winning 30 of them, to the surprise, it is commonly believed, of Winston Field, who now found himself Prime Minister. It was a double misfortune that the R.F. won a majority and that it did so without gaining a single B Roll seat. If their parliamentary caucus had included two or three blacks, or perhaps even one, this might have restrained them from some of the worst examples of their reactionary programme. It might also have made them more sensitive to the feelings of up-and-coming black politicians.

Rhodesia now, for the first time, had a backward-looking government. Huggins had narrowly missed being ousted in 1946 by the misnamed Liberal Party. He owed his political survival, at that time, to the fact that the forces ranged against the United Party were split. The Labour Party skimmed off the white artisan vote, which was predominantly hostile to black advancement whether in industry or in government, while the Liberals catered for other white voters who were obsessively opposed to black advancement. The Rhodesian Front, in 1962, made an appeal to all those elements in the white electorate who were opposed to the advancement of blacks or who were alarmed at Whitehead's signs of accelerating the pace of black advancement. With the R.F. victory, for the first time in Rhodesia's history, the reactionary elements of the former Labour Party began to have a real voice in the government. In 1922, their ancestors had joined forces with Coghlan to block Rhodesia's entry into the Union of South Africa, but, with the referendum behind him, Coghlan discarded these elements when he won the general election which made him Premier. Ian Smith, unlike Coghlan, remained loyal to these supporters, and their influence can be readily seen in much of the backward-looking legislation his government inflicted on the country, notably the Land Tenure Act.

The accrual to Field's banner of erstwhile Labour Party supporters would not in itself have sufficed to give him the victory in 1962. He won the election because of a massive defection of U.F.P. supporters. What were the causes that led them to desert Whitehead in the critical 1962 election? The main reason I have already referred to, namely the British Government's backsliding on Federation and partnership. A contributory cause was the eccentric personality of Whitehead. Lord Home in *The Way the Wind Blows* has noted that Whitehead was very deaf, very blind and able to consume 13 beers in an evening without putting up his hand and asking to leave the room. Added to these peculiarities, he was a bachelor with perhaps even less "charisma" than Edward Heath to attract voters whether male or female. His record with the electorate shows a curious in-and-out pattern. First elected to Parliament in 1939, he was beaten in 1946 but won a by-election; elected in 1948 he lost the by-election in 1958, but won the ensuing general election. He won the 1961 referendum and lost the 1962 general election (though elected himself).

In the years leading up to Federation, Whitehead had never been in the vanguard of multiracialism. In the Hitler War, he served under Lord Swinton in West Africa and became alive to the rising tide of African nationalism. A full awakening only came, I believe, when he went to Washington D.C. as the Federal Government's representative. When he left this post on his birthday, in 1958, to return to politics in Rhodesia, he embarked on a policy of rapid change in the direction of black advancement in all departments of life, including government, and his record in this respect during his term of office far surpasses that of Todd. Lord Home writes off Todd in a brief paragraph, saying that he was evasive on the subject of black political advancement, excusing himself on the ground that the pace must be slow or else repudiation by the predominantly white electorate would follow. "In that respect," says Lord Home, "in spite of his later protestations, he was exactly the same as his predecessors and successors."

Some may think that this sweeping generalisation is unfair to both Todd and Lord Malvern. It is manifestly wrong as regards Todd's immediate successor, Whitehead, whose government made important changes in the Industrial Conciliation Act and other laws directed to improving the position of blacks in industry, and who negotiated the very advanced 1961 Constitution, whereby Africans were given an immediate and substantial voice in Parliament. His election promise to repeal the Land Apportionment Act lost him the votes of many former supporters of the U.F.P., thus showing that Todd's hesitation was understandable.

As to Todd's "later protestations" it is true that his call in 1959 for discrimination to be stopped "massively and immediately" had never been heard in public while he was Prime Minister. In 1954, Todd had ridden into power on the crest of the federal wave. In 1959, Whitehead had scarcely got a firm seat in the saddle when Dr. Banda began to make difficulties for the Federation. When it become necessary to send Federal soldiers and Rhodesian police to Nyasaland, Whitehead sought to anticipate trouble with black nationalists on the home front by banning the A.N.C. and detaining a large number of its members for whom I had to make room in Federal prisons. In my opinion, he detained more of the lesser lights than the circumstances warranted.

However, the A.N.C. cropped up again as the old firm with a new signboard, N.D.P.; and when this, in turn, was banned, Z.A.N.U. and Z.A.P.U. raised their twin heads. After Joshua Nkomo had reneged on the 1961 constitutional settlement, violence became widespread in African townships and tribal trust lands The police wished to ban political meetings at the week-ends. Whitehead thought that this would be unfair to the black community. At this period the ditty "Never on Sunday" was at the top of the hit parade. White military and police reservists and their wives thought that they should never have to be called out on Sunday to preserve order at political meetings, but they were constantly on duty at the week-ends. The U.F.P. undoubtedly lost many votes in 1962 because of Whitehead's refusal to ban Sunday meetings.

Another contributing factor was the R.F.'s crude but effective play on white emotions, a prominent example of which was a full-page advertisement depicting white and black legs mingling on their way to school. Electoral dirty tricks like the Zinovieff letter can sway elections in the U.K. so it is not a matter for wonder that the Rhodesian electorate could be influenced by questionable means. Lord Home gives another factor contributing to Whitehead's defeat, namely the news flowing in from the United Nations.

One of the positive factors in the R.F. victory was the air of respectability lent to it by its leader Winston Field who was a gentleman in all senses of the word. He made the error of taking into his cabinet John Gaunt, a malcontent former District Commissioner from Northern Rhodesia, who was a flamboyant personality and had represented Lusaka in the Federal Assembly. It is said that when Field ultimately recognised his mistake and demanded Gaunt's resignation, Gaunt asked him to leave the matter over till Monday as he had one or two odd jobs to clear up over the week-end. One of these turned out to be a conspiracy to get rid of Field. Subsequently, Ian Smith kicked Gaunt upstairs to Pretoria.

It will be obvious from what I have said that I am no admirer of the Rhodesian Front, but one thing can be said in its favour, namely, that within a year or two it managed to restore law and order which in the latter years of Whitehead's administration had been getting out of hand. Violence was rife in the African townships and the rural areas, mostly in the form of intimidation of blacks by blacks. Prosecutions of the evil-doers often failed because witnesses were intimidated. Under the R.F. regime, order was restored until the time of the Pearce Commission when some of the African political leaders were released from detention. There was an immediate recurrence of violence and intimidation which effectively damned the 1971 settlement in the eyes of the commission. In 1975, Prime Minister Vorster's moves for detente resulted in further releases, with the result that terrorist activity was immediately stepped up.

50

Bar and Bench

A^{S} THE dissolution of the Federation drew near, towards the end of 1963, and my political career was about to come to an abrupt end, I had to give thought to my own future. It was obvious that in the short term there would be no place for me in the political life of Rhodesia, and even in the long run it would only be a remote possibility. Field and his Minister of Justice urged me to accept a judgeship, and, indeed, wished to appoint me to a new Court of Appeal they intended to establish, but their plans ran into constitutional difficulties. For several years before the break-up of the Federation my friend Sir Hugh Beadle had pressed me to join the Bench. This step would have given me an easy way out of several personal problems but a judgeship held little attraction for me. I had always been more interested in the constructive side of the law, that is to say legislation and law reform, rather than the application of existing laws to past events which is the main function of a judge. Moreover, I felt that having been away from the mainstream of those branches of the law with which the courts are mostly concerned, I was not best fitted for the work of a judge. Accordingly, I declined to accept judicial office and decided to return to Bulawayo to resume my practice at the Bar. I remained with Sir Roy Welensky and my other colleagues to the end, and my presence was very necessary to protect the interests of Federal judges and others for whose rights the British Government cared little.

In the closing stages of the Federation, some of its enemies did not scruple to spread the lie that Welensky and his Ministers were trying to keep it alive because our livelihoods depended upon it. Many of the general public, although they may not have attributed such low motives to Federal Ministers, assumed that we would emerge from the break-up with ministerial pensions. Of course, this was not so, nor was there a rush to offer us directorships.

I was confident that I could still make a tolerable living at the Bar. Early in January, 1964, my wife and I returned to Bulawayo, having with considerable difficulty sold our house near Salisbury for about half of what it had cost us. Our eldest son, Ewen, who had recently married was living at Harthill, and we took up residence at Kaya Pezulu as soon as our tenant there was able to vacate it.

I did not have the illusion that it would be easy to regain my former position in a leading practice at the Bar after an absence of over thirteen years. The break-up of the Federation had brought about a recession which was even more marked in Bulawayo than in Salisbury. I did not expect that briefs would be showered on me but I did think that some of the senior attorneys who used to brief me in bygone years would look in at my chambers to welcome me back. A month or more elapsed before I saw any of them, but one who had been on holiday in January called on me in February, and by slow degrees work began to come in.

At Bulawayo, there was almost no litigation of the kind which warrants briefing senior counsel, and not very much chamber work of this sort. However, one case did crop up in Bulawayo, and soon afterwards Salisbury attorneys began to give me occasional briefs which brought me back into the courts in that city. It was not long before Dupont, the Minister of Justice, invited me to fill a new vacancy on the Bench but I again declined. My main source of work was now the Rhodesia Railways, whose attorneys renewed the general retainer I had relinquished in 1950, fortunately, at a fee vastly greater than it used to be. At this time, the Rhodesia Railways continued to operate on both sides of the Zambezi under the direction of a Board whose membership was equally divided between Zambia and Rhodesia. Co-operation between these two countries, even in 1964, was minimal, and the Board could only operate through the casting vote of the chairman, A. R. Kemp, who had been appointed by the Federal Government before the dissolution.

Kemp had an unenviable task which he performed with great courage and ability. Previously, he had been successful in a commercial business at Broken Hill (Kabwe), and he was to a certain extent *persona grata* to the new Zambian Ministers. In Rhodesia, he was consequently viewed by the Ministry of Transport with suspicion verging on open hostility, which I believe was quite unwarranted.

For some unfathomable reason, the Rhodesian Government seemed bent on bringing to an end the unitary railway system, and their Zambian counterparts were only too willing that this should happen, although they were not then in a position to manage their own section of the railway system. The Rhodesian Government proceeded to rush legislation through Parliament without prior consultation with some of those most intimately concerned by it, including Kemp and the general manager, Trevor Wright. On one occasion, I was called in to advise on a Bill which Kemp and Wright had seen for the first time when Friday's Government Gazette reached Bulawayo on Saturday morning, and which was to be debated early the next week in Parliament. Speed seemed always to be of the essence, and we found that the only way to persuade the Government to accept necessary changes was to present them with amendments drafted in Parliamentary form. Fortunately, I had a fair amount of experience in drafting of this sort and was able to deal with it at short notice, like Orton Chirwa's Attorney-General in Malawi. By methods such as these we sometimes got changes made in the nick of time.

Relations between the two governments became increasingly strained and even at official level it was almost impossible to settle differences amicably. The two countries seemed to vie with each other to make regulations designed to embarrass each other. Kemp was constantly seeking my advice, which I did my best to give but it was political rather than legal advice. I told him, on occasion, to ignore certain provisions of the law in one or other or both countries, otherwise the whole system would grind fairly quickly to a halt, with disastrous consequences. As a hardened politician, it was easier for me to give this sort of advice than it would have been for most of my competitors at the Bar whose views on the law were untainted by political expediency.

It is difficult to understand why the Rhodesian ministers and their advisers handled railway matters in this strange fashion. Probably life was made very difficult for them by the wholly uncompromising and unreasonable attitude of their counterparts in the north. This, however, in my opinion, does not justify the way in which they treated Kemp, whose services in keeping the Rhodesia Railways going in both territories, under such difficulties, deserved high praise. He got neither praise nor thanks when his contract expired. Subsequently, the railway system was divided at the Victoria Falls bridge, though I doubt whether the accountancy side of the split has even yet been finalised.

When U.D.I. occurred on 11th November, 1965, there were great heart-searchings among the judges, and much anxiety at the Bar. Advocates in Salisbury and Bulawayo were vitally concerned as to what might happen if the judges should resign or refuse to carry out their normal functions under the new order. Relations between the judiciary and the Government were under great strain, but never quite reached breaking point. It was inevitable that sooner or later the courts would be confronted by a challenge to the legality of the Government. In 1966, such a case arose in which a periodical called *The Central African Examiner* challenged the validity of certain censorship regulations on the basis that having been issued by an illegal government they had no validity. I was briefed with a junior for the Minister, but we had very little time to prepare our arguments. Counsel for *The Examiner* relied, among other points, on legislation promulgated in England immediately after U.D.I. which was designed to render invalid all the purported legislation of what British Ministers regarded as Smith's illegal regime.

A curious feature of the British Government's handling of U.D.I. was the furtive, almost secretive, way they circulated their anti-Smith legislation in Rhodesia itself. I myself received some of the earliest of such legislation from England under cover of an anonymous letter. Lewis J., who tried *The Examiner* case was most scathing in his remarks about the British Government's failure to promulgate their own laws in Rhodesia.

Judgment was eventually given in favour of the Minister, not on the ground of want of promulgation but on another point of a somewhat technical nature. Thus, a direct confrontation between executive and judiciary for the time being was avoided. I was not briefed when the main constitutional issue came squarely before the High Court and was finally disposed of in 1968.

One of the judges on the appeal, J. C. R. Fieldsend, although he upheld the actions of the Rhodesian Government, resigned from the Bench, as he felt that he could not continue to serve under existing conditions. He had begun his legal career as a pupil in my chambers in 1946, and I had a considerable regard for him. Before U.D.I., Dupont had given me a further opportunity to join the Bench which I had declined. When Fieldsend resigned, the Chief Justice pressed me strongly to agree to fill the vacancy, and this I did with extreme reluctance.

I was sworn in on 1st May, 1968. When welcoming me to the Bench, the Chief Justice remarked on the fact that I was the fifth former Minister of Justice to be elevated to the Bench, but the only one of the five who had not appointed himself. I mention this because a scurrilous article appeared in *The Times,* signifying that as I had not fared very well since the dissolution of the Federation I had leapt at the opportunity provided by Fieldsend's departure to get myself a job. I was the first post-U.D.I. judge. The courts in Britain drew a distinction between pre- and post-U.D.I. judges, marriage officers and others. Among my colleagues I was therefore not regarded as being quite kosher because any divorce I granted would be looked upon in the British Courts as invalid. Likewise, a marriage ceremony performed by a clergyman who came to Rhodesia after U.D.I. would be treated as a nullity. When U.D.I. was declared, the British Government urged the judges to remain at their posts. One wonders what they expected to happen as vacancies occurred by retirement, resignation or death. If they expected the surviving judges to carry the extra load they were hardly being realistic.

I did not enjoy my six years on the Bench any more than I had expected to. Conditions of service were congenial but the work consisted mainly of criminal trials, mostly primitive murder cases, and endless reviews of magistrates' decisions in criminal cases. In Bulawayo, where I was stationed, there was little civil litigation except uncontested divorces, with an occasional contested case where the action was based on cruelty. I retired in September, 1974 mainly because of increasing deafness. I got no sympathy when I moaned to a colleague about my inability to hear what a certain advocate was trying to say. My colleague assured me that my deafness was a great advantage.

51

U.D.I.

WHEN the British Government decided to break up the Federation, most of the Rhodesian electorate regarded their action as a cynical breach of trust, and their feelings of resentment were aggravated when independence was withheld from Rhodesia but instantly accorded to Malawi and Zambia. These two countries were at once welcomed into the Commonwealth family and the United Nations while Winston Field was not given even a courtesy seat at the ensuing Commonwealth Conference, a privilege which had been extended to Sir Godfrey Huggins (Lord Malvern) as far back as 1935. It was a shabby way to treat Field, who, above all, had played into the hands of R. A. Butler by co-operating in his plans for dissolution of the Federation at the Victoria Falls in July, 1963.

Small wonder that such treatment of Field and his country rankled in the minds of Rhodesian ministers and voters. As they saw it, Rhodesia had been self-governing for over forty years and her record was sound. She had rallied to the mother country in both World Wars, not to mention the Anglo-Boer War, in each case making a contribution of fighting men of top quality in proportion to the size of the white population that was second to none. White Rhodesians were justifiably proud of what had been done for the black population for whom their government had provided educational, health and other facilities that were vastly better than those provided by the British Colonial Office in any country in Africa north of the Zambezi.

As recently as 1961, the electorate had agreed to constitutional changes which had the effect of enfranchising large numbers of blacks, putting 15 out of 65 seats immediately under the control of black voters. Surely, white Rhodesians thought, their country had fully earned the right to independence. The British Government's excuse for withholding independence was the refusal of the Rhodesian Government to agree to further changes in the 1961 Constitution which would accelerate the pace of black political advancement to a point where black majority rule would come in a very near future. Most of the Rhodesian electorate considered that the pace should be much more gradual. They had seen at close quarters evidence of one-man one-vote leading to dictatorship and chaos. They realised that, notwithstanding the high-sounding phrases and platitudes that Macmillan and other British ministers had used in Federal times, they had now cynically abandoned the principle of partnership enunciated in the preamble to the Federal Constitution and had substituted the concept of black majority rule regardless of the consequences. In the northern territories, the British Government had their own way, but Field and his Ministers refused to be blackmailed into buying independence at the price of a premature extension of voting rights to blacks, which they believed would spell disaster for blacks and whites alike. It would inevitably have led to the erosion of Western standards of justice, liberty, law and order, just as it had done in the Congo and in Ghana. I held no brief for Field but had I been in his place I would not have submitted to the British terms for independence.

Apparently Field's failure to secure independence as part and parcel of the arrangements for dissolution of the Federation lost him the support of all his Ministers except Howman. In April, Ian Smith became Prime Minister in his stead. When he, in turn, failed to reach agreement with Sir Alec Douglas-Home the likelihood of U.D.I. grew by the day. At this stage, Whitehead was leading an opposition of 28, half of whom were white and the other half black. He seemed to be losing grip. In August, Welensky, who was not in Parliament, was prevailed upon to take over the leadership from Whitehead. At an ensuing by-election, on 1st October, the former Federal Prime Minister was heavily defeated, after a campaign in which the tactics of some of the R.F. reached an all-time low level in the annals of Rhodesian politics. To the account of this given by Lord Blake* it may be added that Welensky had been discredited in the eyes of the electorate because he had been unable to prevent the British Government from breaking up the Federation.

After Harold Wilson became Prime Minister of the United Kingdom on 16th October, Smith proceeded to engage in a show of brinkmanship which was very unnerving to those who, like me, thought that a unilateral and final breach with the mother country would be disastrous. At this time, of course, I was in the political wilderness. I strongly sympathised with the Government's desire to make Rhodesia independent if this could be done by constitutional means. I did not subscribe to the view that independence was unimportant. So long as Rhodesia remained, from an international constitutional point of view, a colony, encouragement was given to black nationalists and their supporters at the United Nations to make trouble. They would get a great deal of help from communists and fellow-travellers. In the closing stages of Whitehead's Prime Ministership, we had seen how they had learned from the examples set by Dr. Banda and Mr. Kaunda to mount a campaign of intimidation and violence which got almost beyond the capacity of the police to control.

I was opposed to U.D.I. not because I thought it morally reprehensible but because I thought it had no chance of succeeding, and that its failure would produce results opposite to what its sponsors were striving to achieve. I wrote a letter to Dupont, at that time Minister of Justice but later to become the first President, in which I urged him to dissuade Smith from U.D.I. and suggested, as an alternative, that he should seize every opportunity in relation to external affairs to act as though Rhodesia were independent but to abstain from any formal declaration that would purport to cut the legal bonds with Britain. Dupont sent me a courteous but non-committal reply which served to convince me that U.D.I. was on the way.

*A History of Rhodesia, p.366.

I therefore joined a group of professional and business men in Bulawayo who were meeting together to see what they could do to avert the disaster. All that eventuated was a brief advertising campaign which made no impact. The group soon became dispirited and fizzled out. It was apparent to me that people whom I regarded as the more responsible members of the community were alarmed at the prospects of U.D.I. but the great majority of the electorate were allowing their emotions to govern their judgment. Smith appeared to have for them "charisma"; certainly from the 11th November, 1965 onwards he had the misfortune to receive the adulation of thousands, something no other white Rhodesian politician had previously suffered.

Before taking the final plunge, Smith consulted the opinions of the top civil servants, and the heads of the army and police. Except for Barfoot, the Police Commissioner, they were unanimously against this step. A few months later Barfoot died of a brain tumour. Most of the leading businessmen and industrialists, as far as I could gauge their views, were opposed to U.D.I. but one felt that some of them had correctly assessed the mood of the Government and the electorate so that, in consequence, their opposition was somewhat muted.

Meanwhile, Dr. Verwoerd had sent Smith a mesage by the hand of Welensky not to count on South African support in the event of a break with Britain. I believe that Sir Alec Douglas-Home had advised Smith not to count on the continued stability of the Portuguese African empire. I have no doubt that advice came from the Rhodesian Government's external offices in Washington D.C. and elsewhere regarding the hostility of the United Nations. Right up to the 12th hour, of course, Harold Wilson was issuing dire threats and warnings. It is, therefore, somewhat of a puzzle to understand why Smith and his colleagues took the final plunge.

In the 72 years that elapsed between the overthrow of Lobengula and the declaration of independence, there had been three main turning points in Rhodesia's constitutional development. These were the decisions to reject linking up with South Africa in 1922, to federate with the northern territories in 1953, and to accept the Sandys-Whitehead Constitution in 1961. In each case, the decision was left to the electorate at a referendum. In 1965, however, Smith and his ministers took upon themselves the decision. It is true that about a year before there had been a referendum in which the voters were asked to say "yes" or "no" to the question "Are you in favour of independence for Rhodesia on the basis of the 1961 Constitution?" The vast majority, myself included, answered "yes". U.D.I., of course, was not on this basis. The constitution under which Smith's regime continued was the 1961 Constitution stripped of the more important entrenchments it contained against amendment of vital clauses. In any event, that referendum gave no warrant whatsoever for a unilateral declaration.

The document commonly regarded as "U.D.I." is headed simply "Proclamation". It ends with the affirmation "God Save the Queen", under which are appended the signatures of Smith and his Ministers, including Howman who was now in the fold. At this stage, they were purporting to accept the Queen as the nominal head of the government while rejecting all other ties with the United Kingdom.

The body of the document, after a short preamble, which attempts to draw inspiration from the famous declaration of the 4th of July nearly two centuries before, is somewhat vague and muddled. The nearest it comes to a specific complaint against the United Kingdom is an allegation that its government "persists in maintaining an unwarrantable jurisdiction over Rhodesia, obstructing laws and treaties with other States and the conduct of affairs with other rulers, and refusing to assent to laws necessary for the public good, all this to the detriment of the future peace, prosperity and good government of Rhodesia."

The lack of sovereign independence would certainly restrict Rhodesia in its dealings with foreign States, but few, if any, of these were likely to want to make treaties with Rhodesia after U.D.I., and none did so. The suggestion that Britain "refused to assent to laws" is different to square with the facts unless the reference is to hypothetical laws concerned with external affairs or designed to change the constitution to fit it for independence.

The Prime Minister's address to the nation, broadcast the same day, did little to clarify the matter. He spoke of a "paralysing state of uncertainty" and said "The bitter lesson of the Federation is constantly in the forefront of my mind. In that case matters were permitted to drift and plans for action were formulated too late to prevent the destruction of this noble concept of racial harmony." Was this a hint that Britain's actions could have been halted if Welensky had taken some unspecified course along the lines that he himself was doing?

In 1966, Lardner Burke, who succeeded Dupont as Minister of Justice, wrote a slender book with the blessing of his leader entitled *Rhodesia — The Story of Crisis.** Curiously enough, this was printed in England despite sanctions. In the chapter "Why Independence is necessary", he refers to the 1961 Conference and says that the British Government refused to write into the new Constitution the Convention which is printed in Part I of the White Paper CMND 1399 presented to Parliament before the Constitution was enacted. He went on to draw the inference that the British Government were not prepared to relinquish the power they claimed to legislate for Rhodesia, and implied that they would not scruple to violate the Convention.

In Chapter 35 I have related the history of the Federal Convention of 1957 on which the 1961 Convention was modelled, and I have shown how this arose out of points that Dendy Young had made in connection with Article 29 (7) of the Federal Constitution. Whitehead had withdrawn from the political scene in 1953 and was not involved in this dispute. Even so, in 1961, he or his advisers should have appreciated the likelihood that lawyers in the opposition party might raise a similar bogey in regard to the British enactments giving legal shape to the Constitution that he had negotiated with Duncan Sandys. Perhaps he thought that the Convention would silence them but it did not have this effect, as Lardner Burke's argument demonstrates.

Rhodesia — The Story of Crisis, by Desmond Lardner-Burke, London, Oldbourne Book Co., Ltd, 1966.

The answer to all this is that Smith and his colleagues should not have crossed over to the wrong side of the legal fence in order to anticipate hypothetical sinister designs of the British Government to dishonour the 1961 Convention as it had dishonoured that of 1953 in the case of the Federation. In fact, U.D.I. gave the British Government the excuse it might have wanted, to revoke the 1961 Constitution. The fact that Smith, despite his unconstitutional action, has been able to hold out for twelve years demonstrates very effectively the impotence of the British Government to bring a Rhodesian Government to heel. How much stronger would its position have been if it had kept within the law and left the British Government to violate the Convention.

The real reason for U.D.I. becomes apparent when one considers the actions of the R.F. government in the ensuing years. First, despite the assurance in Smith's broadcast to the nation, the constitution he substituted for the 1961 document did make changes going well beyond what would be required formally to adapt it for independence. The important entrenchments relating to changes in the constitution were dropped, thus enabling the R.F., by a simple two-thirds majority, to make what alterations it liked in the electoral laws and the Land Apportionment Act. They took full advantage of their new-found powers to enact a constitution and electoral laws in 1969 which bear little, if any, resemblance to those of 1961, and to enact the retrogressive Land Tenure Act in place of the Land Apportionment Act. The facts are that Smith had been the leading opponent of the 1961 Constitution at the referendum held that year, and he and his ministers were determined to get rid of it by hook or by crook.

Smith is said to have expressed the view that U.D.I. would prove to be a nine-day wonder. Harold Wilson expressed the opinion that the R.F. government would collapse in weeks rather than months. I confess that I shared Wilson's opinion. I had expected that oil sanctions would have an immediate impact and that there would be black industrial unrest, if not violence, on a scale that would bring the economy to a halt. I would add that these were my fears, not my hopes. Opposed as I was to U.D.I., once it had happened I hoped that the British Government would not become masters of the situation because I felt sure this would spell disaster. Smith and Wilson were both proved wrong. There is no doubt that the R.F. government performed a remarkable feat in holding out for twelve years in the face of worldwide sanctions and hostility. Unfortunately, their record in regard to unnecessary discriminatory legislation and practices has detracted very seriously from their reputation.

As I write, more than a year has elapsed since Smith intimated in September, 1976 that on certain conditions he would accept the Kissinger plan for a hand-over to majority rule within two years. The conditions were not accepted by the black nationalist terrorist movements and as yet a final settlement is not in sight. Smith, however, has virtually acknowledged that U.D.I. has failed and that black majority rule is inevitable. What drove him to this position was the collapse of Portuguese rule in Mozambique, and not British and United Nations sanctions, except to the extent that these, by their effects on the economy of Mozambique and the blockade of the port of Beira, may have contributed to the downfall of Caetano's government.

But Smith should get no comfort from blaming the collapse of the Portuguese dictatorship for his own misfortunes, and the sad state to which he has reduced his country by his foolish blunder. In 1965, any responsible politician of average intelligence should have realised that less than a decade might elapse before Mozambique and Angola were in the same state of chaos as the Congo had seen in 1960 onwards. Smith, having been warned by Sir Alec Douglas-Home, had no excuse for gambling on the stability of the Portuguese dictatorship at a time when the ageing Salazar was soon to depart from the scene.

It is ironical that in 1976 Smith found it necessary to resort to black Members of Parliament to muster the two-thirds majority required to repeal some of the unnecessary discriminatory provisions of the Land Tenure Act, a piece of legislation which could never have been enacted if the 1961 Constitution had been in operation.

Even more ironical is the fact that Smith from a position of extreme weakness is trying to get some safeguards for the white population when black majority rule is substituted for rule by the R.F. What would the majority of white voters in Rhodesia not give to be restored to the 1961 Constitution under which no change adverse to their rights could be made without the approval of themselves and three other racial groupings at separate referenda? Now, instead of a gradual increase in black parliamentary representation Rhodesian whites are faced with the prospect of a one-person one-vote type of democracy which will effectually deprive them of any semblance of political power or even influence. Consequently, they are now faced with the erosion of present standards of administration, justice and liberty which will almost certainly result in a large exodus of those who can afford to go.

What should be said of the attitude and actions of successive British governments towards Rhodesia? I consider that Rhodesian whites are justified in having only contempt for their vindictive and hostile behaviour. Duncan Sandys was perfectly correct when he told Welensky and me, in 1962, that Britain had lost the will to govern in Africa. When a prominent Zambian politician subsequently compared the British Government to a toothless bulldog he was not far short of the mark. Successive British governments have failed to solve the problems of Northern Ireland a good deal nearer their own doorstep than Rhodesia. They are blind to the anomaly of refusing to allow majority rule to operate in Northern Ireland while insisting that it must do so in Rhodesia where it will inevitably be detrimental to both blacks and whites. Willing to wound but afraid to strike, the Labour government of Harold Wilson attempted to shift the responsibility to the United Nations. Under James Callaghan, subsidies are being given to the Marxist regime in Mozambique which affords the main base for terrorist action against Rhodesia. They have used sanctions to try to bring down the R.F. regime, recklessly ignoring the probability of civil war between rival terrorist factions which bid fair to bring about a Congo or Angola type of chaos.

The sinister hand of the United States can be traced in

the background of British dealings with the Federation from the time of the Suez debacle onwards, right up to the time when Kissinger's shuttling diplomacy has brought it into the open.   President Carter's administration seems to have learned little from the intervention in Vietnam about the unwisdom of attempting to sort out the affairs of distant foreign countries.

South Africa has now become the main focus of world attention and American interference to an extent that it almost seems to be taking some of the heat off Rhodesia. It was singularly unfortunate and unfair that South Africa's policy of apartheid, inaugurated by the Nationalist Government of 1948, should have rubbed off on Rhodesia, or to change the metaphor, it is unfortunate that the aroma of the South African polecat should have enveloped Rhodesia. Politicians and journalists remote from the scene were seemingly unable to distinguish between the very different policies of South Africa and Rhodesia that obtained right up to the time when the R.F. came to power in 1962. Admittedly, since then the R.F. government began to make retrogressive moves, but it must be remembered that the British Government had quietly dropped the principle of partnership and plumped for black majority rule which elsewhere has always resulted in reverse discrimination.

As a Rhodesian "white settler" of the 1909 vintage, albeit I was then less than two years old, I have always resented the arrogance of so many British politicians in their assumption that their knowledge of how to conduct the affairs of Rhodesia must be superior to that of people of British stock, or, in the case of Welensky, of pro-British sentiments, who have lived their working lives in Rhodesia and engaged in the conduct of its political affairs.   I have often thought that British governments might well have encouraged some of their own promising Members of Parliament to emigrate to Rhodesia, there to assist in the conduct of her political affairs. Not everyone in Rhodesia believes that Sir Edgar Whitehead was a model Prime Minister. Had he laboured in the company of a few others like Stephen Hastings, Patrick Wall, Victor Goodhew, Biggs Davidson, to name only a few British Members of Parliament, what a difference it might have made, whereas the voices of these reasonable and intelligent men have been lost in the clamour of the ignorant.

The fate of the Federation of Rhodesia and Nyasaland, and impending changes in Rhodesia prompt the thought that Alexander Pope was right when he said :

> *For forms of government let fools contest*
> *What's best administered is best.*

INDEX OF PERSONS

Monckton Commission, 172; Welensky discussion, 174; Mrs. Rosin, 175; Chequers, 198; Whitehead, 233; Todd, 234; U.N.O., 236

Hone, Sir Evelyn, 53, 196, 203

Hove, Mike M., 193

Hudson, Sir Robert, 86

Huggins, Sir Godfrey, later Lord Malvern, 1942 St. Andrew's, 80; 1933 team, 88; 1941 Native policy, 91; *laissez-faire*, 92; Action Group, 92; Liberal Party, 93; 1949 Falls Conference, 100; 1951 Falls Conference, 107; Partnership, 108; Afrikaners, 112; Baxter Report, 116; 1952 London negotiations, 116; Speech, 120; 1953 London Conference, 124; Dendy Young clash, 129 - 30; Federal Party, 133; succession to, 1953, 135-5; Todd's attack, 145; comparison with Welensky, 146; Nyasaland, 167; Blantyre Congress, 168; political survival, 1946, 233

I

Ibbotson, Rev. Percy, 74, 75

Ingham, John, 53

Ismay, Lord, 116

J

Jacob, Sir Claude, 227

K

Kaunda, Kenneth, rejects appeal court, 143; intimidation, 173, 219; 1960 Federal Review, 188; author's Chequers visit, 198; master plan, 204; Barotseland, 209

Keller, L. J. W., 87, 90, 96, 106

Kemp, A. R., 238

Kennedy, Sir John, 106, 133

Kenyatta, 184

Kilmuir, Lord, 140, 141, 197

Kissinger, Henry, 252

Knight, Reginald, 142

L

Lardner-Burke, D., 248

Leask, Rev. A. G., 79

Leggate, W. M., 72, 89

Lennox-Boyd, Alan (Lord Boyd), 1952 London Conference, 117; April 1957, 149, 154; 1958 Northern Rhodesia Constitution, 165; Devlin Commission, 169-70

Lestor, Miss Joan, 90

Lewanika, Godwin, 208, 211

Lewanika, Sir Mwanuwina, 208-211

Lewey, Sir Arthur, 141-142

Lewin, Prof. Julius, 91

Lewis, Justice John, 240

Lewis, Vernon A., 62

Listowel, Lord, 107

Llewellin, Lord, 137, 152, 213

Low, Sir Henry, 48, 59

Lyttelton, Oliver (later Lord Chandos), Afrikaners, 112; 1952 London Conference, 116; Gorell Barnes, 123; 1953 London Conference, pledge, 125-6

M

Macintyre, Sir Donald, 90, 96, 168

Maclean, Ian, 188

Macleod, Iain, Colonial office, 168, 170; whip hand, 180; release of Dr. Banda, 183; 1961 Nyasaland Conference, 184; 1961 Northern Rhodesia Conference, 197; author's dinner with, 198; February 1961 White Paper, 199; June 1961 White Paper, 204; Maudling, 206; Barotseland, 208

Mcleod, Lord, 220

Macmillan, Harold, unflappable, 154; Monckton terms, 172; debate, 177-8; backsliding on partnership, 179; Blantyre demo, 182; 1960 Federal Review, 187, 190; entertains author, 198; tearful appeal to Welensky, 200; intimidation by Kaunda, 204; rough handling of Maudling and Sandys, 207